Surviving Crisis

$2— 1/98

Also by Lee Gutkind

An Unspoken Art: Profiles of Veterinary Life; Henry Holt, 1997.

The Art of Creative Nonfiction: The Literature of Reality; John Wiley, 1996.

Creative Nonfiction: How to Live It and Write It; Chicago Review Press, 1996.

Stuck in Time: The Tragedy of Childhood Mental Illness; Henry Holt & Company, 1994; Owl paperback, 1995.

One Children's Place: Inside a Children's Hospital; A Plume Book by Penguin USA, 1992, published in Japanese language edition.

Many Sleepless Nights: The World of Organ Transplantation; W. W. Norton & Co., 1990, published in Japanese, Korean, Italian editions.

Our Roots Grow Deeper Than We Know (anthology); University of Pittsburgh Press, 1985.

The People of Penn's Woods West (essays about rural America); University of Pittsburgh Press, 1984.

God's Helicopter (a novel); Slow Loris Press, 1983.

Best Seat in Baseball, but You Have to Stand: The Game As Umpires See It; Dial Press, 1975.

Bike Fever: An Examination of the Motorcycle Subculture; Avon Books, Inc., 1974.

Surviving Crisis

Twenty Prominent Authors
Write About Events That
Shaped Their Lives

edited by Lee Gutkind

JEREMY P. TARCHER/PUTNAM

a member of Putnam Penguin Inc.

New York

Most Tarcher/Putnam books are available at special quantity discounts
for bulk purchases for sales promotions, premiums, fund-raising, and
educational needs. Special books or book excerpts also can be created
to fit specific needs. For details, write or telephone Putnam Special
Markets, 200 Madison Avenue, New York, NY 10016; (212) 951-8891.

Jeremy P. Tarcher/Putnam
a member of
Penguin Putnam Inc.
200 Madison Avenue
New York, NY 10016

Library of Congress Cataloging-in-Publication Data

Surviving Crisis : twenty prominent authors write about events that shaped
their lives / edited by Lee Gutkind.
      p.   cm.—(Creative nonfiction reader series)
      ISBN 0-87477-889-1
      1. Authors, American—20th century—Psychology.   2. Authorship—
Psychological aspects.   3. Character.   4. Crises.   I. Gutkind, Lee.
II. Series.
      PS129.C75 1997   97–12387 CIP
      810.9'005—dc21
      [B]

Book design by Ralph L. Fowler
Cover design by Randall Freisen

Printed in the United States of America

10   9   8   7   6   5   4   3   2   1

Acknowledgments

I wish to thank the editorial board of *Creative Nonfiction*, Lea Simonds, Laurie Graham, and Patricia Park, managing editor Leslie Boltax Aizenman, and the Juliet Lea Hillman Simonds Foundation for ongoing support.

Contents

Surviving Crisis

A Search for Sanity

Lee Gutkind

For research into a book about the world of organ transplantation, I was granted unrestricted access to the largest transplant center in the world. Day and night, people literally on the edge of death arrived in ever-increasing numbers for the opportunity to be considered for a rare heart, liver or heart-lung transplant, including a little girl named Kellie Cochran and her mother, Judy. Although Kellie has been dead now for more than a decade, her image returns with unnerving clarity in my dreams.

I am sitting in the hospital playroom watching Rashad, a little Arab boy, attached to an intravenous unit like a puppy on a leash, blowing bubbles. He can't go far, but he covers his ground with nervous quickness. Soon, I turn my attention to Kellie, whose legs and arms are like twigs, but whose blue eyes sparkle with fascination. Instinctively, she reaches out to embrace the floating bubbles, which lazily evade her tiny, awkward grasp. The nurse comes in with Kellie's many medicines, loaded in narrow dispensers, and injects them one by one into her mouth. Kellie accepts each with a glazed-over annoyance. Medicine is nothing new for this little girl; medicine is something she has tolerated from the very beginning of her short and painful life.

A shot of pink drool suddenly spills from Kellie's mouth and rolls down her T-shirt. It is only noon, but this is the third outfit Kellie has ruined today. Kellie is crying as Judy, a preppy-looking woman with reddened eyes and disheveled blonde hair, slowly pushes herself up out of the chair in which she has been momentarily dozing and begins to undress her. This is what the little girl has wanted all along. Kellie's symptoms are not as pronounced as some of the other patients suffering from liver disease whom I have seen, but they are extraordinarily severe, nonetheless. She has the brownish-yellow cast—jaundice—and the bloated belly caused by the buildup of poisonous fluid and ammonia. Her arms and legs are next to nothing in size; my forefinger is nearly as wide as her wrist.

Kellie is two years old. For more than a year, she has weighed fifteen pounds. With her emaciated frame, I can't help thinking of concentration camp victims. For the past few months she has been waiting in the hospital for organs to materialize so that she can be transplanted. Her life is in imminent jeopardy. When her clothes come off, Kellie quiets down, and when Judy takes out the hairbrush, Kellie's eyes brighten slightly. "This," says Judy, "is Kellie's favorite toy."

Judy rubs the hairbrush over Kellie's little body, and for the first time I see more than simple signs of acceptance in Kellie's wondrous blue eyes. She is not capable of much emotion, but there is a flicker of pleasure and relief, at least momentarily. The incessant itching caused by liver disease is the greatest torment; adult patients have described the itching as unrelenting, radiating from the inside out. Kellie is not strong enough to put up much of a struggle, but when Judy attempts to dress her, Kellie begins to squirm and cry. Judy pauses to caress Kellie with the brush once more and then to apply some lotion to the little girl's arms and feet and hands. But every time she tries to put on the little shirt and overalls, Kellie screams louder. It is a slow, tedious process, but Judy knows what she is doing. If only Kellie will give an inch, allow her shirt to be slipped over her head, then Judy will scratch so that Kellie will relax, and Judy can gain more headway. A sleeve, a leg, a button. Sooner or later, Kellie is dressed.

Judy's life here is simple enough—and terrible. She changes Kellie's clothes four or five times a day, tries to snatch a couple of hours of fitful sleep. She talks to the nurses and attempts to feed Kellie, begging and cajoling her to eat. Before and after feeding, there is always bathing, and then oil applied to her skin every few hours. And in between everything, there is scratching with the hairbrush, forever scratching. Kellie also scratches on her own, digging desperately into her nose and ears, raking her tiny fingers through her scalp and picking at her feet. Two or three times a day, Judy lifts Kellie into the portable stroller and wheels her around the corridors—until, invariably, Kellie will spit up the food that has just been coaxed into her, forcing Judy to return to re-change Kellie's outfit and give another soothing session of therapeutic scratching. The rhythm is ongoing and relentless.

Judy and I don't talk too much. After all, I am a writer—what some people refer to as an "immersion journalist," involving myself in a subject or situation as a fly on the wall, observing but not participating. I am not supposed to allow my presence to affect the situation. Mostly, I witness her struggle with her dying daughter with admiring fascination. But once, when I am about to leave, I reach over and touch Judy's shoulder long enough for her to know that I respect her, and then I ask: "Is there anything I can get you? Anything you need?"

As usual, she is smiling, but her smile is now just a tight and twitching line across her pale and desperate face. "A little bit of sanity?" Her reply is posed as a question more than an answer, as if she were questioning her worthiness of such a modest gift.

I stare at her helplessly, drawing my shoulders up tightly against my neck in a slow and nervous shrug.

"Is that too much to ask?"

"No," I reply. "I guess not."

My ongoing memories of Kellie and Judy, and the decade of research I devoted to a hospital setting with people seeking sanity under enormous and unrelenting stress, helped me recognize and appreciate the ways in which strength of character and instinct for survival suddenly emerge in the face of adversity—even death. In many cases, people seem to become stronger and more resolute in their determination to prevail as the situation grows more pressured, dire and dangerous. By "prevail," I don't mean to sustain life, necessarily, but more often to die with dignity or to readjust to a philosophy which transcends frustrating irritations and live life for the moment—sometimes with laughter.

Marjorie Gross, whose *New Yorker* essay "Cancer Becomes Me" appears in this reader, provides five good points about being terminally ill, including: "People don't ask you to help them move" and "Everyone returns your phone calls immediately." You first learn about having cancer, Gross says, when the doctor walks in "and gives you the sympathetic head tilt that right away tells you, 'Don't buy in bulk.'" Gross was a lead writer for "Seinfeld" who died soon after her essay was published. Joan Mikulka Albert ("Counting on the Heart"), who is also terminally ill, clutches desperately to her sanity by refusing to allow the deterioration of her body to erode her spirit. "My body is a mess," she told me. "I'm ill, and I look it. But weirdly, the more damaged I am, the more fond of my body I become . . ."

Although this reader is not generally about death and dying, all of the essays have a special, sometimes subtle link to the search for or development of character. I believe that character is a muscle with which we are all born—a tiny button of flesh that must be flexed, strained, stretched on a regular basis in order for it to self-lubricate and grow. Character is a special muscle in that it is necessarily always taut, a rubber coil ready to spring instinctively into action whenever and wherever required. The unfortunate thing about the character muscle is that it is susceptible to shock and can be overloaded. In other words, it can freeze or lock the moment it is most needed or wanted. Unlocking the character muscle is one of life's greatest challenges, especially if it has been locked up for a long time. The writers and characters in this creative nonfiction reader are often being tested; some characters, such as the shop owners in Sandell Morse's "Canning Jars," fail miserably. Others discover hidden strength and admirable integrity, as did ten-year-old Natalie Kusz who somehow survived a vicious attack by wild dogs deep in the Alaskan wilderness.

Writing books about medicine and children, I have observed many kids like Kellie Cochran and Natalie Kusz under great stress and have been amazed at how simple, straightforward and courageous their responses are to pain, fear and confusion and to a variety of unexpected physical and emotional challenges. Certainly adults can and will respond in such a direct manner, but more so when an enemy or a challenge can be clearly determined and articulated. This scenario is captured quite graphically in the excerpt from John McPhee's paean to Alaska, *Coming Into the Country*, which details the incredible journey of Leon Crane—a lone airman, survivor of a crash landing in the middle of the tundra in the dead of winter. Crane, an engineer in civilian life, with little experience in the wilderness, lived four months on his own and eventually hiked back to civilization—a five-hundred-mile trek. Robert McCrum faced an equally terrifying battle for survival described in his essay, "My Old and New Lives," over the course of a day and night in his own home, alone, when he, a healthy man in his middle thirties, was suddenly, without warning, paralyzed—awake and unable to move.

Leon Crane and Robert McCrum were courageous and heroic; their ability to endure and survive was tested and proven in rare and overwhelming circumstances. Unfortunately, however, adult humans will often face more complicated, less delineated crises to overcome. In "Three Spheres" Lauren Slater returns to the psychiatric hospital in which she, only a few years before, was a long-term patient. But now she is a psychotherapist, assigned to treat a patient with a diagnosis similar to her own. In "The Break" Cynthia Ozick seeks emotional stability through psychic surgery by creating a daring metaphorical procedure in which she separates herself from the negative aspects of her past. Judy Ruiz's "The Mother, the Daughter, and the Holy Horse," which also partially takes place in a psychiatric setting, is a self-described "Trilogy" of incest, indignity and self-destruction that poses an all-encompassing emotional test of character of marathon proportions.

A marathon runner will hit what is called the wall at approximately the twentieth mile of a twenty-six-mile race. That's when the real test of mettle or character begins—or ends. Andre Dubus, who, while coming to the aid of a stranded motorist, is crushed on a darkened highway by a speeding car ("Lights of the Long Night"), hits the wall at the beginning of the essay, the marathon struggle of his entire life—and never stops struggling to prevail.

Survival needn't be represented by the winning of a race or contest or by the denial of death; a test of character measures an ability to prevail in the face of all-consuming crisis and to deal with the often far-reaching consequences of difficult circumstances. Kathy Dobie in "The Only Girl in the Car" survives an eerie and inexplicable obsession with adolescent promiscuity, but not the stinging memories of the indignities of those years, which will forever haunt her. Dominique, the young stripper in Lisa Hay's "immersion" essay, weakened by the sobering brutality of an abusive relationship, is fighting with all of her psychic strength to regain her confidence and emotional equilibrium.

It is no wonder that the heroic mother of my transplant dreams, Judy Cochran, asks for nothing less or nothing more than sanity, which can be the most steadfast and enduring reward—all we can hope for and expect—in the face of unrelenting trauma and suffering. In "Killing a Turtle" Joel Agee captures the dramatic impact of this struggle to remain in control of one's own emotional destiny as he describes a man in rural Kentucky joyfully impaling a turtle, while he (Agee) and the man's daughter are forced to watch. This incident occurred thirty years ago, but Agee is haunted by the memory of the little girl, Emily, "whose shoulders hunched up to her ears, her mouth open, the corners of her lips pulled way down, her arms cramped to her sides, her fingers splayed . . . If I were to paint a soul at the gate of hell, that is how I would picture it; right on the threshold, looking down, with nothing to hold her . . . But there is another figure in this tableau. It is me. I am just looking. Everything in me has turned cold, and in that coldness there is no pity, no pain, only the prayer for an end."

For writers, the genre of creative nonfiction is ideal for such emotionally wrenching scenarios; it demands a special, character-testing effort and challenge and, in contrast to traditional nonfiction, it invites and encourages the writer to become a character in the essay or article—to share emotions, feelings, ideas and to contribute an intellectual and often subjective substance to what can become a dangerously emotionless form. Thus, from both a personal and a literary point of view, creative nonfiction is the ultimate test of a writer's potential and range because it asks so much more in content and technique than any other genre. In addition to a writer's insight and reflection and in contrast to the traditional newspaper journalist, creative nonfiction writers skillfully employ literary techniques like scene-setting, dialogue, description, point of view. The essays in this collection read like short stories—smooth, fluent and powerful, structured with a tight action-oriented plot, fortified with believable and often charismatic characters to which readers will relate.

Of course, the characters are believable and the readers relate because these people are real—not a composite of a number of forms and faces. The people joining John Edgar Wideman at the gates of Western Penitentiary are the members of his family—the real names and faces of his mother, wife and children united by the horrible circumstances of their private reality in which a son, a favorite uncle, Wideman's younger brother, is a convicted murderer, sentenced to life; this is also Wideman's own personal search for sanity behind this gauntlet of gates and security checks. Creative nonfiction is the literature of reality.

Poetry and fiction, although believable and often seemingly very authentic, aren't expected to be true. Creative nonfiction is not only true—at least from the perception of the writer's experience—but also informational. Wideman begins his family's journey with a description and detailed history of the edifice in which his brother is incarcerated, while Reginald Gibbons introduces us to the frightening, ironic reality of Juvenile Court in Chicago a few days before Christmas. Of course, literary truth, in contrast to factual truth, is perceived and re-created through the lens of life experiences and the scars of frustration. In "Fat," Carol Kloss sits in a shopping mall with her charcoal and sketchbook "trying to catch in ten seconds the sling of a belly over a belt or the wobbly scallop of body rolls. The people in the mall get nervous when they see me drawing them," she writes, "but I don't think they know that on paper, they're not fat . . . they're powerful, not flabby; fascinating, not shocking, more human than any unpadded bones could ever be. Sometimes, I look at my own fat and hope that one day someone will draw me." Scott Murphy also draws his own self-portrait, reliving his life in combat in Vietnam ("Cold Sweat"), unable to distinguish between the reality of his life and his visions of what he hoped might have happened, which appear in vivid flashbacks in a string of soldier's nightmares.

Annie Dillard's remarkable "Expedition to the Pole" does not deny reality, as much as it bends and manipulates the genre—and demonstrates its great literary potential. Dillard, employing a parallel narrative, confronts the Catholic church while surveying the history of the exploration of the Arctic Circle, and the decline of the British empire. Throughout, Dillard is daring. At one point, in a flight of fantasy, she blends all of these diverse elements into one wild and brooding stew of ideas and implications in the middle of an ice floe. Inexplicably, she is wearing the uniform of a Keystone Kop.

Age is a theme and a barrier that surfaces in many of these essays—and in the overall revelation and resolution of strength and longevity of character. Florence Epstein's essay begins with her birthday ("Sixty") and the recollection of her dream of writing the great American novel in exile, in the tradition of Hemingway and Fitzgerald, and then returning to the United States in triumph. Epstein fails at both endeavors and suddenly, on her sixtieth birthday, finds herself stranded and nearly destitute in Spain, living with uneducated peasants who do not talk with her, understand her history or recognize her artistic motivations. As a writer, she is a failure—and yet, as a human being, she has found a way to survive; to preserve or to gain sanity which, in this context, can be defined as an acceptance of and a comfort with the circumstances of one's life, however disappointing.

Such is the essence of creative nonfiction generally and the overall objective of the pieces selected for this creative nonfiction reader, the first of many creative nonfiction readers, specifically: To maximize literary potential by telling a story about real people that embraces readers in a three-dimensional perspective, while providing writers the opportunity to push the boundaries of life, literature, philosophy, history, science and their own creative juices to the ultimate.

Kathy Dobie

This essay begins with simplicity and innocence, darkened by a subtle shadow of despair. The reader is intrigued not by what is happening on the first few pages but by the unspoken promise that something will happen — something troubling, and compelling. That promise is fulfilled. Scene after scene, Dobie walks an unnerving tightrope of increasingly promiscuous behavior. Dobie writes with an understated honesty. She combines the passion of the moment with a reflective three-dimensional distance, thus permitting a reader to see the story unfolding and suspend judgment until the very end.

The Only Girl in the Car

As a child, I courted simplicity and goodness. I'd fill a soup bowl with water, add leaves from the hedge, and eat it with a doll's spoon, slowly, until I was calm. The world was gorgeous and terrible—lightning, God, my father in a suit, the mere thought of my mother asleep . . . My passions disheveled me. At dusk, I could be found hiding in the lilac bushes, watching my younger sisters whirl around the yard. Their blonde manes, their shrieks and laughter left silver tracings in the air. My mother would come to the kitchen window to watch, her shadow springing across the lawn. I could feel her thoughts: Where is she? Why isn't she playing with her sisters? Crouched there, I felt unhealthy, crooked, a runt among golden lion cubs. Although my mother told us she wanted each of us to have our own personality, I had trouble finding a good one. I was the dreamer, the sloppy, forgetful girl. My solitude was seen as melancholy. Reluctantly, I would leave the lilacs and join my sisters in their loop-the-loops over the grass, wheeling through the window light and my mother's dark gaze, heavy-footed and grim where my sisters were wild and light.

My mother was nineteen when she married. Before she turned thirty she had six children, and before I turned two I was a big sister. I was the third child, but as the oldest daughter I was responsible for my two younger sisters and my baby brother. My responsibility plucked me from the happy, bloody tribe of my siblings, stripped me of innocence. I fretted and worried, held them and bossed them around. "This one's the oldest girl," my parents would say, and something would click shut in the eyes regarding me.

I was achingly aware of my mother's youth and big-boned beauty, the full lips painted red right before my father came home from his work as an administrator at Yale, the slender fingers playing "Try to Remember" on the piano, playing with such sadness I'd clutch myself and rock back and forth, wishing she would stop. My father came home with stories, comic and heroic adventures starring janitors and professors, politicians and cops. What a world lay outside our door! And my father was the man in the sharp suit gliding through cocktail parties and student riots, not a shadow of anxiety or doubt on him. On Sundays he took us to Yale. We wore our Sunday best, our prettiest smiles, and the rowdy, dangerous world my father knew would straighten itself up and smile politely back.

In a photo he took, my two sisters and I sit on the living-room floor by the fire, wearing lacy dresses. We've been caught dreaming; our faces are milky, stunned—caught in that vague sadness children sometimes feel when they've been kept up too late, too long in the adult world. It's a beautiful portrait, only I'm at the very edge and half my face is cut out. The camera was focused elsewhere. I didn't exist in Daddy's gaze; therefore, I was not a girl.

When my youngest brother, Stephen, was born, I carried him around for hours on my hip. I had a nanny's secret tenderness, her bitter pride; a fear of the day when others would see his value and take him from me. Except with Stephen, a kind of coldness surrounded me, a moat that couldn't be breached. When I was in my teens, my mother told me that I didn't seem to like being held or touched as a child—I cringed, I grew stiff—so she and my father made a decision not to. They would wait until I came to them. And they waited and waited. For it seems the touch I wanted wasn't familial, wasn't even "loving." That affection was for good little girls, and it made me feel like an impostor, made me lonelier.

In the attic bedroom I shared with three of my brothers and sisters, I caressed and kissed my pillow, calling it "Mark, honey, baby" after a crazy, vicious boy at St. Rita's grammar school. Mark was the only kid in the entire history of fourth grade to have shaved his head, tattooed himself with Nazi insignia, and worn rubber boots and a trench coat to school. I licked Mark Honey Baby, kissed him like I was sucking oranges. All the kids hated him. He was powerful and lonely. His glasses were broken and heavily taped, but he wore them like they were something dangerous: a car wreck, a baseball bat. I can see him now—little

Nazi prince clumping home from the schoolyard alone, his trench coat swirling around him like a cape. He was my ally in a world that seemed increasingly cold. Family barbecues, cars baking on the black tar of the mile-long shopping plaza, the endless stream of women and carts, exhortations to be happy, to join in the games . . . Life went cheerfully around and around while my visions grew monstrous. I wanted out. I wanted company.

I imagined the landscape outside family in part by watching my father's work life and in part by the books I read. I used to babysit for a family that had a huge library of porn. (In a *Playboy* cartoon, a doctor says it's time for a shot and if she's a good girl and doesn't cry, heh, heh, he'll give her something to suck on.) The idea of being an object of discussion, of lust, of trickery, of winks between men aroused me. My favorite books were written by women. I read for those moments when the sex kitten, the queen bee, the happy hooker caught his glance at the party, and she and he threaded their way out of the polite company and met panting, fumbling, straining in the dark hallway. These were my Cinderella stories.

Imagine us rolling across the country that summer of my fourteenth year, my father at the wheel of the huge motor home, Mother and my oldest brother playing co-pilot, Henry Mancini blaring from the speakers. I sat on the couch at the very back of the motor home by the window. Truckers blasted their horns. Men followed in their cars. I carried on conversations with them, first mouthing words, then writing notes. They rode our bumper so that we could read each other's words. In the middle of one such conversation with two men, they held up a sign that read: "JAILBAIT." I wrote a reply: "WANT TO GO FISHING?" There was a brief astonishment on their faces, and then they broke into laughter. They followed us for miles and miles of sunlit highway until we turned into a campground. They turned in after us, paying the campground fee, and then I got nervous. They were drawing into the family zone, too close.

They parked in the campsite next to ours, and when my father went out to hook up the electricity and water, the men started chatting with him, their eyes roving over the trailer door. My father noticed nothing, not even the fact that they were trailerless, tentless, extraordinarily idle. It was painful, this dumbness of his. Before I stepped from the motor home, I grabbed my baby brother's hand and dragged him with me like a prop. The men lit up like flares, but I bent down to Stephen and talked intently to him. I played with him, keeping close to the motor home, occasionally casting a look at the men, a look like a rope that said, "Hold on." I stroked Stephen's hair lingeringly. I hoped some courage or form of action would occur to me. Perhaps by nighttime, when my family had fallen asleep. But the two men left the campground in an angry scud of pebbles and exhaust smoke, and I'd gone from being the most desirable bit of jailbait in the world to a stupid tease.

Back home, in August, my father's friend from work sat on our couch as my father showed him photos from our vacation. He came to one of me, posed on a rock in a black bathing suit. "Cheesecake," the man said. And the word hung there, porous, crumbling, glittering over the coffee table, the blue-green shag carpet, the piano. My father cleared his throat. His laugh was startled, embarrassed. He didn't send a glance my way. He pulled out the next photo.

"Cheesecake" was a door opening, but I walked through it alone. "Cheesecake" was stamped on my flesh in an ink that glowed. My parents, my sisters and brothers, seemed to notice nothing. But men heard my message loud and clear; they understood it perfectly.

One morning I missed the bus and walked to school, late and happy about it. I was wearing my Catholic schoolgirl uniform, the plaid skirt and kneesocks, but I pushed the socks down around my ankles, rolled the skirt up short, and undid the top three buttons on my blouse. A man stopped his car—did I want a ride? He was in his forties and dressed for golf. His dress was corny to me, even creepy, but his confidence was laid on thick. His eyes were bold, blue, and amused.

He drove me to school and picked me up that afternoon, suggesting we get ice-cream cones. He wore a belt, drove a car, had a thick wallet—how can I capture what a grown man feels like to a girl? He was a man, and his flesh was pale and heavy, disgusting and exciting. He was incredibly casual about his maleness. Even when he wasn't looking at me, even when he was busy ordering the cones and paying and driving the car, I felt his awareness of me, his plans for me on my skin. It was more exciting than being touched.

The next time we went out, I wore a black, backless sundress. I laced my wedged-heel shoes up my ankles. I wore the dress without jewelry so that I wouldn't hide its true intent. After he picked me up (I no longer remember his name), he brought me directly to his condo. He didn't work, he played golf; he lived on a trust fund. The rooms were pin neat—no dust, no music, no windows cracked open to the outside—and the things he talked about left me tongue-tied: golfing tournaments, tennis, money. Except for the huge mystery of what might happen next, an event completely in his hands, I would have been extraordinarily bored. But I was too nervous to be bored; my whole body was humming.

He suggested a massage and told me to take my shoes off and lie down on the bed. I couldn't see his face when he said sarcastically, "Aren't you going to take your pantyhose off?" He said it like I was being a scared prude. To pull them off was to shed feminine cowardice, male disgust. So I did. Then he told me to loosen my dress. And that seemed to be enough for him, to massage me as I lay there in my girl's white underwear.

At home, I opened the venetian blinds to let in the sun. Spring, summer, beaches, parks, barbecues, back-slapping sunshine—my family thrived in bright light, warm days, togetherness. A desire for darkness, for aloneness, was sick. I was sick. So when the time came, none of the ugliness of sex astonished me: the hickey made with sour breath and brown teeth that became infected a few days later, the hands shoving my legs into the right position, the grunt of loveless coming. I cringed at none of it. "Jailbait," the men named me, laughing together. And the thing they named tried out its new voice. "Want to go fishing?" Bait asked slyly. I became as oily and dirty as the moment called for. Rarely did a boy have to make it pretty for me.

I remember a moment of absolute clarity before the storm of boys, fingers, dirty words whispered hotly in my ear, then howled to my face. One Saturday morning I stepped out the door of my parents' house in Hamden, Connecticut, wearing a candy-striped halter top, hiphugger jeans, and platform shoes, went out the front door, and sat down in the middle of the lawn. If my mother was watching, I was, finally, unaware of her. I was going to lose my virginity. The family dog sat at my side. I stroked and knotted his fur. Cars sped by, honking. Boys hissed, whistled, blew kisses, yelled. If they were caught at the red light, they became shy, though one boy wagged his tongue at me like a pendulum, and then ran it, slowly, up the window.

It was a full-grown man who finally stopped. He did a U-turn, parked in front of the house, and got out. He made his way over to me, long hair swinging, eyes pretending friendliness. Robert was thirty-three.* It didn't matter that I wasn't attracted to him. He was what other girls would have called "sleazy," a loser: he still lived with his mother, he was picking up fourteen-year-olds. But to see that man's tight-jeaned, T-shirted form gliding through the grass, intent on me and *mine* in ways that I didn't yet understand . . .

He smiled cagily, nodded at the house. "You live here?" Then, "Your parents home?" He crouched down in the grass and picked at a blade. "So you're just hanging out with your dog?" He circled me with questions, patronizing, nervous as a thief. "Do you want to go to the movies sometime?" he asked. And when I said sure, he said, "Uh, what are you doing tonight?" And he came and picked me up at my parents' house.

I don't know how I dressed for the occasion. I know that I had no idea what sex might be like, though I had the vocabulary. I thought sex was going to be something you'd like no matter who you did it with. We left the movie right after it started and drove to a small empty lot behind a brick building. He had trouble getting it in and kept asking, "Are you sure you aren't a virgin?"

"I've had lots of boys," I told him. I wasn't just lying, I was bragging. He told me to stay still.

I could say my first sexual experience was disappointing, but that misses the point. I had posed and passed my own initiation rite into the world—losing my virginity. Now I was free. I walked down Treadwell Street the next day licking my lips. That was a signal, too. I wanted boys to know that I'd had sex, and that I was now open to them.

* For obvious reasons, some names have been changed.

I walked the three blocks to the Teen Center, a small brick building that used to be a firehouse, owned and operated by the town of Hamden. I sat down on the curb across the street and waited until the kids drifted over. The boys came first. They had shaggy heads and wore dungaree jackets. They invited me across the street, and we hung out in front of the center. The girls eyed me more closely, but there was no trouble that night. I sat there smoking while the laughter and talk closed in around me. Just like that, I was taken in.

Even that night, it was the boys who made me feel at home—the way they goofed around and told tall tales of cops and drugs and cars and someone's father chasing one of them with a baseball bat. Their scattered, coarse energy warmed me, entertained me, let me in but asked no questions, made no examination. There was something very democratic about the boys, and from then on I always hung out with a group of them, the only girl in the car.

Men had ushered me into my sexuality, but I wanted boys—boys with light in their eyes, hoarse voices, hard arms, silky chests, bodies that were my size. And the boys I wanted were the bad ones—the confident, aggressive, dirty-minded ones. They put me at ease, and the willfulness of their desire turned me on. Timidity, efforts to converse, dates for pizza, the nicely dressed boy at the door made me feel awkward and dirty. The bad boy was sneaky, clever, always thinking one step ahead. He was kissing me, whispering, "Baby, baby," while he raised his hips to unzip his pants, and then fiddled with the snap on my jeans, all the time acting as if I might be so preoccupied with his tongue and his voice that I wouldn't notice what was going on below. I didn't even mind that they assumed they were tricking and pushing me into sex. I was dangerously careless about their opinion of me.

At the Teen Center there was a group of boys who were rougher, rowdier, cooler than the rest. Most of them were high-school dropouts and had juvenile records—drunk and disorderly, vandalism, maybe a few B&Es. Usually they just shot their mouths off, got drunk, fought, ran their cars into things. Once they set one of the couches in the center on fire and pushed it down the stairs into the basement.

The girlfriends of these boys hung out together, all very pretty girls. It was their boyfriends I was messing around with. I was so new to the center, so swept away by the boys themselves, that I didn't even know they had girlfriends. And although I must have heard these girls talk happily about "kicking ass," I didn't think it had anything to do with me. I spent very little time at the center, and I wasn't there to make new girlfriends. I'd arrive, and a few minutes later I'd be taking off with a boy or a gang of them.

Tony was my first boy. He was Puerto Rican, but everything about him said white frat boy. He had black wiry hair and thick lips, a squat wrestler's build. Tony never bothered with any preliminaries. He picked me up, went straight to the park, kissed me, got my clothes off, and got on top of me.

Every night for nine nights we were in the back seat of Tony's car. One day I skipped school and we went into the woods across from my parents' house, and he spread out a blanket. I thought Tony and I were girlfriend and boyfriend then. I must have mentioned that idea to him, because he sneered, "You're not my girlfriend. I've got a real girlfriend and she won't even let me *kiss* her." I was shocked that he had a girlfriend and that *not* kissing made her real. It was exactly the opposite of what I fiercely believed to be true. There was the daytime world, the public world, in which we all had families, went to school, took directions from adults, and lied all the time without even thinking about it. We had faces, not thoughts or feelings. Sex blew this world open, and the blank-faced boy lit up, stuck out his tongue, and wagged it at me. I thought that boy was the real boy. When Tony told me I wasn't his girlfriend I felt a hurt, a humiliation that I immediately tossed out, rode over. I went on to the next boy.

How many boys altogether? It doesn't seem like all that many, not if you watch the talk shows. Maybe nine or ten in seven months' time. Almost all of my early sexual experiences were with boys who wanted me and hated me for it, boys who thought their desires were dirty and were quick to put that dirtiness on me. That peculiar mix of lust and loathing, the light in their eyes, the brusqueness of their hands, the begging and then sneering, the whimpering and then boasting—that was sex as I knew it. Not what I had expected, but there was a striking kind of shamelessness to me, and I took all comers. I was looking for experience and that feeling of being in the middle of things. I liked the rush, the willfulness of boys' desire. I admired them for it. I liked to feel them hard under their pants, the tender urgency, the focus on me that disregarded me. And if I wasn't concerned with what the others were thinking of me, it was because I wasn't seeing myself from their point of view. It never would have occurred to me that sex was only a boy's adventure. I just kept going, hungry and excited, despite the talk around me, the approaching trouble.

I must have driven the other girls mad. They heard what the boys said, the contempt in their voices; they shrieked at the dirty jokes. And then they'd see one of those boys come into the Teen Center to get me, and off I'd go with a grin and a wave. They hated me for getting away with it.

One night, the four black boys at the Teen Center told me they wanted to talk to me and asked me to take a ride with them. I only remember Craig and Fat Roscoe. Craig was tall, whiplike, genial. Fat Roscoe was indeed fat, wrinkled with it, like a bulldog. He had gold teeth and carried a walking stick. Roscoe made ugly cool, cooler than any white-boy prettiness. Behind his back, the other kids constantly referred to him as "the coon." They were afraid of him, and they loved him. He was like some kind of mascot, he so perfectly fulfilled their idea of a nigger.

Craig drove that night, Roscoe sat in front, and I got in the back with the other two boys. As soon as we hit Hamden's main drag, they began. "Kath, everybody's talking about you," Roscoe said. Craig added, "You've got to be careful, you're getting a rep." They told me not to trust the others, but I was sticking my face out the window, letting the wind push my smile away. A rep. A shadow, a ripple. Something's there before you enter a room and after you're gone. I couldn't have been happier. My name would have the force, the thunder of Roscoe's walking stick, thumped down every time he took a step.

He and Craig advised me to slow down, watch out. There was nothing judgmental in their words, nothing that said I was wrong and dirty, or that having sex was. It was all about the treacherous company I was keeping. To this day, I marvel at their goodness; I still don't understand it. Four boys in a car with me? They could have done anything they wanted—that's the kind of girl I was—and yet all they tried to do was protect me.

Joey was the last Teen Center boy with whom I had sex willingly. Joey with his crazy, movie-star grin, his stubbly jaw, and his many fuckups. There wasn't a mean bone in Joey's body. He was just a hapless bad boy.

Joey and I drove around in his beat-up Chevy for hours, usually with a gang of boys. I sat next to him under the curve of his arm, being pulled into his body every time he took a corner. I had the usual schoolgirl crushes—on his brown, scarred leather jacket, his blue-green eyes and dark lashes, the Marlboro hanging from his lips. With one hand on the wheel and the other around me, he couldn't very well hold his cigarette, and he didn't have to. He squinted his eyes and smoked. I took it from him once in a while, tapped out the ashes, and, taking a drag, put it back in his mouth, holding my fingers against his lips as he puckered for it.

He worked in his father's gas station, and we spent every night together. On Sundays, we used to go visit a woman named Patty, who worked at the Teen Center. She was big and fleshy with hair down to her hips, and had a black boyfriend from New Haven. They were always in bed when we arrived, me and Joey and a few of the boys. We'd raid their refrigerator and then, Cokes in hand, pull chairs up around their bed.

Patty and her lover spoke in the laziest tones, and you could feel their pleasure, naked under the white sheets and our gaze. She'd lean back against him and he'd reach over her to grab the menthols from her night table, pausing, it seemed, to let us see his black arm against her marshmallow skin. He was all ripples, lean and long, and she was a mountain of whipped cream. That was our Sunday service, Joey and me, worshiping at their bed. (She got fired shortly after the boys burned the couch and threw it down the stairs. An earnest and tousled-looking man named Steve took her place.)

Then we just tooled around town, Gladys Knight on the tape deck, Joey singing the words to me. He called me "babe," and I tried out all the names I'd been keeping on the tip of my tongue: "sugar," "honey," "baby," "lover." He had a girlfriend, too, but she was like his mother, something we both disregarded.

At the end of the night, the boys would be dropped off somewhere, and Joey and I would head to East Rock Park. I can still remember his hard jaw, the stubble underneath my hand, and his lips, kind of hard, a *man's* lips, his tongue smoky and muscular inside my mouth. After we had sex, he'd drive me home and be there again the next afternoon. If he ran into my parents, he'd be as charming and clumsy as a shaggy dog, but to me he was the epitome of masculinity.

That last night with Joey began as all our nights began, a car full of boys and me. Joey at the wheel, me by his side. Pete and Bob and another boy in the back with a bottle of gin, a case of beer in the trunk. For many years I couldn't remember the fourth boy, though I think it was Ronny. And I'll never be sure of the order. I know we drove into the park and it was filled with snow and Joey's car was a boat rocking over drifts, plowing through the woods, churning up clouds. We drank, we told war stories, we laughed. Then Joey began to kiss me in front of the boys, his hand sliding up my shirt, his breathing coming harder. He wanted us to have sex. He said the boys could leave the car, and the boys said they would.

Everybody got out, and Joey and I slipped into the back seat. They took the bottle, and while Joey was on top of me I could hear them talking and laughing. After a while, they started stamping their feet in the snow and shouting for us to hurry up. I can only imagine their excitement, only imagine what it felt like to stand outside that car, its windows steamed over, the music pumping, picturing what was going on inside. They must have thought of themselves in Joey's place and why couldn't they be there?

Joey was shining when we finished, and after he let the boys back in he kept calling me his baby with that happy, grateful look on his face. Then the negotiations began to let his friends have a taste. What exactly was said, how long it went on, I don't know. I only remember his saying, "I want them to see how good you are, babe" and, "Do it for me, babe. Don't you love me?" It doesn't matter what was said, only that it came out of Joey's mouth and that no other world existed for me that night—just those boys, that car in the snowy woods. That was the moment when everything that had been said about me became real, when I gave up.

I think Pete must have gone first. He was in his thirties, and bolder than Ronny or Bob. I got into the back seat again, Ronny and Bob crowded in front with Joey, and Pete climbed in after me. When Pete was on top of me, Joey held my hand and told me he loved me. I cried. After Pete came inside me, he sat next to me and pushed my head down. I threw up. Pete jumped out of the car, cursing me, and the boys broke into laughter. The next boy wasn't hard and had to take his fingers and push himself inside of me. When the fourth one was on top of me, huffing in my hair, I began to scream that I couldn't breathe, and then they stopped.

More beers were cracked open. I dressed. Bent down in the back seat, into the darkness near the floor, I pulled my pantyhose up over each foot. Above me, the boys laughed and talked loudly, exhilarated—and, perhaps, nervous. I stayed hidden in the dark well of the floor, stretching the hose up over my legs, feeling that it was incredibly ugly, the pale pasty color of it, called "nude," the white pad at the crotch so sanitary, so modest.

The boys drove me home, swearing no one would know about that night, and I stepped out of the car, out of the back seat this time, headed up the driveway toward the dim kitchen light, tripped and fell over a snowbank.

The next day, I put on my fake leather jacket with its fake fur collar, walked the three blocks to the Teen Center, and when I entered the place broke apart. The girls sitting on the floor began to open and shut their legs in some grotesque imitation of sex. Kids crowded in from the pool room in back. "Look who's fucking here!" "Look at the bitch, coming in here after . . ." "Gang bang!" Their astonishment and delight couldn't have been keener. My vision refracted (a problem I'd have from then on), and as bizarre as the scene was it became more so, with faces split in two and revolving in front of me, wagging tongues, eyes, legs bouncing and snapping back and forth. Steve, the new director of the center, came hurrying in, pulled me into his office in back, and told me I'd have to leave—the kids had spent the day planning to beat me up.

He said he'd drive me home but we had to go *now.* He didn't understand why I'd come back there after last night, but he told me to stick close, and he rushed us through the throng of bodies, out the front door to where his car was parked. The kids massed outside, screaming "douche bag!" and "cunt!" A snowball hit my back, and some old movie, a western perhaps, came to me, and I turned around and faced them, looked them straight in the eye— whap! a snowball hit my chest and splattered on to my face. Then there was a torrent of them, and I ducked into the car and Steve drove me to my house, dropping me off with the advice that I no longer needed: not to return.

I went through the kitchen—"hi, honey!" and straight up-stairs, and began to count the years, the months, then the weeks before I could leave Hamden.

I spent a lot of time over the next two years perched on my bed, looking out the attic window at the intersection and its blinking traffic light. My youngest sister says I carried a switchblade when I went out, and told her I had enemies, but I don't remember that. I still had to go to school and do errands; everything had changed but the family routine. I'd hop on my bicycle and pedal to the grocery store as fast as I could, telling myself that if I could run the wheel straight over a leaf in the road it meant I could win a fight with half a dozen girls.

They found me on street corners. They came piling out of cars, howling, "We're gonna kick your ass!" I never got used to it, though that particular look on their faces—the lively disgust, the sheer joy of hating—became very familiar. Strange boys sprouted from the sidewalk (always with a gang of friends) and announced, "I fucked you." What good was it saying, "I don't even know who you are"? I tried that once and got machine-gun laughter, and the reply, "Well, then how the fuck do I know you?" I became the route by which timid boys lost their virginity without losing their timidity.

When I finally got to drive, I drove fast, dressed down, and hung out at old men's bars where no one would find me. I began to listen to classical music, though only Rachmaninoff was sweeping and sentimental enough for my teenage heart.

. . .

Without sex I felt deaf, dumb, and blind. So in spite of the heavy shame I now felt, the attacks of panic and guilt that often overtook me, I kept on, though now my lovers were older; they were men, white, black, and Puerto Rican men, men from New Haven. At sixteen and seventeen, I worked in the kitchens at Yale, trying to make enough money to move to New York as soon as I finished high school. I was a pot-washer, a prep cook, a stockroom girl, and a general service assistant, unloading hundred-pound bags of rice and potatoes from trucks and sweeping up storerooms. Although they bordered each other, New Haven seemed worlds away from Hamden. The physical labor was a relief from my dark thoughts, and I was the only girl in a crew of men.

I went out with a work-study student from Brooklyn. He would hop on his battered bicycle and pedal out of Yale's lit courtyards, down Whitney Avenue, past the reservoir, the darkened pharmacy and beauty parlor, the graveyard at the end of Treadwell Street, and in twenty minutes arrive at the kitchen door when my family was asleep. I loved him, but I wouldn't let him go all the way. In his medieval dorm room, we took off our T-shirts and traded them with each other. We compared our bodies; we clutched and rolled around his bed for hours, limbs aching, blood thudding.

A grizzled, gray-haired biker guessed something about me, and when we pulled out of my parents' driveway, he stopped the bike, turned to me, and said, "Kath, you've got to hold on to me or you'll fall off the bike. I don't know what the boys did to you, but I'm not going to do anything, okay?" And he would sweep me far away from Hamden and into farm fields. After all our rides, we went to his rented room and drank tea.

But the white boys of Hamden had one last message for me. The summer was steaming to a close, and I was going to New York in a week. Because I was leaving town, because of my job and the men of New Haven, I took a chance. I had the audacity to believe that I was finally free of Hamden, that my sexuality belonged to me, that people forget.

I finished up my work and went to the basement lockers to change out of my uniform. I put on the black backless sundress, the wedge-heeled shoes that laced up my ankles—no jewelry, but a bag to carry my other clothes in. On the New Haven green,

Stan Kenton was playing and families were picnicking on the grass. I sat on a bench at the border of the green, a sidewalk running between the families and me. I saw the boys coming from far away. "Don't be stupid. It can't be," I told myself. "It was so long ago. Nobody cares anymore."

There were eight of them, and they headed straight across the green, stepping around blankets, children, never looking down, until they stood in front of me. Their leader had a rubbery, clam-shaped face that I recognized but couldn't place. (Years later, I'd remember he was my oldest brother's friend, someone who went on family picnics with us when we were kids and had once almost drowned me in a lake; a Catholic schoolboy.) He had an ugly grin on his face. He named my brother and asked if I was his sister. I shook my head rapidly. "I don't know who you're talking about." He laughed and asked again, and again I denied it.

They were all laughing now, their faces filled with disgust, and the ringleader said, "Come on, we know who you are!" And he dug into his pocket, fished up some change, and held it out to me. "There's only eight of us," he said. "This should be enough for you to do each of us." I got up and walked away fast. "Fucking dirtbag!" "Go back to Howe Street where you belong, you cunt," they shouted, naming the street in New Haven where the prostitutes worked. The coins came flying at me, some of them hitting my bare back. On the green, people stared, and I thought they clutched their children to them. Even then, I knew these boys were still virgins and that they hated me for going, again and again, to the place they feared to tread. I knew how much pleasure it gave them to hurt a girl, to poke her and see her twitch, more pleasure than making love to her. I told myself to walk, just keep walking out of that town, that present, and into the future. I told myself the world was out there, just a little farther out than I'd thought at fourteen—New York, not Hamden—and that I still had a chance to enter it.

John McPhee

In a career spanning three decades at The New Yorker magazine and with more than twenty published books, John McPhee, perhaps more than any other writer, has been instrumental in elevating creative nonfiction, a fact-based genre, to an art form. McPhee's work is grounded in reality, as is any reporter's; yet he possesses an uncanny ability to unearth marvelous true stories that have never been told. When he writes these stories, McPhee will rarely include himself as a character — only when his insight adds substantially to the narrative, as in this excerpt from his book about Alaska, Coming into the Country, which describes in sparkling and uncanny detail the incredible journey of Leon Crane.

The Incredible Journey of Leon Crane

The country is full of stories of unusual deaths—old Nimrod Robertson lying down on a creek in overflow and letting it build around him a sarcophagus of ice; the trapper on the Kandik who apparently knocked himself out when he tripped and fell on his own firewood and froze to death before he came to—and of stories also of deaths postponed. There are fewer of the second. I would like to add one back—an account that in essence remains in the country but in detail has largely disappeared.

On a high promontory in the montane ruggedness around the upper Charley River lies the wreckage of an aircraft that is readily identifiable as a B-24. This was the so-called Liberator, a medium-range bomber built for the Second World War. The wreckage is in the dead center of the country, and I happened over it in a Cessna early in the fall of 1975, during a long and extremely digressive flight that began in Eagle and ended many hours later in Circle. The pilot of the Cessna said he understood that the crew of the Liberator had bailed out, in winter, and that only one man had survived. I asked around to learn who might know more than that—querying, among others, the Air Force in Fairbanks, the Gelvins, various old-timers in Circle and Central, some of the river people, and Margaret Nelson, in Eagle, who had packed parachutes at Ladd Field, in Fairbanks, during the war. There had been one survivor—everyone agreed. No one knew his name. He had become a symbol in the country, though, and was not about to be forgotten. It was said that he alone had come out—long after all had been assumed dead—because he alone, of the widely scattered crew, was experienced in wilderness, knew how to live off the land, and was prepared to deal with the hostile cold. Above all, he had found a cabin, during his exodus, without which he would have died for sure.

"And the government bastards try to stop us from building them now."

"Guy jumped out of an airplane, and he would have died but he found a cabin."

If the survivor had gone on surviving for what was now approaching thirty-five years, he would in all likelihood be somewhere in the Lower Forty-eight. When I was home, I made a try to find him. Phone calls ricocheted around Washington for some days, yielding only additional phone numbers. The story was just too sketchy. Did I know how many bombers had been lost in that war? At length, I was given the name of Gerard Hasselwander, a historian at the Albert F. Simpson Historical Research Center, Maxwell Air Force Base, Alabama. I called him, and he said that if I did not even know the year of the crash he doubted he could help me. Scarcely two hours later, though, he called back to say that he had had a free moment or two at the end of his lunch hour and had browsed through some microfilm. To his own considerable surprise, he had found the survivor's name, which was Leon Crane. Crane's home when he entered the Army Air Forces had been in Philadelphia, but Hasselwander had looked in a Philadelphia directory and there was no Leon Crane in it now. However, he said, Leon Crane had had two brothers who were also in service—in the Army Medical Corps—during the Second World War. One of them was named Morris. In the Philadelphia directory, there was a Dr. Morris Crane.

When I called the number, someone answered and said Dr. Crane was not there.

I asked when he would return.

"I don't know," was the reply. "He went to Leon's."

The Liberator, making cold-weather propeller tests above twenty thousand feet, went into a spin, dived toward the earth, and, pulling out, snapped its elevator controls. It then went into another spin, and the pilot gave the order to abandon ship. There were five aboard. Leon Crane was the co-pilot. He was twenty-four and he had been in Alaska less than two months. Since the plane was falling like a swirling leaf, he had to drag himself against heavy centrifugal force toward the open bomb bay. He had never used a parachute. The outside air temperature was at least thirty degrees below zero. When he jumped, he forgot his mittens. The day was December 21st.

The plane fiercely burned, not far away from where he landed, and he stood watching it, up to his thighs in snow. He was wearing a hooded down jacket, a sweater, winter underwear, two pairs of trousers, two pairs of socks, and felt-lined military mukluks. He scanned the mountainsides but could see nothing of the others. He thought he had been the second one to go out of the plane, and as he fell he thought he saw a parachute open in the air above him. He shouted into the winter silence. Silence answered. Months later, he would learn that there had been two corpses in the aircraft. Of the two other fliers no track or trace was ever found. "Sergeant Pompeo, the crew chief, had a hell of a thick set of glasses. He must have lost them as soon as he hit the airstream. Without them, he really couldn't see. What was he going to do when he got down there?"

For that matter, what was Crane going to do? He had no food, no gun, no sleeping bag, no mittens. The plane had been meandering in search of suitable skies for the tests. Within two or three hundred miles, he had no idea where he was.

Two thousand feet below him, and a couple of miles east, was a river. He made his way down to it. Waiting for rescue, he stayed beside it. He had two books of matches, a Boy Scout knife. He started a fire with a letter from his father, and for the first eight days he did not sleep more than two hours at a time in his vigilance to keep the fire burning. The cold awakened him anyway. Water fountained from a gap in the river ice, and that is what he lived on. His hands, which he to some extent protected with parachute cloth or in the pockets of his jacket, became cut and abraded from tearing at spruce boughs. When he spread his fingers, the skin between them would split. Temperatures were probably ranging between a high of thirty below zero and a low around fifty. The parachute, as much as anything, kept him alive. It was twenty-eight feet in diameter, and he wound it around him so that he was at the center of a great cocoon. Still, he said, his back would grow cold while his face roasted, and sparks kept igniting the chute.

He was telling me some of this on a sidewalk in Philadelphia when I asked him how he had dealt with fear.

He stopped in surprise, and looked contemplatively up the street toward Independence Hall, his graying hair wisping out to the sides. He wore a business suit and a topcoat, and he had bright, penetrating eyes. He leaned forward when he walked. "Fear," he repeated. "I wouldn't have used that word. Think about it: there was not a hell of a lot I could do if I were to panic. Besides, I was sure that someone was going to come and get me."

All that the search-and-rescue missions had to go on was that the Liberator had last been heard from above Big Delta, so the search area could not be reduced much below forty thousand square miles. Needless to say, they would not come near finding him. He thought once that he heard the sound of an airplane, but eventually he realized that it was a chorus of wolves. In his hunger, he tried to kill squirrels. He made a spear, and threw it awkwardly as they jumped and chattered in the spruce boughs. He made a bow and arrow, using a shroud line from his parachute, but when he released the arrow it shot off at angles ridiculously oblique to the screeching, maddening squirrels. There was some rubber involved in the parachute assembly, and he used that to make a slingshot, which was worse than the bow and arrow. When he fell asleep by the fire, he dreamed of milkshakes, dripping beefsteaks, mashed potatoes, and lamb chops, with lamb fat running down his hands. Awake, he kicked aside the snow and found green moss. He put it in his mouth and chewed, and chewed some more, but scarcely swallowed any. Incidentally, he was camped almost exactly where, some twenty-five years later, Ed and Virginia Gelvin would build a cabin from which to trap and hunt.

Crane is a thoroughly urban man. He grew up in the neighborhood of Independence Hall, where he lives now, with an unlisted number. That part of the city has undergone extensive refurbishment in recent years, and Crane's sons, who are residential builders and construction engineers, have had a part in the process. Crane, more or less retired, works for them, and when I visited him I followed him from building to building as he checked on the needs and efforts of carpenters, bricklayers, plumbers. He professed to have no appetite for wild country, least of all for the expanses of the north. As a boy, he had joined a city Scout troop, and had become a First Class Scout, but that was not to suggest a particular knowledge of wilderness. When he flew out of Fairbanks that morning in 1943, his lifetime camping experience consisted of one night on the ground—with his troop, in Valley Forge.

He decided on the ninth day that no help was coming. Gathering up his parachute, he began to slog his way downriver, in snow sometimes up to his waist. It crossed his mind that the situation might be hopeless, but he put down the thought as he moved from bend to bend by telling himself to keep going because "right around that curve is what you're looking for." In fact, he was about sixty miles from the nearest human being, almost a hundred from the nearest group of buildings large enough to be called a settlement. Around the next bend, he saw more mountains, more bare jagged rock, more snow-covered sweeps of alpine tundra, contoured toward another river bend. "Right around that curve is what you're looking for," he told himself again. Suddenly, something was there. First, he saw a cache, high on legs in the air, and then a small cabin, with a door only three feet high. It was like the lamb chops, with the grease on his fingers, but when he pushed at the door it was wood and real. The room inside was nine by ten: earth floor, low ceiling, a bunk made of spruce. It was Alaskan custom always to leave a cabin open and stocked for anyone in need. Split firewood was there, and matches, and a pile of prepared shavings. On a table were sacks of dried raisins, sugar, cocoa, and powdered milk. There was a barrel stove, frying pans on the wall. He made some cocoa, and, after so long a time without food, seemed full after a couple of sips. Then he climbed a ladder and looked in the cache, lifting a tarp to discover hammers, saws, picks, drills, coiled rope, and two tents. No one, he reasoned, would leave such equipment far off in the wilderness. "I figured civilization was right around the corner. I was home free."

So he stayed just a night and went on down the river, anxious to get back to Ladd Field. The moon came up after the brief light of day, and he kept going. He grew weak in the deep cold of the night, and when the moon went below the mountains he began to wander off the stream course, hitting boulders. He had been around many corners, but no civilization was there. Now he was sinking into a dream-hazy sleepwalking numbed-out oblivion; but fear, fortunately, struck through and turned him, upriver. He had not retraced his way very far when he stopped and tried to build a fire. He scraped together some twigs, but his cut and bare hands were shaking so—at roughly fifty below zero—that he failed repeatedly to ignite a match. He abandoned the effort, and moved on through the snow. He kept hitting boulders. He had difficulty following his own tracks. He knew now that he would die if he did not get back to the cabin, and the detached observer within him decided he was finished. Left foot, right foot—there was no point in quitting, even so. About noon, he reached the cabin. With his entire body shaking, he worked at a fire until he had one going. Then he rolled up in his parachute and slept almost continuously for three full days.

In his excitement at being "right around the corner from civilization," he had scarcely looked in the cache, and now he found rice, flour, beans, powdered eggs, dried vegetables, and beef— enough for many weeks, possibly months. He found mittens. He found snowshoes. He found long johns, socks, mukluks. He found candles, tea, tobacco, and a corncob pipe. He found ammunition, a .22. In the cabin, he mixed flour, peas, beans, sugar, and snow, and set it on the stove. That would be his basic gruel— and he became enduringly fond of it. Sometimes he threw in eggs and vegetables. He covered his hands with melted candle wax, and the bandage was amazingly effective. He developed a routine, with meals twice a day, a time for hunting, a fresh well chopped daily through the four-foot river ice. He slept eighteen hours a day, like a wintering bear—not truly hibernating, just lying there in his den. He felt a need to hear a voice, so he talked to himself. The day's high moment was a pipeful of tobacco puffed while he looked through ten-year-old copies of *The Saturday Evening Post*. He ransacked the magazines for insights into the woods lore he did not know. He learned a thing or two. In a wind, it said somewhere in the *Post*, build your fire in a hole. He shot and ate a ptarmigan, and had the presence of mind to look in its stomach. He found some overwintering berries there, went to the sort of bushes they had come from, and shot more ptarmigan. Cardboard boxes, the magazines, and other items in the cabin were addressed to "Phil Berail, Woodchopper, Alaska." Contemplating these labels, Crane decided that Alaska was a fantastic place—where someone's name and occupation were a sufficient address. One day, an old calendar fell off the wall and flipped over on its way to the floor. On the back was a map of Alaska. He stared at it all day. He found Woodchopper, on the Yukon, and smiled at his foolishness. From the terrain around him, the northward flow of the stream, the relative positions of Fairbanks and Big Delta, he decided—just right—that he was far up the Charley River. The smile went back where it came from.

He decided to wait for breakup, build a raft, and in late May float on down to the Yukon. After five or six weeks, though, he realized that his food was going to give out in March. There was little ammunition with which to get meat, and he had no confidence anyway in his chances with the rifle. If he stayed, he would starve. He felt panic now, but not enough to spill the care with which he was making his plans. He had set off willy-nilly once before and did not want to repeat the mistake. He patched his clothes with parachute cloth, sewing them with shroud lines. He made a sled from some boards and a galvanized tub. He figured closely what the maximum might be that he could drag and carry. On February 12th, he left. The sled would scarcely budge at first, and snow bunched up before it. Wearing a harness he had made, he dragged the sled slowly downriver. Berail's snowshoes had Indian ties. Try as he would, he could not understand how to secure them to his feet. The snowshoes were useless. Up to his knees, and sometimes to his hips, he walked from dawn until an hour before dark each day. He slept beside bonfires that burned all night. Blizzards came up the river some days, and driving williwaws—winds of a force that could literally stop him in his tracks. He leaned against the wind. When he could, he stepped forward. Once, at the end of a day's hard walking, he looked behind him—on the twisting mountain river—and saw where he had started at dawn. The Charley in summer—clear-flowing within its canyon walls, with grizzlies fishing its riffles, Dall sheep on the bluffs, and peregrines above it in the air—is an extremely beautiful Alaskan river (it has been called the loveliest of all), but for Leon Crane it was little more than brutal. He came to a lead one day, a patch of open water, and, trying to use some boulders as stepping stones, he fell in up to his armpit. Coming out, barging through snowdrifts, he was the center of a fast-forming block of ice. His matches were dry. Shaking as before, he managed this time to build a fire. All day, he sat steaming beside it, removing this or that item of clothing, drying it a piece at a time.

After a couple of weeks on the river, he found another cabin, with a modest but welcome food cache—cornmeal, canned vegetables, Vienna sausage. He sewed himself a backpack and abandoned his cumbersome sled. Some seven or eight days on down the river, he came around a bend at dusk and found cut spruce tops in parallel rows stuck in the river snow. His aloneness, he sensed, was all but over. It was the second week of March, and he was eighty days out of the sky. The arrangement of treetops, obviously, marked a place where a plane on skis might land supplies. He looked around in near darkness and found a toboggan trail. He camped, and next day followed the trail to a cabin—under smoke. He shouted toward it. Al Ames, a trapper, and his wife, Neena, and their children appeared in the doorway. "I am Lieutenant Leon Crane, of the United States Army Air Forces," he called out. "I've been in a little trouble." Ames took a picture, which hangs on a wall in Philadelphia.

Crane remembers thinking, Somebody must be saving me for something, but I don't know what it is. His six children, who owe themselves to that trip and to Phil Berail's fully stocked Charles River cabin, are—in addition to his three sons in the construction business—Mimi, who is studying engineering at Barnard; Rebecca, who is in the master's program in architecture at Columbia; and Ruth, a recent graduate of the Harvard Medical School. Crane himself went on to earn an advanced degree in aeronautical engineering at the Massachusetts Institute of Technology, and spent his career developing helicopters for Boeing Vertol.

"It's a little surprising to me that people exist who are interested in living on that ground up there," he told me. "Why would anyone want to take someone who wanted to *be* there and throw them out? Who the hell could *care?*"

Al Ames, who had built his cabin only two years before, harnessed his dogs and mushed Crane down the Yukon to Woodchopper, where a plane soon came along and flew him out.

Crane met Phil Berail at Woodchopper, and struggled shyly

to express to him his inexpressible gratitude. Berail, sixty-five, was a temporary postmaster and worked for the gold miners there. He had trapped from his Charley River cabin. He was pleased that it had been useful, he said. For his part, he had no intention of ever going there again. He had abandoned the cabin four years before.

Lauren Slater

My first contact with Lauren Slater was when I received her book manuscript, a thin collection, seven essays in all, two hundred pages, barely. I sat down for a quick skim, which is part of my usual routine, just to see if a work is actually worth pursuing. Four hours later, I finished the entire book and looked up, feeling breathless and amazed that such a wonderful writer (and an extraordinary human being) could somehow exist, basically unpublished and undiscovered. But she was not undiscovered for long.

Lauren Slater's book, Welcome to My Country, *was published by Random House in 1996. "Three Spheres," the lynchpin essay in that book, was first published in the magazine* Creative Nonfiction. *Lauren Slater currently teaches creative nonfiction writing in Goucher College's low-residency program while living in Cambridge, Massachusetts.*

Three Spheres

Ms. Cogswell is a 37-year-old SWF who has had over 30 hospitalizations, all for suicide attempts or self-mutilation. She scratches her arms lightly when upset. Was extensively sexually abused as a child. Is now requesting outpatient therapy for bulimia. Ms. Cogswell says she's vomiting multiple times during the day. Teeth are yellowed and rotting, probably due to stomach acids present during purges.

Client has been in outpatient therapy with over 70 (!) social workers, psychologists and psychiatrists. She has "fired" them all because she cannot tolerate their limit-setting. She has threatened to sue "at least eight, maybe more," because "they never gave me what I needed. They were a menace to the profession." Please note: Client has never carried through with any of her threats to sue. She does, however, demand complete access to her health-care providers. Has a history of calling her therapists in the middle of the night, screaming that she needs to see them right away, and self-mutilating when her requests are refused.

During her intake and evaluation appointment, client presented as teary and soft-spoken. She wore large hoop earrings and much makeup. She said she believes she has gout and asked to be prescribed medication for it. Became belligerent when refused. Possibly this client is delusional, although she was fully oriented to all three spheres—person, place and time—knowing who and where she was, and demonstrating capacity to locate historical figures in their appropriate periods. Proverb interpretation: somewhat concrete. Serial sevens: intact. Recommendation: psychological testing; 1x weekly behavioral therapy to address eating disorder; possible admission as an inpatient if she cannot get bulimia under control.

"So who wants to take the case?" Dr. Siley, the director of the outpatient portion of the unit where I work, asks. He folds the initial intake evaluation from which he's been reading back into its green file.

None of the other clinicians offer. A woman as outrageously demanding and consistently suicidal as this one is would add a lot of pressure to anyone's job. Ellen looks away. Veronica busies herself with the pleats on her skirt. The staff room stays quiet.

"What about you?" Dr. Siley says, looking in my direction. He knows my numbers are down. My job description states I'm responsible for seeing at least twenty outpatients, in addition to the chronic schizophrenics in the residential program.

"Well," I say, "she sounds like a lot of work."

"Who isn't?" Veronica says.

"Why don't you take her then?" I say.

"I'm full," Veronica says.

"And you aren't," Dr. Siley adds, pushing the file across the table toward me.

The phone rings six, maybe seven times, and then I hear a tiny voice on the other end—"Hello," it whispers, and I announce myself, the new therapist, let's make an appointment, look forward to meeting you, here's where the clinic is, in case you forgot—

"Can't," the voice weeps. "Can't can't." I hear the sound of choking, the rustle of plastic. "Ten times a day," the voice says. "Into thirty three-gallon bags. I've spent," and sobbing breaks out over the line, "I've spent every last penny on frozen pizzas. There's blood coming up now."

"You need to be in a hospital then," I say.

"Oh please," the voice cries. "Put me in a hospital before I kill myself. I'm afraid I'm going to kill myself."

I tell her to sit tight, hang on, and then I replace the receiver. I know the routine by heart. I call 911, give the ambulance company her name and address, tell them there's no need to commit her because she said she'd go willingly. Next they'll take her to an emergency room and after that she'll be placed on an inpatient unit somewhere in this state. She can't come into our own program's inpatient unit because she's neither schizophrenic nor male, the two criteria for admission. She'll stay wherever she is put anywhere from three days to four weeks, enough time, probably, for her to forget I ever called, to forget she ever wandered into the clinic where I work. At the hospital they'll likely set her up with an aftercare psychologist affiliated with their own institution, and he, or she, will have to deal with what sounds like her enormous neediness. And I, lucky I, will be off the case. Or so I think.

· · ·

Two days later a call comes through to my office. "Ms. Linda Cogswell tells us you're her outpatient therapist. Could you come in for a team meeting next Monday afternoon?"

"Well, I don't even know her, actually. I was assigned the case but before I could meet her she had to be hospitalized. Where is she?"

"Mount Vernon. I'm her attending psychologist here. Would you be willing to meet with us regarding her aftercare plans?"

Mount Vernon, Mount Vernon. And suddenly, even though it's been years, I see the place perfectly all over again, the brick buildings, the green ivy swarming the windows. The nurses who floated down the halls like flocks of seagulls, carrying needles in their beaks. My heart quickens; a screw tightens in my throat.

"Mount Vernon?" I say. Of all the hundreds of hospitals in Massachusetts, why did it have to be *this* one? And another part of me thinks I should have been prepared, for eventually past meets present; ghosts slither through all sealed spaces.

"Look, I don't know the woman at all," I repeat, and I hear something desperate in my voice. I try to tamp it down, assume a professional pose. "I mean," I say, "the patient, although technically assigned to me, has not begun a formal course of psychotherapy under my care."

A pause on the line. "But *technically*," the voice retorts, "she is under your care, yes? You have some sort of record on her? Your clinic agreed to take the case?"

"Yes," I say. "Well . . . yes."

"Next Monday then, one o'clock, Wyman—"

"Two," I interrupt bitterly. "Wyman Two."

"Good," she says. "We'll see you then."

What else can I do? Technically, I *have* been assigned the case. But this isn't any longer about the case; my hesitations now don't have to do with Linda Cogswell and her stained teeth, but with ivy on the brick, the shadow of a nurse, a needle, the way night looked as it fell beyond the bars and the stars were sliced into even segments. I remember looking out the windows on Wyman Two; I remember Rosemary swallowing her hidden pills, how she danced the Demerol onto her tongue and later sank into a sleep so deep only the slamming cuffs of a cardiac machine could rouse her. Liquid crimson medicines were served in plastic cups. The rooms had no mirrors.

But the reflections came clear to me then, come still in quiet moments when past meets present so smoothly the seams disappear and time itself turns fluid. Sometimes I wish time stayed solid, in separable chunks as distinct as the sound of the ticking clock on my mantel right now. In truth, though, we break all boundaries, hurtling forward through hope and backward on the trail made by memory.

But what else can we do except reach, except remember? What else can I do, having been assigned this case? I will go in, go down. Go back.

American culture abounds with marketplace confessions. I know this. And I know the criticisms levied against this trend, how such open testifying trivializes suffering and contributes to the narcissism polluting our country's character. I agree with some of what the critics of the confessional claim. I'm well aware of Wendy Kaminer's deep and in part justified scorn for the open admissions of Kitty Dukakis, who parades her alcoholism for all to observe, or for Oprah, who extracts admissions from the soul like a dentist pulls teeth, gleefully waving the bloodied root and probing the hole in the abscessed gum while all look, without shame, into the mouth of pain made ridiculously public. Would it not be more prudent to say little, or nothing, to hold myself back like any good doctor, at most admitting some kind of empathic twinge? For what purpose will I show myself? Does it satisfy some narcissistic need in me—at last I can have some of the spotlight? Perhaps a bit, yes? But I think I set aspects of my own life down not so much to revel in their gothic qualities, but to tell you this: that with many of my patients I feel intimacy, I feel love. To say I believe time is finally fluid, and so are the boundaries between human beings, the border separating helper from the one who hurts always blurry. Wounds, I think, are never confined to a single skin but reach out to rasp us all. When you die, there's that much less breath to the world, and across continents someone supposedly separate gasps for air. When—Marie, Larry, George, Pepsi, Bobby, Harold—when I weep for you, don't forget I weep as well for me.

· · ·

I have to drive out of the city to get there, down forty miles of roads I've avoided for the past eight years. Where there was once farmland, horses spitting sand as they galloped, wide willow trees I sat under when the nurses let me out on passes, there are now squat square houses dotting the hills. But the building's bubbled dome rises unmistakably over a crest as I round the corner, floating there in the distance like a glittering spaceship, looking exactly the same as it did almost a decade ago. Walking back from passes I would see that domed bubble, that silver blister bursting against a spring sky, and I would count *one, two, three*, getting closer, my heart hammering half with fear, half with relief. Safe again. Trapped again. Safe again. Trapped aga—

And I have the same heart in the same socket of chest, and it hammers like it used to and I find myself thinking the same words *safe again, trapped again.* My palms sweat on the steering wheel. I remind myself: I am *not* that girl. I am *not* that girl. I've changed. I've grown. I am now a psychologist who over the years has learned to give up her Indian print sundresses and bulky smocks for tailored skirts, who carries a black Coach leather briefcase. How often, though, I've marveled at the discrepancy between this current image of me and the tangled past it sprang from. Sometimes I've imagined shouting out in staff meetings, in front of all my colleagues who know me as a spunky, confident doctor, how often I've wanted to say *Once I too* . . .

And what I would tell them goes something like this. On five separate occasions, spanning the ages from fourteen to twenty-four, I spent considerable portions of my life inside the very hospital whose graveled drive I am now turning into. Until what could be called my "recovery" at twenty-five or so, I was admitted to this institution on the average of every other year for up to several months. And even today, at thirty-one years old, with all of that supposedly behind me, with chunks of time in which to construct and explain the problems that led me to lock-up, I find myself at a loss for words. Images come, and perhaps in the images I can illuminate some of my story. I am five years old, sitting under the piano, as my mother, her face a mask of manic pain, pummels the keys. Beneath the bench I press the golden pedals, hold them all down at the same time so our house swells with raw and echoing sounds, with crashing crescendos and wails that shiver up in-side my skin, lodging there a fear of a world I know is impossible to negotiate, teetering on a cruel and warbling axis. And later, lying in my bed, she murmurs Hebrew while her fingers explore me and a darkness sprouts inside my stomach. A pain grows like a plant and when I'm twelve, thirteen, I decide to find the plant, grasping for its roots with a razor blade. Stocked solid with the romance of the teenage years, with the words of the wounded Hamlet and the drowned Virginia Woolf, whom I adored, I pranced on the lawn of my school, showing off the fresh gashes— Cordelia, a dwarf, a clown, Miss Havisham. I loved it all. I wept for the things inserted into me, the things plucked out of me. And I knew, with the conviction of adolescence, that pain confers a crown. I was removed to the hospital, then a foster home, then the hospital, again and again. Later on, in my late teens and early twenties, I starved myself, took pills to calm me down, wanted a way out. And finally I found one, or one, perhaps, found me.

I am *not* that girl any longer. I tell that to myself as I ride up the hospital's elevator. I *found* some sort of way into recovery. But I know, have always known, that I could go back. Mysterious neu-rons collide and break. The brain bruises. Memories you thought were buried rise up.

I rise up in the elevator and the doors part with a whisper. Stepping off, I find myself face to face with yet another door, this one bolted and on it a sign that says: Enter With Caution. Split Risk.

And now I am standing on the other side of that door—the wrong, I mean the right, side of the door, and I ring the buzzer. I look through the thick glass window and see a nurse hustle down the hall, clipboard in hand. I recognize her. Oh my god, I recog-nize her! I hunch, dart back. Impossible, I tell myself. It's been over eight years. Staff turnover in these places is unbelievably high. But it could be her, couldn't it? And what happens if she recognizes me? My mouth dries and something shrivels in my throat.

"Dr. Slater?" she asks, opening the door. I nod, peer into her eyes. They're the blue of sadness, thickly fringed. Her lips are painted the palest sheen of pink. "Welcome," she says, and she steps back to let me pass. I was wrong, I've never seen this woman in my life. I don't know those eyes, their liquid color, nor the voice, in whose tone I hear, to my surprise, a ring of deference. Doctor, she actually calls me doctor. She bends a bit at the waist, in greeting, acknowledging the hierarchies that exist in these places—nurses below psychologists, psychologists below psychiatrists. Patients are at the bottom of the ladder.

With a sudden surge of confidence, I step through. The reversal is remarkable, and for a second makes me giddy. I'm aware of the incredible elasticity of life, how the buckled can become straight, the broken mended. Watch what is on the ground; watch what you step on, for it could contain hidden powers and, in a rage, fly up all emerald and scarlet to sting your face.

And here I am, for the briefest moment, all emerald, all scarlet. "Get me a glass of water," I imagine barking to her. "Take your pills or I'll put you in the quiet room."

Then the particular kind of dense quiet that sits over the ward comes to me. Emerald goes. Scarlet dies down. I am me again, here again. I grip my briefcase and look down the shadowy hall, and it's the same shadowy hall, loaded with the exact same scents, as it was so many years ago. The paint is that precise golden green. The odor is still undefinable, sweet and wretched. Another woman comes up, shakes my hand. "I'm Nancy," she says, "charge nurse on the unit."

"Good to meet you," I say. And then I think I see her squint at me. I've the urge to toss my hair in front of my face, to mention a childhood in California or Europe, how I've only been in this state for a year.

"We're meeting in the conference room," Nancy says. Clutching my briefcase, I follow her down the corridor. We pass open doors and I hold my breath as we come to the one numbered 6, because that was my bedroom for many of the months I stayed here. I slow down, try to peer in. Heavy curtains hang, just as they used to, over a large, thickly meshed window. *There are the stars* I want to say, for in my mind it's night again, and someone is rocking in a corner. Now, in the present time, a blond woman lies in what used to be my bed. On that mattress swim my cells, the ones we slough off, the pieces of ourselves we leave behind, forever setting our signatures into the skin of the world. As she sleeps, my name etches itself on her smooth flesh, and my old pain pours into her head.

And just as we are passing her by completely, the woman leaps out of bed and gallops to the door. "Oh Nancy," she keens. "I'm not safe, not safe. Get my doctor. I want my doctor."

"Dr. Ness will be up to see you at four," Nancy says.

Suddenly the woman snarls. "Four," she says, "Dr. Ness is always late. Always keeps me waiting. I want a new doctor, someone who'll really care. A new doctor, a new . . ."

Her voice rises and she sucks on her fist. "Stop it, Kayla," Nancy says. "Take your fist out of your mouth. You're twenty-nine years old. And if you want a new doctor, you'll have to bring it up in community meeting."

Kayla stamps her foot, tosses her head like a regal pony. "Screw you," she mutters now. "Screw this whole fucking place," and then she stomps back into her bed.

When we're a few feet beyond the scene, Nancy turns to me, smiles conspiratorially. I feel my mouth stretched into a similar smirk, and it relieves yet bothers me, this expression toward a patient. "Borderline," Nancy says matter-of-factly, giving a crisp nod of her head.

I sigh and nod back. "They're exhausting patients, the ones with borderline personalities." I pause. "But I prefer them to antisocials," I add, and as I say these words I feel safe again, hidden behind my professional mask. I am back on balance, tossing jargon with the confidence of a Brahmin in a village of untouchables. There is betrayal here, in what I do, but in betrayal I am finally camouflaged.

Of all the psychiatric illnesses, borderline personality disorder may be the one professionals most dislike to encounter. It's less serious than, say, schizophrenia, for the borderline isn't usually psychotic, but such patients are known for their flamboyant, attention-getting, overly demanding ways of relating to others. Linda, according to her intake description, is surely a borderline. These patients are described with such adjectives as "manipulative" and "needy," and their behaviors are usually terribly destructive, and include anorexia, substance abuse, self-mutilation, suicide attempts. Borderlines are thought to be pretty hopeless, supposedly never maturing from their "lifelong" condition. I myself was diagnosed with, among other things, borderline personality disorder. In fact, when I left the hospital for what I somehow knew would be the very last time, at twenty-four years of age, I asked for a copy of my chart, which is every patient's right. The initial intake evaluation looked quite similar to Linda's, and the write-ups were full of all kinds of hopeless projections. "This young woman displays a long history marked by instability in her interpersonal and intrapsychic functioning," my record read. "She clearly has had a long career as a mental patient and we will likely encounter her as an admission again in the future."

I recall these words now, as we enter the conference room, where several other nurses and doctors sit around a table with a one-way mirror on the far wall. I scan their faces quickly, praying I look as unfamiliar to them as they do to me. I don't recognize any of the people in here, and I'm hoping against hope they don't recognize me. Still, even if we've never met, I feel I know them somehow, know them in a deep and private part of me. "Ta da," I have the angry urge to shout out, bowing to the bearded psychiatrist at the oval's head, standing arms akimbo, twirling so my skirt swells out. "Here I am," I'd like to yell, "yes sireee, encountered again. Guess who you're looking at; guess who this is. The Borderline! And sure enough folks, I *did* mature out, at least a little . . ."

But of course I won't say such a thing, wouldn't dare, for I would lose my credibility. But the funny thing is, I'm supposedly in a profession that values honesty and self-revelation. Freud himself claimed you couldn't do good analytic work until you'd "come clean" with yourself in the presence of another, until you'd spoken in the bright daylight your repressed secrets and memories. Freud told us not to be so ashamed, to set loose and let waltz our mothers and fathers, our wetness and skins. Training programs for psychologists like me, and the clinics we later work in, have as a credo the admission and discussion of countertransference, which by necessity claims elements of private conflict.

At the same time though, another more subtle yet powerful message gets transmitted to practitioners in the field. This message says *Admit your pain, but only to a point. Admit it but keep it clean. Go into therapy, but don't call yourself one of us if you're* anything *more than nicely neurotic.* The field transmits this message by perpetuating so strongly an *us* versus *them* mindset, by consistency placing a rift between practitioners and patients, a rift it intends to keep deep. This rift is reflected in the language only practitioners are privy to, in words like *glossolalia* and *echolalia* instead of just saying *the music of madness,* and then again in phrases like *homicidal ideation* and *oriented to all three spheres* instead of *he's so mad he wants to kill her* or *he's thinking clearly today, knows who, what, and where he is.* Along these same lines, practitioners are allowed to admit their *countertransference* but not the *pain pain pain the patient brings me back to, memories of when I was five, your arms my arms and the wound is one.* No. To speak in such a way would make the rift disappear, and practitioners might sink into something overwhelming. We—I—hang onto the jargon that at once describes suffering and hoists us above it. Suddenly, however, here I am, back in an old home, lowered.

I recognize the conference room as the place where, when I was fourteen, I met with my mother and the social worker for the last time. My father had gone away to live in Egypt. My mother was wearing a kerchief around her head and a heavy bronze Star of David wedged between the hills of her breasts. Years later, seeing the mountains of Jerusalem, cupping the scathing sand of the desert, hearing the primitive wails of the Hasids who mourned the Temple's destruction, I would think of my mother's burning body, a pain I could never comprehend.

This is the conference room where she, unstable, prone to manic highs and depressive lows, shot through with a perpetual anxiety that made her hands shake, this is the same conference room where she told me she was giving me over to the care of the state, giving me up to become a foster child. "I can't handle you anymore," she'd said to me, spit at me. "I no longer want you with me."

I bow my head in deference to something I cannot name, and enter the room. Things are screaming inside me and my eyes feel hot. Nancy introduces me all around and I take a seat, pull out a notebook, try to act as calm and composed as possible. "The patient Ms. Cogswell," the bearded psychiatrist begins, "is not able to make good use of the hospital. She's an extreme borderline, wreaking havoc on the unit. We suspect her of some factitious posturing as well." He pauses, looks at me, clears his throat. I smile back at him but my mouth feels uncoordinated, tightness at its corners. I won't cry, won't cry, even though in the one-way mirror, in the criss-crossing of the creamy branches beyond the ward's windows, I see my mother again, her face coming to me clearly, her eyes haunted with loneliness and rage. I feel her fingers at my breasts and flinch.

"We think," a social worker named Miss Norton continues, "that we'll be discharging her in a matter of days, as soon as we get her stabilized on some meds. We take it you'll be picking up her case on an outpatient basis. Any ideas of how you'll work with her?"

I nod, pretend to make some notes on the pad. As my voice rises through my throat, I'm surprised at how smooth it sounds, a sleek bolt of silk. "Lots of limits," I say. "We know borderlines do well with lots of limits. This is the only context in which a workable transference can begin."

The bearded doctor nods. In the tree, my mother tongues her teeth and wind lifts her lovely skirt, embroidered with fragile flowers. And then she is not my mother anymore, but a little girl whose legs are white, a single ruby scar on scrubbed knee. And while part of me sits in the conference room, part of me flies out to meet this girl, to touch the sore spot, fondling it with my fingers.

For I have learned how to soothe the hot spots, how to salve the soreness on my skin. I can do it so no one notices, can do it while I teach a class if I need to, or lead a seminar on psychodiagnosis. I can do it while I talk to you in the evenest of tones. "Shhhh," I whisper to the hurting part, hidden here. You can call her borderline—call me borderline—or multiple, or heaped with post-traumatic stress—but strip away the language and you find something simple. You find me, part healthy as a horse and part still suffering, as are we all. What sets me apart from Kayla or Linda or my other patients like George, Marie, Pepsi—what sets me apart from these "sick" ones is simply a learned ability to manage the blades of deep pain with a little bit of dexterity. Mental health doesn't mean making the pains go away. I don't believe they ever go away. I do believe that nearly every person sitting at this oval table now has the same warped impulses, the same scarlet id, as the wobbliest of borderlines, the most florid of psychotics. Only the muscles to hold things in check—to channel and funnel—are stronger. I have not healed so much as learned to sit still and wait while pain does its dancing work, trying not to panic or twist in ways that make the blades tear deeper, finally infecting the wounds.

Still, I wonder. Why—how—have I managed to learn these things while others have not? Why have I managed somehow to leave behind at least for now what looks like wreckage, and shape something solid from my life? My prognosis, after all, was very poor. In idle moments, I still slide my fingers under the sleeves of my shirt and trace the raised white nubs of scars that track my arms from years and years of cutting. How did I learn to stop cutting and collapsing, and can I somehow transmit this ability to others? I don't know. It's a core question for me in my work. I believe my strength has something to do with memory, with that concept of fluid time. For while I recall with clarity the terror of abuse, I also recall the green and lovely dream of childhood, the moist membrane of a leaf against my nose, the toads that peed a golden pool in the palm of my hand. Pleasures, pleasures, the recollections of which have injected me with a firm and unshakable faith. I believe Dostoyevsky when he wrote, "If man has one good memory to go by, that may be enough to save him." I have gone by memory.

And other things too. Anthony Julio wrote in his landmark study, *The Invulnerable Child*, that some children manage to avoid or grow out of traumatic pasts when there is the presence in their lives of at least one stable adult—an aunt, a neighbor, a teacher. I had the extreme good fortune to be placed in a foster home where I stayed for four years, until I turned eighteen, where I was lovingly cared about and believed in. Even when my behavior was so bad I cut myself in their kitchen with the steak knife, or when, out of rage, I swallowed all the Excedrin in their medicine cabinet and had to go back to the unit, my foster parents continued to believe in my abilities to grow, and showed this belief by accepting me after each hospital discharge as their foster child still. That steady acceptance must have had an impact, teaching me slowly over the years how to see something salvageable in myself. Bless those people, for they are a part of my faith's firmness. Bless the stories my foster mother read to me, the stories of mine she later listened to, her thin blond hair hanging down in a single sheet.

The house, old and shingled, with niches and culverts I loved to crawl in, where the rain pinged on a leaky roof and out in the puddled yard a beautiful German shepherd, who licked my face and offered me his paw, barked and played in the water. Bless the night there, the hallway light they left on for me, burning a soft yellow wedge that I turned into a wing, a woman, an entire army of angels who, I learned to imagine, knew just how to sing me to sleep.

At a break in the conference, a nurse offers me a cup of coffee. "Sure," I say, "but first the ladies' room." And then I'm off, striding down the hallway I know so well, its twists and turns etched in subterranean memory. I go left, then right, swing open the old wooden ladies' room door, and sit in a stall.

When I come back, the nurse is ready with a steaming Styrofoam cup. She looks at me, puzzled, as she hands me my hot coffee. "You've been here before?" she asks.

My face must show some surprise, for she adds, "I mean, the bathrooms. You know where they are."

"Oh," I say quickly. "Right. I've visited some of my patients on this ward before, yes."

"You don't have to use the patient bathroom," she says, smiling oddly, looking at me with what I think may be suspicion. "We don't recommend it," she adds. "Please use the staff bathroom, through the nurse's station."

"OK," I say. I bend my face into the coffee's steam, hoping she'll think the redness is from the rising heat. Of course. How stupid of me. What's she thinking? Can she guess? But in a way I am one of the patients, and she could be too. I'm not ready to say it yet though, weak one. Wise one. This time, memory has led me astray.

The conference resumes. I pay little attention. I'm thinking about the *faux pas* with the bathroom, and then I'm watching the wind in the tree outside the window. I am thinking about how we all share a similar, if not single pain, and the rifts between stalls and selves is its own form of delusion. And then I hear, through a thin ceiling, wails twining down, a sharp scream, the clattering of footsteps. I sit up straight.

"Delivery rooms," the social worker says, pointing up. "We're one floor under the maternity ward."

I smile and recall. That's right. Wyman Two is just one floor of what is an old large public hospital. The psychiatric unit we're on has always been wedged between labor rooms upstairs and a nursery downstairs. When I was a patient I could often hear, during group therapy or as I drifted into a drugged sleep, the cries of pushing women as their muscles contracted and in great pain their pink skins ripped, a head coming to crown.

"Why don't you meet with Linda now?" the psychiatrist says, checking his watch and gathering his papers. Everyone stands, signaling the end of the conference. "You can take one of the interview rooms," Nancy, the charge nurse, adds. "They're nice places for doing therapy, comfortable."

I nod. I've almost forgotten about Linda and how she is the reason for my return here today. Now I walk with the rest out of the conference room and Nancy points down the long hall. "There," she says, her finger aiming toward a door on the left. "The third room. We'll bring Linda to you." And then, to my surprise, Nancy fishes deep into her pocket and pulls out a large steel ring of keys, placing them in my hand. They're the same keys, I know, from all those years ago, keys I was not allowed to touch but which I watched avidly whenever I could, the cold green gleam and mysterious squared prongs opening doors to worlds I didn't know how to get to. Keys, keys, they are what every mental patient must dream of, the heart-shaped holes keys fit into, the smart click as they twist the secret tumblers and unlatch boxes, velvet lined and studded with sea-jewels. Keys are symbols of freedom and power and finally separateness. For in a mental hospital, only one side has the keys; the others go to meals with plastic forks in their fists.

Slowly, I make my way down the hall to the interview room, stand outside the locked door holding the key ring. It feels cool, and I press it to my cheek. A hand there once, feeling me for a fever, stroking away my fear. Bless those who have helped.

A woman who looks far older than her thirty-seven years is now making her way down the hall. Stooped she is, with tired red ringlets of hair. As she gets closer I see the dark ditches under her eyes, where years of fatigue and fear have gathered. I would like to put my finger there, sweep away the microscopic detritus of suffering.

"Linda," I say, and as she comes close to me, I extend my hand. "Hello," I say, and I can hear a gentleness in my voice, a warm wind in me, for I am not only greeting her, but myself.

We stand in front of the locked interview room and I fumble for the correct key. I start to insert it in the lock, but then halfway done, I stop. "You," I say to my new patient, Linda. "You take the key. You turn the lock."

She arches one eyebrow, stares up at me. Her face seems to say *Who are you, anyway?* I want to cry. The hours here have been too long and hard. "You," I say again, and then I feel my eyes actually begin to tear. She steps forward, peers closely, her expression confused. Surely she's never seen one of her doctors cry. "It's OK," I say. "I know what I'm doing." And for a reason I cannot quite articulate at the moment, I make no effort to hide the wetness. I look straight at her. At the same time, for the first time today, my voice feels genuinely confident. "Take the keys, Linda," I say, "and open the door."

She reaches out a bony hand, takes the keys from me, and swings open the door. The interview room is shining with sun, one wall all windows. I've been in this room, too, probably hundreds of times over the years, meeting with the psychiatrists who tried to treat me. I shiver with the memory. Ultimately it was not their treatments or their theories that helped me get better, but the kindness lodged in a difficult world. And from the floor above comes the cry of a protesting baby, a woman ripped raw in birth. She is us. We are her. As my mother used to say, rocking over the Shabbat candles, chanting Jewish prayers late, late into the night, "Hear O Israel. The Lord is God, The Lord is one, and so are we as a people."

She would pause then, her hands held cupped over the candlesticks. "We are one," she would repeat to me after a few moments, her strained face peering at me through shadows. "As a people we are always one."

Sometimes I miss her.

My patient and I sit down, look at each other. I see myself in her. I trust she sees herself in me.

This is where we begin.

Reginald Gibbons

When I first started the magazine Creative
Nonfiction, the venture which led to this reader, I
expected submissions primarily from journalists
who had been stifled for years by conservative editors
bent on objectivity and formulaic prose. Creative
Nonfiction would provide the opportunity for
journalists to extend themselves and write
nonfiction as literature, I reasoned. However, most
of the best work I received, initially, came from
poets crossing genres and experimenting.

Reginald Gibbons, editor of one of the oldest and
most prestigious literary journals in the world—
TriQuarterly—is one of those increasing numbers
of poets, in addition to Mary Karr (The Liars'
Club) and Diane Ackerman (A Natural
History of the Senses), who have broadened
their perspective by writing creative nonfiction. In
describing his work, Stuart Dybek has said that
Gibbons's prose "has arrived at what seems an
effortless emotional directness and a voice that is
extraordinary for its intense intimacy."

Christmas at Juvenile Court

The juvenile court complex, amidst damaged, decayed and dangerous neighborhoods, is very difficult to get to by public transportation, but that's what most of its visitors must use. It consists of a new building, an older building to which the new one is grafted, and a new parking garage for those who drive their cars to court. In addition to courtrooms and offices, the complex houses a juvenile temporary detention center with its own school—said by some to be one of the better schools in the Chicago public school system.

There are two entrances to juvenile court. The security checks have electronic works tuned so fine that a dollar's worth of change will set off warning beeps. At the delinquency-side entrance, the guards are loud, peevish, brusque. Men and women, mostly black, who are coming to court for the hearings and trials of their children, stand in sluggish separate lines to take their turns through the sensitive devices and enter. Public defenders, private attorneys, states' attorneys, guardians ad litem, judges, case workers, and others, mostly white, flash their i.d. cards—or don't bother—and pass without even slowing down. On the delinquency side, the building is bare—hard, cold. On the other side of the building, at the abuse-and-neglect entrance, there are lots of Christmas decorations.

A typical hearing or trial in juvenile court is like a brief, highly organized dance. The public defenders work from a table to one side of the small courtroom, the states' attorneys from another, at the other side. The clerk calls the next case. Someone steps out of the closed doors, to the waiting area, and calls out the name of the "minor respondent." The child himself is also brought in. A long moment. ("Someone is approaching, judge," says an attorney, to placate the impatient man behind the bench.)

In come three women. The judge says, "Is mother here?" "Yes, judge," the public defender says, indicating one of the women. "And who is with mother?" the judge asks. "Grandmother and aunt," says the attorney. The judge says, "Aunt, please sit at the back of the courtroom," and the woman goes there, without saying a word. The other two wait, also silent.

Like the women who are here to stand with him, the child is black, this time. Everyone else in the courtroom is white. Handcuffs have been removed from his wrists at the side door to the courtroom, and as instructed by the uniformed officer who accompanies him, he stands at the center of the bench, before the judge, his hands clasped behind his back, and holding, in this case, a jacket, a tube of toothpaste and a toothbrush.

This legal episode takes only three minutes. The states' attorney speaks; the judge speaks; the public defender speaks; the person of whom they are speaking is not asked to speak, and does not speak. Although they have had time, in their service, to learn somewhat the language that *he* speaks, they do not speak a language that is intelligible to *him*.

Something having been decided, he is taken out of the courtroom. There are far too many cases to be heard before each day is over. And the judge wants to deal with each one quickly.

The public defender gathers some papers, whispers a few moments to one of his colleagues, about another matter, while the next three-minute hearing or trial begins—perhaps to be postponed, broken off or concluded—and then he goes out the same door through which his client was taken.

That door leads to a hidden corridor. Along it are the chambers of seven or eight judges. At one end is a police desk. To one side of the raised police desk, where five or six officers are on duty, talking loudly among themselves, is the holding tank—a single large room with a glass wall facing the police desk. About fifty boys aged sixteen or younger are waiting—standing, talking, yelling, sitting, remaining silent, staring out through the glass wall and the glass door.

The public defender meets his client in a small bare interview room. The client is fourteen years old, and has been held for two weeks so far on a very serious charge. A violent crime. His hearing, which will take place in two more weeks, will determine whether he will be tried as a juvenile in this building, and have some chance to straighten out and go free again, eventually, or whether he'll be sent to the criminal court at 26th Street to be tried as an adult.

The child does not understand why he has behaved as he has behaved. He does not have an adult's understanding of himself, of other people, or of the world—not even of his own tiny world of the street. In his whole life so far, he has never been downtown to the Loop or North Michigan Avenue, where those immense buildings stand so impassively, erected at such inconceivable cost, sustained by such astonishing wealth. In his world, he does what his friends do.

This boy is short, thin; he does not look directly at the public defender, his attorney, who is explaining to him what happened in the courtroom in those three minutes of the judge's time. It was decided that something will be decided. But this explanation, too, is in the language of courts. It does not make sense to the child. So in response to the explanation, which is that he is going to be given psychological tests, and he needs to be completely honest with the doctor, and then there will be another session before the judge, to determine where he will be tried, the boy says, "How long am I going to be in here?" For his crime, if he is convicted as an adult, he'll probably remain in prison for the rest of his life. In his particular case, the crime was to have accompanied another boy who killed another boy with bullets from a pistol belonging to another boy. So many boys, wandering through the desolations of aimlessness, agitation, rage, fear and bravado.

His attorney says, "That depends. But it's gonna be a while. We have to convince the judge not to send you to 26th Street, right?"

"Right."

"You know how we do that?"

"Oh, man."

"You know how we do that? You have to do two things—you have to not get written up for anything while you're here, and you have to do well in school, upstairs. Are you doing well in school, here?"

The child is not doing well. And he has already been written up once. People get in his face, he says. He says he has a temper. All he really wants to know is, how long will he be in here?

"It could be a long time," his attorney says.

"*How* long? Am I going to get out for Christmas?"

"No."

"No?" He doesn't believe this man is an attorney. He says he wants a *good* lawyer, he wants to pay five hundred dollars and have a *good* lawyer.

His sleeves are too long. His pants are too big. He shifts in his chair, again and again. The small, windowless, brick-walled room doesn't fit him either.

Even here, coming faintly from some corner, from behind one of these bricks, there are echoes of voices which—whether they're endangered or dangerous—are still free, on the street. That's the world he knows. He doesn't know any of all the other worlds. He and his friends are suspicious of other worlds. "Is it more important to you," the attorney is saying, "to react when someone is on you, so they *know* you won't tolerate that, *or* to not spend the rest of your life in jail? If the judge hears that you got written up, he's gonna think that you're not taking this seriously, and if that's what he thinks, then he'll decide that you need to go to 26th Street. Right?"

The child fidgets violently in his chair and flings his arms to one side, then the other. He looks at every corner of the room and not at his attorney.

His attorney says, "Someone gets in your face, you have to walk away from it. Right? And in school, you need A's and B's. OK? So we can ask one of the teachers to come down to the courtroom and *tell* the judge that you shouldn't be tried at 26th Street. As an adult. Right?"

The child is taken back into the part of the building that is behind locks. After he is gone, his attorney says of him, "He isn't going to make it. What he has to do is more than any adult could be reasonably expected to be able to do, and he's only fourteen."

The day proceeds. More trials, more hearings. The courthouse empties. The worlds, here and everywhere around here, go dark early at this time of year. After rush hour, whether at the known street corners where traffic goes steadily by, slowly, or at the safe corners where nothing should be happening, the snow falling since late afternoon makes everything quiet. And the street is bright in that strange, nighttime snow-lit way, from the light of a few streetlamps, home lights, headlights, reflected up off the soft whiteness. Quiet.

But inside the juvenile detention center, still noisy. People are getting in other people's faces. Taunting the weak. Threatening. Outside the dirty unbreakable windows, the snow is falling in the night, falling freely, softly, steadily, slowly.

Carol Kloss

The evolution of "Fat," according to Carol Kloss, began with visits to the local shopping mall and the medical library. "I researched fat in the human body, with special inspiration coming from a photographic guide to dissecting cadavers. I also looked at Lane Bryant catalogs."

Kloss's sketchbook and charcoal are pivotal elements in this essay, specifically, and in her writing generally: "The best thing I ever did for my development as a writer was to learn how to draw. Drawing training, done well, enables writers to recognize the perceptual shift that allows them to really see details and frees them from their conscious mind."

Fat

I suck heavy, sweet, dark sauce from chopped-up bones in the food court at the mall: baby back ribs from the Oriental Express, scraps of pork too charred to bite. While I eat, I watch people. A puffy-haired woman whose bottom and thighs droop off the seat of her chair. A saggy globe of a man with knees that will never touch and arms that can't hang straight; a skinny-legged little girl floats from the end of his hand. Three blocky women in shorts, no space between them and their big purses—boulders in the people-stream, their eyes focused on some solitary distance. We have each other, their faces say. I watch people and I watch fat: It rolls and jiggles under baggy shirts, shivers on over-bared thighs, swells the hand eating a sundae at the Dairy Queen.

"I hate cellulite," my husband told me once.

"Did you ever see your mother naked?" I asked.

"No, but there's such a thing as bathing suits," he said. "I dated a girl who was all cellulite; my mother fixed me up with her. She was just cellulite hanging on bones."

I watch the fat and wonder what's really inside, how deep it goes, how far away the bones are. Cushioned and pillowed, some people look boneless anyway, like boneless roasts, boneless pork roasts. Twist them slowly on a giant rotisserie and all the fat would drip off, dribble into the fire with every turn, drip and spurt and flame. Roast away all that fat—I'll take my gut well-done—and how much meat would be left? Maybe about as much as the shreds on the chopped-up Oriental Express bones. Maybe it depends on what you call the meat.

The fruit theory of fat says that pear fat is better than apple fat, this referring to the distribution of fat on the body: Store it in the legs and hips, not the belly, for less heart disease, cancer, diabetes, etc. Advertising and television and movies pick their bodies by the vegetable theory of fat: celery stalks. A lot of people are fruits trying to become vegetables, which is funny because most diets stuff you with vegetables and celery-stick nausea never dies. My mother-in-law, for instance, has been on a diet since 1962, and when she comes to my house for dinner she doesn't touch the salad.

Theory meets reality: Slap us in the diet pen, crack the whip of exercise, and pretty soon the calories counted and calories burned drift behind the television set while we cram into Slimmaire belts or ankle-length Spandex or blue jeans, the unisex girdle. Ah, support. That's what corsets were for. Where did they go? Maybe we should drag the whalebone out of the landfills. Or easier, order a floater from Lane Bryant, settle under your vertical-striped tent, and stay out of the wind.

Mostly we worry about it in guts, spare tires, balloon butts and saddlebags. But it also plumps cheeks, triples chins, inflates breasts, thickens ankles, and pads our feet and hands. Strip the skin from a pickled body and you'll see fat plastered everywhere, yellowed and chunky like margarine half-mixed with eggs. It bulges from the bottoms of kneecaps, hangs from arms and earlobes, swaddles the lymph nodes that cluster in armpits. The right coronary artery is wrapped in it, and the eyeballs lie on it.

Inside our nice coat of fat, with our little extra cushions tucked here and there, we have built-in protection from life's everyday shocks and jolts. Some people seem to need more protection than others. Like my friend Lana, a three-hundred-pound secretary who corrects her boss's grammar and improves his strategic plans but won't get a college degree. A person as fat as she, she says, couldn't go higher anyway. Or the man who lived in his bed except for the day he was supposed to leave on a free trip to Dick Gregory's fat farm. He got to the door but couldn't make himself go out and instead went back to the cushiony, crumb-covered pit of his specially reinforced mattress. Or my mother, who spent her days on a brown couch in a brown-carpeted room with brown-paneled walls, watching soap operas on a brown plastic television set. She built her protection from sardines and anchovies and pork and beans, cookies and day-old doughnuts and deep-fried onion rings. She dropped cigarette ash on her solitaire games and wrapped supper's potato peelings in the ads for the jobs she said she didn't know how to do.

Some fat is invisible. You see legs that look great in miniskirts; I see thighs that need the fat beaten out of them. You might think that you can get right up close and touch the edge of my size twelve body. But I feel the hidden tingle of my real edge a foot or two beyond your hand. The fat that you don't see tells me to strip my insides with laxatives and tells my husband's sister Trudi that she should only eat farina. It makes her wake her neighbors at four in the morning with the rumbling of her NordicTrack, and sometimes it throws her on the floor for 250 sit-ups while her parents watch from the dinner table. So, invisible fat has a lot of power. But it doesn't protect the back of Trudi's hand from her teeth when she shoves her finger down her throat. And it doesn't hide the sharpness of the shoulder blades that cut into my arms when I give her a hug.

Even though we try, we can't live without fat, and the more you have the luckier you are, really: all that adipose tissue bulging with future fatty acids, potential bits of muscle food, an internal portable Armageddon food cellar. If you happen to have accumulated an extra 220 pounds of it, you'd be able to live a theoretical year without going grocery shopping—quite a time-saver.

My grandmother swelled her fat cells with a special ethnic blend: Polish sausage fat, bacon fat, sour cream fat and cheesecake fat. About nine months of reserve lipids, I would guess she had, stored mostly between her neck and belly and carried around on fine muscled legs that her short, skinny beer-drinking husband admired. He died forty years before she did, and she fed five kids from the full-fat Polish meatcases in her three grocery stores. When she retired she became the baker for the St. John Berchmans bingo nights: cream cheese *kolacki* and deep-fried, jelly-filled *paczki* and all-butter poundcakes baked in pans so big that I was sure it would be a sin to keep a cake like that just for herself. She sold cheesecakes to her relatives and afghans to the priests. Then her doctor said she was too fat, and her daughters made her lose weight. When she got skinny she went into a nursing home, where she sat in a chair waiting for salt-free skinless chicken and begging quarters for the candy machine. And I brought her chocolate-frosted doughnuts from Amy Joy until she didn't remember who I was any more.

Sometimes I sit by the fountain in the mall with my charcoal and sketchbook, trying to catch in ten seconds the sling of a belly over a belt or the wobbly scallop of body rolls. I have to go to the mall to find fat people to draw because they don't seem to want to model. Day after day in figure-drawing class, I drew skinny young people with straight-line bodies—bony hips, meatless thighs, hardly a bump at the biceps. If those models only knew how boring I thought their bodies were—until the day we got a blonde woman with breasts that actually shook, a belly that pushed out from her ribs and thighs that showed no muscles. She glided through the quick poses, holding her chest as still as possible, but it was hard to pay attention to the movement I was supposed to be drawing. The curves and volume of her gold-lit body, the kind of figure Rubens would have molded with red and orange and yellow, made motion, and bones, irrelevant. She arranged herself on a faded old easy chair for the long pose. Cellulite dimpled the thigh that sagged over the chair seat, her belly flopped on her hip, and a shoulder without a clavicle blended into her swelled upper arm. She was big and loose, and I couldn't draw any part of her with a straight line. I followed her curves with my eyes and arm and felt my charcoal sinking into her flesh. I shaded her thighs and hips and shoulders; as I moved from dark to light, the energy of her mass softened the touch of my hand on the drawing. I looked at the paper and found lines that I didn't know I could draw—the dangle of her arm over the chair seat, the droopy fullness of her breast. The lines connected me with her, made me see and feel her solid and beautiful whole.

Fat people at the mall get nervous when they see me drawing them, but I don't think they know that on paper they're not fat. On paper, where I take away their three dimensions and put them into two, they're powerful, not flabby; fascinating, not shocking; more human than any unpadded bones could ever be. Black and white and shades of gray strip away suffering, take the flesh out of flesh, make bigness bounty. Sometimes I look at my own fat and hope that someday someone will draw me.

Robert McCrum

"My Old and New Lives" begins with a nightmare
we all might secretly fear. We open our eyes in the
morning — and soon realize that we cannot get out
of bed. In fact, we are alone in our house and we
can barely move. This is what happened to forty-
one-year-old Robert McCrum who, married only
two months, had recently passed a complete physical
examination. For the reader, McCrum's battle to
save himself through the next forty-eight hours and
subsequently over the months (and years) in his
"new life" is electrifying — and terrifying.

Originally published in The New Yorker, and
currently being expanded into a book, "My Old and
New Lives" is classic creative nonfiction. McCrum's
story is taut and true, yet very informational. The
reader learns exactly what happened to McCrum;
he shares the relevant science behind the incident
(cause, diagnosis, treatment) and explains it in
easy-to-understand language. Voice is a major
strength in this essay; it's as if we're settled into an
easy chair in his living room, listening intently as
he relates exactly what happened, in intimate
detail, when, in the course of a night, his life was
changed forever.

My Old and New Lives

No one will ever know exactly what happened in my head on the night of last July 28th, but probably it went something like this: First, a surreptitious clot began to form deep inside one of my cerebral arteries, cutting off the blood supply to the one organ in the body that, next to the heart, is greediest for blood. Eventually, perhaps some hours later, the clot burst in the right side of my brain—an uncontrolled "bleed" that would result in irreversible destruction of the brain tissue.

I was unaware of this cerebral drama; all I knew was that when I went to bed I had a raging headache, and then, the next morning, I could hardly move. Overnight, I had suffered what a specialist later called a "right-hemisphere hemorrhagic infarct," or what the world knows as "a stroke"—a word whose Old English origin connotes "a blow" and "a calamity."

Actually, it's a calamity that befalls some four hundred and fifty thousand Americans each year, killing about a third of them. But when it happened to me I was completely ignorant of the affliction, which Sherwin B. Nuland, the author of "How We Die," calls "the third most common cause of death in the developed countries of the world."

It was just another Saturday morning, and I was in bed, unable to get up—alone at home, a four-story town house in Islington, North London. My wife, Sarah Lyall, a journalist, was away in San Francisco. We had been married less than two months, and it was odd to be solo again. It was odder still to be so helpless, but I was in no pain, and, in retrospect, I realize that I was barely half conscious. Downstairs, the grandfather clock was chiming the hour: eight o'clock. I could see that beyond the heavy maroon curtains it was a lovely day. Through the open window, the sounds of the street filtered in, sharp and echoey in the stillness of the weekend.

I was supposed to drive to Cambridge that morning to visit my parents. So, time to get up. But there it was—I could not move. More accurately, I could not move my left side. Overnight, my body had become a deadweight of nearly fifteen stone. I thrashed about in bed trying, and failing, to sit upright, and wishing that Sarah were with me. For some unknown reason, I experienced no anxiety about my condition—just irritation and puzzlement. Why should I, who had recently sailed through a full medical examination, be unable to do as I pleased?

It was my dentist, Mr. Glyn, who, a year earlier, had first questioned my immortality. "Teeth," he observed, studying the X-rays of root-canal work to my upper-right quadrant, "were not designed to last more than forty years." He snapped the light off. "And, frankly, nor were we." I was forty-one then, and when I was occasionally reminded of Mr. Glyn's wisdom by some ache or twinge I would wonder when some other body part might follow the example set by my teeth and protest, "Enough!"

As my forty-second birthday approached, Sarah, a New York doctor's daughter, was anxious for independent verification that she was not marrying a crock. She'd witnessed enough of my candle-at-both-ends lifestyle to believe that this was a desirable prenuptial precaution; my assurances that McCrums lived forever (all my grandparents died in their eighties) cut no ice. So, at her insistence, I made an appointment with Dr. Guy O'Keeffe, who has a pretty little surgery near Eaton Place. From Dr. O'Keeffe's examination room, the world seems secure, a place for healthy young women to bring up big, bouncy babies: the air is flavored with Johnson's baby powder, and highbrow Muzak tinkles in the background.

Dr. O'Keeffe himself—sandy-haired, trim, and boyish—seemed a promising recipient for intimate disclosures. Good health, his manner says, is our birthright; everything can be diagnosed, treated, and cured. So he poked and prodded and pricked. He took blood and urine. He weighed and measured. He eavesdropped on the secret colloquy of my vital organs. In half an hour or so, he was asking me to put my clothes on again. The tests would be sent for analysis, but, according to all the visible signs, I was fit. "For a tall guy, you're OK, but keep an eye on your cholesterol," he said. It was good that I didn't smoke, but I'd be wise to watch the drink.

Of course. We chatted about "units." (I am a lifelong subscriber to the British media maxim that "white wine is not a drink.") Dr. O'Keeffe nodded competently and made another little note. A daily half bottle of wine was OK with him.

I returned to the street, ready for anything. Jungle warfare? Cross-country skiing? I could hack it. I blessed my hardy, long-lived ancestors. No question, mine were a better class of genes.

That was in June. In the meantime, Sarah and I had come back to London from our wedding, in Philadelphia, and our honeymoon seemed to segue into a month of dinner parties, at which my American wife was introduced to some part of my circle for the first time. Clearly, we were going to live forever and then happily ever after.

In July, Sarah flew to San Francisco to interview the novelist Amy Tan. We were to be apart for eight days. I remember taking her to the airport and, as I watched her in the rearview mirror— a small, blond figure with an oversized red suitcase waving good-bye from the curb—praying that no harm would befall her.

Now here I was, a week later, unable to get out of bed. I have relived this moment a thousand times in a fruitless quest for some explanation—the moment my life divided into "old" and "new."

Strangely, I had felt ready for a change, though I could not say what kind. For seventeen years, I'd earned my living as the editorial director of the publishers Faber & Faber, working with writers from Kazuo Ishiguro and Peter Carey to Paul Auster and Milan Kundera; I also write fiction and have sometimes combined this with freelance journalism in troubled parts of the world— Peru during Mario Vargas Llosa's Presidential campaign, Cambodia during the UNTAC election, and, most recently, East Timor. Like many of my generation, I'd envied those, like my parents, who had lived through wars and revolutions. Consciously or not, I'd always hoped my trips would yield a *frisson*—a moment of danger from which I'd nonetheless emerge unscathed. Mentally, I wore a flak jacket and jeans under my yuppie suit, and I liked to think I was more at home on the road than in the chic, heartless salons of Thatcher's London, though in truth I had begun confiding to Sarah a vague dissatisfaction with my working life. Indeed, on the evening of my collapse I'd done something I now think of as typical of my "old" life: I'd gone out for dinner at the Ivy, a restaurant in Covent Garden, with the literary agent Kathy Robbins, specifically to discuss Life (mine and hers). Before taking the taxi to the West End, I'd swallowed a couple of Nurofen tablets for the headache that had been troubling me all day, and at the Ivy I ordered a glass of champagne while I waited for Kathy to arrive. (In that life, a glass of champagne would dispel most troubles. How often, as editor-in-chief, had I downed champagne with Faber authors in the Ivy's upstairs dining room.)

By the time Kathy and I were sitting with our coffees, kvetching about the world, I was conscious that I still had a headache. I remember yawning with unaccountable weariness, wondering why, after only two glasses of champagne, my speech was so muddy and indistinct. My American Express receipt shows that I paid for our meal at 22:38 hours; my signature is steady. Then we rose from the table and made our way to the street. But something was not quite right. My legs felt spongy, as though I were walking through treacle. But I said nothing to Kathy. Whatever it was would pass.

Opposite the Ivy, in the St. Martin's Theatre, "The Mousetrap" was playing—"the world's longest-ever run," now in its forty-third year. I had occasionally observed that Agatha Christie's thriller and I had aged well together, but tonight I was ready to call in the understudies. We reached St. Martin's Lane—a walk of perhaps a hundred yards, during which every step had become more difficult for me. I said good night to Kathy and, desperate to be home, hailed a taxi, articulating the address with some effort. The driver repeated it contemptuously, as if he were picking up a drunk. I climbed heavily on board and sank into the back seat.

When we reached Islington, my legs felt like lead, and I was walking like a deep-sea diver, but I made the front door without falling over, and let myself in. I was plainly unwell, but my symptoms were unfamiliar. So I turned to that sovereign English remedy: a cup of tea.

Downstairs in the kitchen, I listened to a cheery message from Sarah on our answering machine. It included a hotel number to call, but, feeling quite extraordinarily tired, I decided to wait until morning. Then, clutching my comforting mug of herb tea, I climbed upstairs to bed. I remember resolving, as I drifted off to sleep, to rise early to beat the weekend traffic on the Cambridge road.

When a stroke occurs and the brain suffers "a hemorrhagic infarct," the body experiences a colossal disturbance of its innate sensory equilibrium. Literally overnight, I went from being someone who could order an expensive meal in a fashionable restaurant to being an incontinent carcass, unable to make any sense of my body. I was conscious and alert (I thought), but my limbs were not responding. My recollection of the first phase of the morning is disconnected and hallucinatory. Perhaps I passed out or fell asleep, because the next thing I remember is the clock in the hall chiming ten. Ten o'clock! I would never get to Cambridge! I rolled, with difficulty, to the edge of our big brass bed.

Then I was falling heavily to the floor, dragged over the edge of the bed by the deadweight of my left side. I was shocked and dismayed, and my first thought was to telephone for help. There was a phone on the bedside table, but, of course, that was now out of reach, and anyway I'd left Sarah's hotel number downstairs in the kitchen. So there I was: cut off. My feelings at first were ones of mild frustration: "Oh, no!" rather than "Jesus Christ!" At worst, I felt like Alice under the glass table, trying to reach the key that would open the door to the magic garden. I tried in vain to remember the name of Sarah's hotel. Wentworth? Grand Western? Nothing came. Even if I could reach the phone, what good would it be?

A new anxiety was distracting me. I was desperate to pee. Suddenly, there was a hot cascade of urine on my chest. (I was lying on my back, naked.) Afterward, I suppose I passed out, because when I came to again it was much later. The street was noisier and busier, and I sensed from the light on the ceiling that the sun was high. When the telephone rang briefly, maddeningly, and stopped, I knew that downstairs in the kitchen the answering machine would be clicking into action. Up here in the bedroom, it was out of earshot.

Time blurred. When I heard the clock chime again, it was three. As the afternoon wore on, the phone rang several more times. We had set the machine to respond after two rings, and in that other life, which now seems so distant, I had often, to Sarah's amusement, hurled myself across our bed to pick up and answer before the machine clicked on. Today, the score was British Telecom 7, McCrum 0.

What did I think about, lying on the floor? My missed rendezvous with my parents became an obsession, and I entertained all sorts of explanations for the cause of my immobility. Perhaps, like Stephen Hawking, I was suffering from motor-neuron disease. Perhaps I had a brain tumor. My cousin Jane had died of a brain tumor. At times, bizarrely persuaded by the remaining strength in my right side, I imagined hobbling across the street to my car, somehow driving with one arm. I was like a rat on a wheel, revolving desperate escape plans.

Then the phone rang again, and stopped, as before. I felt I had to do something decisive. I knew there was a phone on the floor downstairs in the living room. Somehow, I had to get there. With what I now see must have been an extraordinary effort, I dragged myself under the frame of our big brass bedstead with my right arm, noticing with interest the little flergs of dust and the debris that collect in such places—forgotten books, discarded Kleenex, Sarah's tights—and then I squirmed, commando style, over the carpet to the head of the stairs.

Here, reaching out to the bannister, which, fortunately, was on my right side, I pulled myself forward over the top step. Again, my deadweight took control, and I found I was sliding helplessly and painfully head first down the carpeted stairs to the mezzanine landing, where I had a borrower's-eye view of my library of modern first editions: *A Pale View of the Hills,* by Kazuo Ishiguro; *The Rachel Papers,* by Martin Amis; *A Good Man in Africa,* by William Boyd; and Raymond Carver's *Will You Please Be Quiet, Please?*

I vividly remember this part of the day, on the stair landing. For some hours, I lay on my back staring up at a framed brown-and-green school map of French Indochina—a souvenir of a trip I had made to Phnom Penh in 1993. I had then been looking for an adventure. Now I seemed to be caught up in one. I had crossed by night from what Susan Sontag (in *Illness as Metaphor*) calls "the kingdom of the well" to "the kingdom of the sick," and, though I still had no name for this new country I was in, it was dawning on me that I was no longer the person I'd been twenty-four hours ago.

I was puzzled and curious. It was almost as though I weren't in my body—the body that seemed to have let me down so badly. (I still wonder if the "I" who is typing this with my "good" right hand is the same "I" who used to peck away, two-handed, at fifty words per minute.) From time to time, my thoughts, such as they were, would be interrupted by the phone: two brief rings, then silence. In the stillness of the afternoon, and from my position on the stairs, I thought I could detect, far away in the kitchen, the faint whir and click of the machine and then Sarah's voice. But I was too far off to distinguish her message, and anyway how could I answer? I was terribly frustrated. I wanted to call out, "Darling, I'm here, please come and help me."

But *could* I do this? To test my speech and memory, I began, weirdly, to recite "Jabberwocky" out loud, forming the words with difficulty: "'Twas brillig, and the slithy toves Did gyre and gimble in the wabe; All mimsy were the borogoves, And the mome raths outgrabe."

As evening drew on, I maneuvered myself on the mezzanine landing for the descent down the final flight of stairs, to the living room. I did not want a repetition of that painful and undignified slide. I did not want carpet burns. Controlling my weight with my right hand on the bannister, I inched head first down to the hallway. It was gloomy here, and pleasantly cool. The clock whose chimes had punctuated my day was ticking steadily nearby. More squirming, and I was in the sitting room—and there, across the carpet on the floor, was the downstairs phone. I felt like a pioneer who, crossing the Rockies, finally arrives in California.

British Telecom records show that I called my parents—it never occurred to me to call Emergency—at 19:53 and that the call lasted two minutes. My mother, who was by now thoroughly alarmed at my failure to appear in Cambridge, picked up. Apparently, I told her I could not move. She tried to keep me on the line, but I had already rung off.

I felt incredibly happy.

Now things began to happen fast. When the phone rang again, it was my brother Stephen. He and his fiancée, Emily, were on their way from Camden Town; they had already phoned the police. I heard a siren outside in the street, the heavy boots of authority clomping up to my front door, and then a voice through the letter box. I replied, with difficulty, "No, I can't open the door."

Another siren; the sound of splitting wood. The police had climbed into the garden and were coming through the back door. I remember worrying that I was naked, but exhaustion was stronger than modesty. After my long day, it felt good to have people—there seemed to be rather a lot of them—taking an interest in my situation. Paramedics in green overalls were towering over me with the cheery bonhomie of furniture movers, rattling out questions to establish the state of my consciousness: "What's your date of birth, Robert? What's your address?"

Quite a crowd had gathered outside the house—curious neighbors alerted by the arrival of the police. Perhaps they hoped for a murder. (Noel Road, where the playwright Joe Orton was bludgeoned to death, is just around the corner.) Soon I was propped up in the ambulance. I took Emily's hand and felt her answering squeeze. The doors closed, the siren began to wail, and we were on our way. I was so happy. I was with my family. I was going to the hospital. I had survived. Through the window I could see the weekend world, which now seemed extraordinarily remote and unimportant, carrying on: shoppers crowding; cars maneuvering through traffic; people with pints standing outside pubs.

One moment, I was in the ambulance on the way to Casualty; the next, I was lying on a gurney listening to two young doctors discuss my case in an undertone. From time to time, a young medic with garlic on his breath would shine a light into my eyes, a standard test for brain function. (Stroke victims are very likely to suffer swelling of the brain, which is often what kills them.) When I heard that a specialist had been reached on the telephone, I became afraid that before my parents arrived from Cambridge this surgeon would trundle me into his operating theatre and slice the top off my head like a watermelon. A phone conference ensued. I lay there expecting the worst. But the specialist never appeared, and I was eventually wheeled into Intensive Care for the night. By then, all I wanted to do was sleep. Huge, yawning waves of tiredness carried me down into a dreamless darkness. Sarah tells me that my life was in the balance at this time, but all I felt was a blissful detachment and serenity. If I was going to die, this was not such a bad way to go.

I did not die, of course, and when, soon after this first night of my "new" life, someone used the phrase "an insult to the brain"—a commonplace of stroke care—I couldn't help imagining a gang of rogue neurons viciously hissing "Your mother is a water buffalo" to my sensitive cortex. Physically, I'd been poleaxed. My left leg was immobilized, and my left arm hung from its socket like a dead rabbit; the left side of my face, which drooped badly for about a week, felt frozen, as if Mr. Glyn had just given it a massive Novocain injection. I could not stand; my speech was slurred; my penis was attached to a Convene, a condomlike device that drained my urine into a plastic bag; and every few hours a team of three nurses would turn me over in bed, as if I were a slow-cooking roast. I was not in pain, but I was oppressed with an overwhelming fatigue. The smallest thing left me wanting to lie down and go to sleep, and the muscles on my left side were so weak that even sitting in a chair—which I was able to do after a few days—was exhausting.

After the first, immediate crisis, with which the National Health Service had coped superbly, I was moved to a private room in the National Hospital, Queen Square. The irony of this was that the headquarters of Faber & Faber overlook the imposing red brick façade of this world-famous center for neurology and neurosurgery. For seventeen years, I'd stared out of my window at the patients—shaved, shuffling figures in pajamas—and wondered about their fate. It was intriguing, finally, to be wheeled into the National's shabby, cavernous Victorian interior.

Sarah arrived from San Francisco, white and hollow-faced with worry and loss of sleep. For the next week, she stayed on a camp bed in a corner of my room, jumping up in alarm whenever I stirred in my sleep, though I do not remember this. She had endured her own drama en route. "Robert isn't feeling very well," my mother had said, and her ominous telephone manner, Sarah told me later, had led her to believe that I was likely to die at any moment. In a daze she had got on a flight to London, and had spent the eleven-hour trip huddled under a blanket, drinking shots of whiskey. She says she had never felt so alone as she did that night, surrounded by people in the darkened plane. At one point, she had turned in desperation to her neighbor. "Do you mind if I talk to you a moment? My husband's just had a stroke," she said. The woman looked at her. "I don't know anything about strokes," she replied, and went back to her *Cosmopolitan*.

Later, when I was on my own again, I found that of all my conscious moments at the National the nights were the worst. No one talks about the nights in a hospital. If you sleep, fine. Lie awake, and you think about dying. If I had a headache at night (like the harbinger of the stroke itself), I would think, I shall be dead in the morning; I'll never see Sarah again.

Headaches, often quite severe, were part of the first phase of recovery. My doctor, Andrew Lees, advised me to think of the bleed in my head as a kind of bruise; over time, the scavenging macrophage cells would literally eat up the damage to the cerebral tissue, leaving that part of my brain permanently scarred. I could see for myself what Lees was talking about: an early M.R.I. scan located the bleed, a menacing black blot, deep in the brain, at what the medical report said was "the proximal right middle cerebral artery at its trifurcation." The sinister stain would gradually shrink and fade, but, despite this brilliant pictorial representation, I am, even now, no nearer a reliable explanation of why the stroke occurred in the first place.

Indeed, about forty percent of all strokes are unexplained. This is unnerving for patients and doctors alike. Usually, the contract between doctor and patient is based on a supposition of expertise, of knowledge. When my rehabilitation specialist, Dr. Richard Greenwood, confessed to me that doctors are actually quite ignorant about the brain, it was oddly comforting to know that one of the best minds in the field was also baffled.

None of this, however, discouraged the Queen Square doctors from returning obsessively to the scene of the crime. Had a clot originated in the arteries of the heart? I was sent off for a transesophageal echocardiogram. Was the thyroid to blame? I gave another sample of blood for analysis. These investigations occupied much of my attention during that first month in the hospital, but no one was able to identify an obvious cause, or to tell me how long I would be incapacitated. In the absence of reliable data, the experts took refuge in a studied vagueness: "probably" I'd be fit in "about a year"; after six months, it would be "fairly clear" how much movement would return to my left side; then "perhaps" my arm would become "useful." Meanwhile, I was still profoundly restricted, anxiously watching for evidence of brain repair; the day the big toe on my left foot began to move, it was as though I had discovered a sixth dimension.

Such moments of joy were rare; I cried a lot in the hospital. Sometimes the tears were slow and weepy; at others, uncontrolled and desperate. I could cry for any reason and none; I have since read that this is characteristic of stroke victims. Dr. Lees had assured me that the parts of my brain which control memory, thought, and personality were unaffected, but Sarah was naturally concerned that I might have suffered a change of identity. I noticed, with some amusement, that she was surreptitiously leafing through the pages of my journal. I feigned sleep and watched her checking the latest entries, presumably looking for telltale gibberish. I resisted the temptation to fill a folio or two with "All work and no play makes Jack a dull boy."

I did not pray. Several visitors later asked if, having "looked into the abyss," I had experienced any religious emotions—to which I can honestly reply that I did not. What I did find was that the world seemed almost unbearably precious. Shut away in my room, with the finest English summer of the century scorching outside, I had a craving for sky, earth, and sea—a craving I satisfied, in part, by watching sports and nature programs on television.

In the hours of reflection that followed the end of "Channel Four Racing," I would brood on the paper-thin gap between health and sickness, and take phone calls. One morning in August the bedside phone rang at nine-thirty. "The Holloway Police here. We have to identify a dead body. Where is Queen Square?" Me: "I'm not dead; I'm just a patient." Cop: "I'm sorry, sir, but we have orders to identify this body and I was given this extension. Can you tell me how to find Queen Square?" Me: "I'm not a corpse, thank you very much. Don't you have a map?" Cop: "I was hoping for a bit of cooperation and politeness." Me (*suddenly furious*): "The kind of politeness, I suppose, for which the Metropolitan Police are renowned!" I slammed the phone down.

Sometimes I wondered when I was going to open the newspaper and read my own obituary. I discovered that in the outside world my stroke had caused something of a stir—it was a memento mori to the media dwellers, writers, journalists, and editors who lived as I once had. The chairman of Faber & Faber, Matthew Evans, joked to me that he was becoming so fed up with answering questions about my state of health that he wanted to wear a lapel button reading, "Robert McCrum is dead."

To while away the long hours of August, Sarah began to read aloud to me. Together, we went back to *Alice in Wonderland, The Lion, the Witch, and the Wardrobe*, and *Charlotte's Web*. There was something profoundly consoling about these old friends. I found my thoughts returning to childhood (the rooks caw-cawing in the beech trees of Ashton House, in Cambridge, where I grew up) and then moving forward through the years. It was a self-examination reinforced by the visitors to my bedside. A novice to hospital life, I discovered that the patient must submit to a parade of parents, siblings, friends, ex-girlfriends, and co-workers, each presenting a tiny fragment of lost time for renewal. The patient is the star of the show, but the audience varies: lame-duck specialists; true friends; compassion junkies; hypochondriacs. (It amused me to see the relief on my friends' faces when they discovered that, as one put it, I was "not a drooling vegetable.") And each post brought new letters of sympathy and encouragement, some of them from people I hadn't spoken to or heard from in years.

When I wasn't bombarded by the past, I found I was alone with a rather interesting person, someone I had not spent much time alone with: myself. So while summer turned to fall I eagerly monitored the tiny external changes that constitute convalescence. My physical restrictions lessened, but with excruciating slowness. For the first twelve weeks, I had to move around, if at all, in a wheelchair, pushed by Sarah or by one of the nurses. My sense of helplessness in this situation was very difficult to come to terms with: I had no control over my feelings, particularly when we were outside, and I would rage horribly against whoever was pushing me. Sarah and I had some of our worst moments when, for instance, the wheelchair got stuck in a rut in the road. Nobody would say when, exactly, I'd be well enough to walk again, and at moments like those I saw a vista of infuriating confinement stretching out before me. Sometimes I wondered how I could possibly cope, and more than once I thought that if this was to be my life I would be better dead.

Fortunately, in the universe I could control—the restricted orbit of my hospital bed—I was not completely out of action. I could scribble in my diary, and write letters or postcards with my right hand; I could see friends and take an interest in the outside world, even though the world itself seemed terrifyingly noisy and overpowering whenever I was in it. Once I was into the routine of daily physiotherapy, I had to face up to the slow process of recovery, which, in the case of a stroke, offers a moving target: one is constantly and imperceptibly getting better. I had to learn to adjust, and also to wait.

Six months ago, I could slip across the street to post a letter in the time it takes to type this sentence. Now I would have to raise myself up from my chair, find my cane, limp to the front door (say, three minutes), negotiate the steps to the street, and make my way to the corner (roughly five minutes), and then hobble back and collapse, exhausted, on the sofa, as though I had just run a marathon. Every day, I am acutely reminded that there is a world out there, a world I cannot be part of in quite the same way. One tangible effect of my illness, however, has been a more Zen-like response to the pressures and anxieties of the world, and in my new mood of self-examination I am inclined to say, "So what?"

The truth is that in my "old" life as a fit person I had become a monster of irresponsibility. For years, I had lived for my freedom. I would look up and see the jets circling over London and say to myself, "There is no reason I shouldn't be on a plane to anywhere in the world, given an hour's notice." I reveled in the idea of escape. Psychologically speaking, I carried a passport and a wallet full of international credit cards. Before my stroke, I'd been dissatisfied with my lot; in the hospital, I came to recognize that I'd been ambushed by the "adventure" I was looking for, and was traveling into a new and strange interior: my heart. Today, my passport is in a drawer and I have not made even a domestic credit-card transaction in six months.

In my new and vulnerable condition, I became dependent on my wife, and we have since discovered an intimacy that might, if things had been different, have taken years to establish. Sarah, who had married me, she says, in part because I seemed "strong and vigorous," was now seeing me at my weakest. At first, this was hard for both of us, and it has demanded constant readjustment. Once I came home, I needed Sarah for so many humble, everyday tasks: to help me in and out of the bath in the morning, to make our bed, to get me ready for the day. Strictly speaking, I can dress myself, but in practice I cannot do it without her: I cannot tie a tie or button a shirt cuff. When, finally, I put on my shoes, it is Sarah who eases my feet into my socks and then, with the "splint" that supports my left ankle and foot, into my shoes, and ties the laces. If the morning post brings medical bills to pay, it is Sarah who tears the checks off at the stub, and seals and stamps the envelope. What else? It is Sarah who has to put the breakfast on the table and bring home the food for our evening meal.

I have become friends with slowness, both as a concept and as a way of life. In the past, I was noted for the impressionistic speed with which I could accomplish things. At first, the contrast was a source of great frustration. I had to learn to be patient. In English, the adjectival and nominal meanings of "patient" come from the Latin for "suffering" or "endurance"—*patientia*. A patient is by definition "long-suffering." Dr. Greenwood, on one of his evening visits to my bedside, coined a phrase for this post-crisis stage of recovery. "You are about to go through the rapids," he said.

Dr. Greenwood was right. The fragile vessel of my personality was swamped and buffeted from all sides, and the months after I realized I would survive and began to understand that I'd never be quite the same again were among the worst of my life— beset with depression, frustration, irritation, and fear of failure. At the age of forty-two, I appeared to be reduced to the condition of an old man with a cane, watching the world go by, musing sadly on the past. I had been dumped unceremoniously into the land of the unwell (to me, it is no "kingdom"), and it was not until I got here that I realized what a charmed life I'd led. For forty years, I had hardly seen a doctor or been inside a hospital. Suddenly, my physical condition was at the top of the agenda every day. What's more, I am not going to wake up one morning and find myself magically restored to health. The changes in my condition are infinitesimal—visible only to those who, like Sarah, observe me from day to day.

The frustration of this, I've decided, is a bit like losing your wallet—it's like losing your wallet *every day*. Your wallet *and* your Filofax. The same sense of "Goddammit!" and "Oh, no!"—all those numbers to ring, all those connections to remake, all those little shortcuts that make everyday life bearable. Occasionally, when I lie in bed—the bed in which I awoke on that summer morning so long ago—I think, Perhaps I am dreaming. Sometimes I say it out loud: "Am I dreaming? Did that really happen? Is this really the case?" But no, I am not dreaming. I am changed forever.

Sometimes it is difficult for me to acknowledge the importance of what has happened—to admit that the stroke was an irrevocable event in my personal history. I come from a tight-lipped culture in which the standard response to misfortune is to assert that one is "fine," that one is "perfectly OK." It is, of course, a form of massive denial to claim that one is coping when, plainly, one is not. For me to admit that I have been scared and lonely these last several months is as difficult as it is to admit that I can sometimes feel a profound anger toward the world that has done this to me.

But then I recognize that I have this consolation: I suffered my stroke less than two months after getting married. I was absolutely sure of Sarah in a way I had never been absolutely sure of anyone before, and yet who knows what this crisis might have done to our relationship as newlyweds? We knew and loved each other well, but no better than two people who had crisscrossed the Atlantic for a year in a highly charged romantic daze and had spent barely a calendar month in each other's company. When Sarah was summoned back from San Francisco, she did not know what she might find at the other end of the plane ride. Her new husband might be a vegetable. He might be dead. As it happened, I was conscious and alive, and she, for her part, rose to the occasion with grace, humor, and determination. Now when I wake and find her next to me, every day seems like a blessing. In recent weeks, I have discarded my wheelchair, have begun to drive my car, and have gone back to work. With a cane, I can sustain a very short, leisurely stroll. I am getting out and about in the world, the world that I thought I had lost, and which, with Sarah, seems to me more precious than ever.

SURVIVING CRISIS

Annie Dillard

Annie Dillard's prose is rich and lyrical, like poetry,
but crammed with an abundance of stimulating
ideas and compelling information. This is the essence
of the best creative nonfiction — to introduce readers
to subjects for which they lack a natural inclination
and to make them want to read and learn simply
by the power of the prose and the selection and
re-creation of scene and detail. Dillard is a scholar,
as well as a writer. She once told me that she read
three hundred books in preparation for writing her
most recent novel, The Living.

As you read "An Expedition to the Pole" note
how much Dillard has to say about the plethora of
subjects she chooses to confront — from the Catholic
Church to the decline of the British empire. Note
too, in the tradition of the best reportage, that she is
eager to immerse herself in the experience about
which she writes by attending Catholic services on a
regular basis, as do all good Catholics, which she is
not, and by launching her own expedition to the
Arctic. Note her parallel narrative — two basically
unrelated stories told simultaneously — and
subsequently converged. Dillard bends the genre and
it explodes into a fantasy that is both surreal and
at the same time quite believable.

An Expedition to the Pole

I

There is a singing group in this Catholic church today, a singing group which calls itself "Wildflowers." The lead is a tall, square-jawed teenaged boy, buoyant and glad to be here. He carries a guitar; he plucks out a little bluesy riff and hits some chords. With him are the rest of the Wildflowers. There is an old woman, wonderfully determined; she has long orange hair and is dressed country-and-western style. A long embroidered strap around her neck slings a big western guitar low over her pelvis. Beside her stands a frail, withdrawn fourteen-year-old boy, and a large Chinese man in his twenties who seems to want to enjoy himself but is not quite sure how to. He looks around wildly as he sings, and shuffles his feet. There is also a very tall teenaged girl, presumably the lead singer's girlfriend; she is delicate of feature, half serene and half petrified, a wispy soprano. They straggle out in front of the altar and teach us a brand-new hymn.

It all seems a pity at first, for I have overcome a fiercely anti-Catholic upbringing in order to attend Mass simply and solely to escape Protestant guitars. Why am I here? Who gave these nice Catholics guitars? Why are they not mumbling in Latin and performing superstitious rituals? What is the Pope thinking of?

But nobody said things were going to be easy. A taste for the sublime is a greed like any other, after all; why begrudge the churches their secularism now, when from the general table is rising a general song? Besides, in a way I do not pretend to understand, these people—all the people in all the ludicrous churches—have access to the land.

The Land

The Pole of Relative Inaccessibility is "that imaginary point on the Arctic Ocean farthest from land in any direction." It is a navigator's paper point contrived to console Arctic explorers who, after Peary and Henson reached the North Pole in 1909, had nowhere special to go. There is a Pole of Relative Inaccessibility on the Antarctic continent, also; it is that point of land farthest from salt water in any direction.

The Absolute is the Pole of Relative Inaccessibility located in metaphysics. After all, one of the few things we know about the Absolute is that it is relatively inaccessible. It is that point of spirit farthest from every accessible point of spirit in all directions. Like the others, it is a Pole of the Most Trouble. It is also—I take this as given—the pole of great price.

The People

It is the second Sunday in Advent. For a year I have been attending Mass at this Catholic church. Every Sunday for a year I have run away from home and joined the circus as a dancing bear. We dancing bears have dressed ourselves in buttoned clothes; we mince around the rings on two feet. Today we were restless; we kept dropping onto our forepaws.

No one, least of all the organist, could find the opening hymn. Then no one knew it. Then no one could sing anyway.

There was no sermon, only announcements.

The priest proudly introduced the rascally acolyte who was going to light the two Advent candles. As we all could plainly see, the rascally acolyte had already lighted them.

During the long intercessory prayer, the priest always reads "intentions" from the parishioners. These are slips of paper, dropped into a box before the service begins, on which people have written their private concerns, requesting our public prayers. The priest reads them, one by one, and we respond on cue. "For a baby safely delivered on November twentieth," the priest intoned, "we pray to the Lord." We all responded, "Lord, hear our prayer." Suddenly the priest broke in and confided to our bowed heads, "That's the baby we've been praying for the past two months! The woman just kept getting more and more pregnant!" How often, how shockingly often, have I exhausted myself in church from the effort to keep from laughing out loud? I often laugh all the way home. Then the priest read the next intention: "For my son, that he may forgive his father. We pray to the Lord." "Lord, hear our prayer," we responded, chastened.

A high-school stage play is more polished than this service we have been rehearsing since the year one. In two thousand years, we have not worked out the kinks. We positively glorify them. Week after week we witness the same miracle: that God is so mighty he can stifle his own laughter. Week after week, we witness the same miracle: that God, for reasons unfathomable, refrains from blowing our dancing bear act to smithereens. Week after week Christ washes the disciples' dirty feet, handles their very toes, and repeats, It is all right—believe it or not—to be people.

Who can believe it?

During communion, the priest handed me a wafer which proved to be stuck to five other wafers. I waited while he tore the clump into rags of wafer, resisting the impulse to help. Directly to my left, and all through communion, a woman was banging out the theme from *The Sound of Music* on a piano.

The Land

Nineteenth-century explorers set the pattern for polar expeditions. Elaborately provisioned ships set out for high latitudes. Soon they encounter the pack ice and equinoctial storms. Ice coats the deck, spars, and rigging; the masts and hull shudder; the sea freezes around the rudder, and then fastens on the ship. Early sailors try ramming, sawing, or blasting the ice ahead of the ship before they give up and settle in for the winter. In the nineteenth century, this being "beset" in the pack often killed polar crews; later explorers expected it and learned, finally, to put it to use. Sometimes officers and men move directly onto the pack ice for safety; they drive tent stakes into the ice and pile wooden boxes about for tables and chairs.

Sooner or later, the survivors of that winter or the next, or a select polar party, sets off over the pack ice on foot. Depending on circumstances, they are looking either for a Pole or, more likely, for help. They carry supplies, including boats, on sledges which they "man-haul" on ropes fastened to shoulder harnesses. South Polar expeditions usually begin from a base camp established on shore. In either case, the terrain is so rough, and the men so weakened by scurvy, that the group makes only a few miles a day. Sometimes they find an island on which to live or starve the next winter; sometimes they turn back to safety, stumble onto some outpost of civilization, or are rescued by another expedition; very often, when warm weather comes and the pack ice splits into floes, they drift and tent on a floe, or hop from floe to floe, until the final floe lands, splits, or melts.

In 1847, according to Arctic historian L. P. Kirwan, the American ship *Polaris* "was struck by an enormous floe. And just as stores, records, clothing, equipment, were being flung from the reeling ship, she was swept away through the Arctic twilight, with most, but not all, of her crew on board. Those left behind drifted for thirteen hundred miles on an ice-floe until they were rescued, starving and dazed, off the coast of Labrador."

Polar explorers were chosen, as astronauts are today, from the clamoring, competitive ranks of the sturdy, skilled, and sane. Many of the British leaders, in particular, were men of astonishing personal dignity. Reading their accounts of life *in extremis,* one is struck by their unending formality toward each other. When Scott's Captain Oates sacrificed himself on the Antarctic peninsula because his ruined feet were slowing the march, he stepped outside the tent one night to freeze himself in a blizzard, saying to the others, "I am just going outside and may be some time."

Even in the privacy of their journals and diaries, polar explorers maintain a fine reserve. In his journal, Ernest Shackleton described his feelings upon seeing, for the first time in human history, the Antarctic continent beyond the mountains ringing the Ross Ice Shelf: "We watched the new mountains rise from the great unknown that lay ahead of us," he wrote, "with feelings of keen curiosity, not unmingled with awe." One wonders, after reading a great many such firsthand accounts, if polar explorers were not somehow chosen for the empty and solemn splendor of their prose styles—or even if some eminent Victorians, examining their own prose styles, realized, perhaps dismayed, that from the look of it, they would have to go in for polar exploration. Salomon Andrée, the doomed Swedish balloonist, was dying of starvation on an Arctic island when he confided in his diary, with almost his dying breath, "Our provisions must soon and richly be supplemented, if we are to have any prospect of being able to hold out for a time."

The People

The new Episcopalian and Catholic liturgies include a segment called "passing the peace." Many things can go wrong here. I know of one congregation in New York which fired its priest because he insisted on their passing the peace—which involves nothing more than shaking hands with your neighbors in the pew. The men and women of this small congregation had limits to their endurance; passing the peace was beyond their limits. They could not endure shaking hands with people to whom they bore lifelong grudges. They fired the priest and found a new one sympathetic to their needs.

The rubric for passing the peace requires that one shake hands with whoever is handy and say, "Peace be with you." The other responds, "Peace be with *you*." Every rare once in a while, someone responds simply "Peace." Today I was sitting beside two teenaged lugs with small mustaches. When it came time to pass the peace I shook hands with one of the lugs and said, "Peace be with you," and he said, *"Yeah."*

The Technology: The Franklin Expedition

The Franklin expedition was the turning point in Arctic exploration. The expedition itself accomplished nothing, and all its members died. But the expedition's failure to return, and the mystery of its whereabouts, attracted so much publicity in Europe and the United States that thirty ships set out looking for traces of the ships and men; these search parties explored and mapped the Arctic for the first time, found the northwest passage which

Franklin had sought, and developed a technology adapted to Arctic conditions, a technology capable of bringing explorers back alive. The technology of the Franklin expedition, by contrast, was adapted only to conditions in the Royal Navy officers' clubs in England. The Franklin expedition stood on its dignity.

In 1845, Sir John Franklin and 138 officers and men embarked from England to find the northwest passage across the high Canadian Arctic to the Pacific Ocean. They sailed in two three-masted barques. Each sailing vessel carried an auxiliary steam engine and a twelve-day supply of coal for the entire projected two or three years' voyage. Instead of additional coal, according to L. P. Kirwan, each ship made room for a 1,200-volume library, "a hand-organ, playing fifty tunes," china place settings for officers and men, cut-glass wine goblets, and sterling silver flatware. The officers' sterling silver knives, forks, and spoons were particularly interesting. The silver was of ornate Victorian design, very heavy at the handles and richly patterned. Engraved on the handles were the individual officers' initials and family crests. The expedition carried no special clothing for the Arctic, only the uniforms of Her Majesty's Navy.

The ships set out in high dudgeon, amid enormous glory and fanfare. Franklin uttered his utterance: "The highest object of my desire is faithfully to perform my duty." Two months later a British whaling captain met the two barques in Lancaster Sound; he reported back to England on the high spirits of officers and men. He was the last European to see any of them alive.

Years later, civilization learned that many groups of Inuit—Eskimos—had hazarded across tableaux involving various still-living or dead members of the Franklin expedition. Some had glimpsed, for instance, men pushing and pulling a wooden boat across the ice. Some had found, at a place called Starvation Cove, this boat, or a similar one, and the remains of the thirty-five men who had been dragging it. At Terror Bay the Inuit found a tent on the ice, and in it, thirty bodies. At Simpson Strait some Inuit had seen a very odd sight: the pack ice pierced by the three protruding wooden masts of a barque.

For twenty years, search parties recovered skeletons from all over the frozen sea. Franklin himself—it was learned after twelve years—had died aboard ship. Franklin dead, the ships frozen into the pack winter after winter, their supplies exhausted, the remaining officers and men had decided to walk to help. They outfitted themselves from ships' stores for the journey; their bodies were found with those supplies they had chosen to carry. Accompanying one clump of frozen bodies, for instance, which incidentally showed evidence of cannibalism, were place settings of sterling silver flatware engraved with officers' initials and family crests. A search party found, on the ice far from the ships, a letter clip, and a piece of that very backgammon board which Lady Jane Franklin had given her husband as a parting gift.

Another search party found two skeletons in a boat on a sledge. They had hauled the boat sixty-five miles. With the two skeletons were some chocolate, some guns, some tea, and a great deal of table silver. Many miles south of these two was another skeleton, alone. This was a frozen officer. In his pocket he had, according to Kirwan, "a parody of a sea-shanty." The skeleton was in uniform: trousers and jacket "of fine blue cloth . . . edges with silk braid, with sleeves slashed and bearing five covered buttons each. Over this uniform the dead man had worn a blue greatcoat, with a black silk neckerchief." That was the Franklin expedition.

Sir Robert Falcon Scott, who died on the Antarctic peninsula, was never able to bring himself to use dogs, let alone feed them to each other or eat them. Instead he struggled with English ponies, for whom he carried hay. Scott felt that eating dogs was inhumane; he also felt, as he himself wrote, that when men reach a Pole unaided, their journey has "a fine conception" and "the conquest is more nobly and splendidly won." It is this loftiness of sentiment, this purity, this dignity and self-control, which makes Scott's farewell letters—found under his body—such moving documents.

Less moving are documents from successful polar expeditions. Their leaders relied on native technology, which, as every book ever written about the Inuit puts it, was "adapted to harsh conditions."

Roald Amundsen, who resumed in triumph from the South Pole, traveled Inuit style; he made good speed using sleds and feeding dogs to dogs on a schedule. Robert E. Peary and Matthew

Henson reached the North Pole in the company of four Inuit. Throughout the Peary expedition, the Inuit drove the dog teams, built igloos, and supplied seal and walrus clothing.

There is no such thing as a solitary polar explorer, fine as the conception is.

The People

I have been attending Catholic Mass for only a year. Before that, the handiest church was Congregational. Week after week I climbed the long steps to that little church, entered, and took a seat with some few of my neighbors. Week after week I was moved by the pitiableness of the bare linoleum-floored sacristy which no flowers could cheer or soften, by the terrible singing I so loved, by the fatigued Bible readings, the lagging emptiness and dilution of the liturgy, the horrifying vacuity of the sermon, and by the fog of dreary senselessness pervading the whole, which existed alongside, and probably caused, the wonder of the fact that we came; we returned; we showed up; week after week, we went through with it.

Once while we were reciting the Gloria, a farmer's wife—whom I knew slightly—and I exchanged a sudden, triumphant glance.

Recently I returned to that Congregational church for an ecumenical service. A Catholic priest and the minister served grape juice communion.

Both the priest and the minister were professionals, were old hands. They bungled with dignity and aplomb. Both were at ease and awed; both were half confident and controlled and half bewildered and whispering. I could hear them: "Where is it?" "Haven't you got it?" "I thought *you* had it!"

The priest, new to me, was in his sixties. He was tall; he wore his weariness loosely, standing upright and controlling his breath. When he knelt at the altar, and when he rose from kneeling, his knees cracked. It was a fine church music, this sound of his cracking knees.

The Land

Polar explorers—one gathers from their accounts—sought at the Poles something of the sublime. Simplicity and purity attracted them; they set out to perform clear tasks in uncontaminated lands. The land's austerity held them. They praised the land's spare beauty as if it were a moral or a spiritual quality: "icy halls of cold sublimity," "lofty peaks perfectly covered with eternal snow." Fridtjof Nansen referred to "the great adventure of the ice, deep and pure as infinity . . . the eternal round of the universe and its eternal death." Everywhere polar prose evokes these absolutes, these ideas of "eternity" and "perfection," as if they were some perfectly visible part of the landscape.

They went, I say, partly in search of the sublime, and they found it the only way it can be found, here or there—around the edges, tucked into the corners of the days. For they were people—all of them, even the British—and despite the purity of their conceptions, they man-hauled their humanity to the Poles.

They man-hauled their frail flesh to the Poles, and encountered conditions so difficult that, for instance, it commonly took members of Scott's South Polar party several hours each morning to put on their boots. Day and night they did miserable, niggling, and often fatal battle with frostbitten toes, diarrhea, bleeding gums, hunger, weakness, mental confusion, and despair.

They man-hauled their sweet human absurdity to the Poles. When Robert E. Peary and Matthew Henson reached the North Pole in 1909, Peary planted there in the frozen ocean, according to L. P. Kirwan, the flag of the Dekes: "the colours of the Delta Kappa Epsilon Fraternity at Bowdoin College, of which Peary was an alumnus."

Polar explorers must adapt to conditions. They must adapt, on the one hand, to severe physical limitations; they must adapt, on the other hand—like the rest of us—to ordinary emotional limitations. The hard part is in finding a workable compromise. If you are Peary and have planned your every move down to the last jot and tittle, you can perhaps get away with carrying a Deke flag to the North Pole, if it will make you feel good. After eighteen years' preparation, why not feel a little good? If you are an officer with the Franklin expedition and do not know what you are doing or where you are, but think you cannot eat food except from sterling silver tableware, you cannot get away with it. Wherever we go, there seems to be only one business at hand—that of finding workable compromises between the sublimity of our ideas and the absurdity of the fact of us.

They made allowances for their emotional needs. Overwintering expedition ships commonly carried, in *addition* to sufficient fuel, equipment for the publication of weekly newspapers. The brave polar men sat cooling their heels *in medias* nowhere, reading in cold type their own and their bunkmates' gossip, in such weeklies as Parry's *Winter Chronicle and North Georgia Gazette*, Nansen's *Framsjaa*, or Scott's *South Polar Times* and *The Blizzard*. Polar explorers also amused themselves with theatrical productions. If one had been frozen into the pack ice off Ross Island near Antarctica, aboard Scott's ship *Discovery*, one midwinter night in 1902, one could have seen the only performance of *Ticket of Leave, a screaming comedy in one act*. Similarly, if, in the dead of winter, 1819, one had been a member of young Edward Parry's expedition frozen into the pack ice in the high Arctic, one could have caught the first of a series of fortnightly plays, an uproarious success called *Miss in her Teens*. According to Kirwan, "'This,' Parry dryly remarked, 'afforded to the men such a fund of amusement as fully to justify the expectations we had formed of the utility of theatrical entertainments.'" And you yourself, Royal Navy Commander Edward Parry, were you not yourself the least bit amused? Or at twenty-nine years old did you still try to stand on your dignity?

The Land

God does not demand that we give up our personal dignity, that we throw in our lot with random people, that we lose ourselves and turn from all that is not him. God needs nothing, asks nothing, and demands nothing, like the stars. It is a life with God which demands these things.

Experience has taught the race that if knowledge of God is the end, then these habits of life are not the means but the condition in which the means operates. You do not have to do these things; not at all. God does not, I regret to report, give a hoot.

You do not have to do these things—unless you want to know God. They work on you, not on him.

You do not have to sit outside in the dark. If, however, you want to look at the stars, you will find that darkness is necessary. But the stars neither require nor demand it.

The Technology

It is a matter for computation: how far can one walk carrying how much silver? The computer balks at the problem; there are too many unknowns. The computer puts its own questions: Who is this "one"? What degree of stamina may we calculate for? Under what conditions does this one propose to walk, at what latitudes? With how many companions, how much aid?

The People

The Mass has been building to this point, to the solemn saying of those few hushed phrases known as the Sanctus. We have confessed, in a low, distinct murmur, our sins; we have become the people broken, and then the people made whole by our reluctant assent to the priest's proclamation of God's mercy. Now, as usual, we will, in the stillest voice, stunned, repeat the Sanctus, repeat why it is that we have come:

> Holy, holy, holy Lord,
> God of power and might,
> heaven and earth are full of your glory . . .

It is here, if ever, that one loses oneself at sea. Here, one's eyes roll up, and the sun rolls overhead, and the floe rolls underfoot, and the scene of unrelieved ice and sea rolls over the planet's pole and over the world's rim wide and unseen.

Now, just as we are dissolved in our privacy and about to utter the words of the Sanctus, the lead singer of Wildflowers bursts onstage from the wings. I raise my head. He is taking enormous, enthusiastic strides and pumping his guitar's neck up and down. Drooping after him come the orange-haired country-and-western-style woman; the soprano, who, to shorten herself, carries her neck forward like a horse; the withdrawn boy; and the Chinese man, who is holding a tambourine as if it had stuck by some defect to his fingers and he has resolved to forget about it. These array themselves in a clump downstage right. The priest is nowhere in sight.

Alas, alack, oh brother, we are going to have to *sing* the Sanctus. There is, of course, nothing new about singing the Sanctus. The lead singer smiles disarmingly. There is a new arrangement. He hits a chord with the flat of his hand. The Chinese man with sudden vigor bangs the tambourine and looks at his hands, startled. They run us through the Sanctus three or four times. The words are altered a bit to fit the strong upbeat rhythm:

Heaven and earth
(Heaven and earth earth earth earth earth)
Are full (full full full)
Of your glory . . .

Must I join this song? May I keep only my silver? My backgammon board, I agree, is a frivolity. I relinquish it. I will leave it right here on the ice. But my silver? My family crest? One knife, one fork, one spoon, to carry beneath the glance of heaven and back? I have lugged it around for years; I am, I say, superlatively strong. Don't laugh. I am superlatively strong! Don't laugh; you'll make *me* laugh. The answer is no. We are singing the Sanctus, it seems, and they are passing the plate. I would rather, I think, undergo the famous dark night of the soul than encounter in church the dread hootenanny—but these purely personal preferences are of no account, and maladaptive to boot. They are passing the plate and I toss in my schooling; I toss in my rank in the Royal Navy, my erroneous and incomplete charts, my pious refusal to eat sled dogs, my watch, my keys, and my shoes. I was looking for bigger game, not little moral lessons; but who can argue with conditions?

"Heaven and earth earth earth earth earth," we sing. The withdrawn boy turns his head toward a man in front of me, who

must be his father. Unaccountably, the enormous teenaged soprano catches my eye, exultant. A low shudder or shock crosses
our floe. We have split from the pack; we have crossed the Arctic
Circle, and the current has us.

The Land

We are clumped on an ice floe drifting over the black polar sea.
Heaven and earth are full of our terrible singing. Overhead we see
a blurred, colorless brightness; at our feet we see the dulled, swift
ice and recrystallized snow. The sea is black and green; a hundred
thousand floes and bergs float in the water and spin and scatter in
the current around us everywhere as far as we can see. The wind is
cool, moist, and scented with salt.

I am wearing, I discover, the uniform of a Keystone Kop. I
examine my hat: a black cardboard constable's hat with a white
felt star stapled to the band above the brim. My dark Keystone
Kop jacket is nicely belted, and there is a tin badge on my chest. A
holster around my hips carries a popgun with a cork on a string,
and a red roll of caps. My feet are bare, but I feel no cold. I am
skating around on the ice, and singing, and bumping into people
who, because the ice is slippery, bump into other people. "Excuse
me!" I keep saying, "I beg your pardon woops there!"

When a crack develops in our floe and opens at my feet, I
jump across it—skillfully, I think—but my jump pushes my side
of the floe away, and I wind up leaping full tilt into the water. The
Chinese man extends a hand to pull me out, but alas, he slips and
I drag him in. The Chinese man and I are treading water, singing,
and collecting a bit of a crowd. It takes a troupe of circus clowns
to get us both out. I check my uniform at once and learn that my
rather flattering hat is intact, my trousers virtually unwrinkled,
but my roll of caps is wet. The Chinese man is fine; we thank the
clowns.

This troupe of circus clowns, I hear, is poorly paid. They are
invested in bright, loose garments; they are a bunch of sponta-
neous, unskilled, oversized children; they joke and bump into
people. At one end of the floe, ten of them—red, yellow, and
blue—are trying to climb up on each other to make a human
pyramid. It is a wonderfully funny sight, because they have put

the four smallest clowns on the bottom, and the biggest, fattest clown is trying to climb to the top. The rest of the clowns are doing gymnastics; they tumble on the ice and flip cheerfully in midair. Their crucifixes fly from their ruffled necks as they flip, and hit them on their bald heads as they land. Our floe is smaller now, and we seem to have drifted into a faster bit of current. Repeatedly we ram little icebergs, which rock as we hit them. Some of them tilt clear over like punching bags; they bounce back with great splashes, and water streams down their blue sides as they rise. The country-and-western-style woman is fending off some of the larger bergs with a broom. The lugs with the mustaches have found, or brought, a Frisbee, and a game is developing down the middle of our floe. Near the Frisbee game, a bunch of people including myself and some clowns are running. We fling ourselves down on the ice, shoulders first, and skid long distances like pucks.

Now the music ceases and we take our seats in the pews. A baby is going to be baptized. Overhead the sky is brightening; I do not know if this means we have drifted farther north, or all night.

The People

The baby's name is Oswaldo; he is a very thin baby who looks to be about one. He never utters a peep; he looks grim, and stiff as a planked shad. His parents—his father carrying him—and his godparents, the priest, and two acolytes, are standing on the ice between the first row of pews and the linoleum-floored sacristy. I am resting my bare feet on the velvet prie-dieu—to keep those feet from playing on the ice during the ceremony.

Oswaldo is half Filipino. His mother is Filipino. She has a wide mouth with much lipstick, and wide eyes; she wears a tight black skirt and stiletto heels. The father looks like Ozzie Nelson. He has marcelled yellow hair, a bland, meek face, and a big, meek nose. He is wearing a brown leather flight jacket. The godparents are both Filipinos, one of whom, in a pastel denim jump suit, keeps mugging for the Instamatic camera which another family member is shooting from the aisle.

The baby has a little red scar below one eye. He is wearing a long white lace baptismal gown, blue tennis shoes with white rubber toes, and red socks.

The priest anoints the baby's head with oil. He addresses to the parents several articles of faith: "Do you believe in God, the Father Almighty, creator of Heaven and earth?" "Yes, we believe."

The priest repeats a gesture he says was Christ's, explaining that it symbolically opens the infant's five senses to the knowledge of God. Uttering a formal prayer, he lays his hand loosely over Oswaldo's face and touches in rapid succession his eyes, ears, nose, and mouth. The baby blinks. The priest, whose voice is sometimes lost in the ruff at his neck, or blown away by the wind, is formal and gentle in his bearing; he knows the kid is cute, but he is not going to sentimentalize the sacrament.

Since our floe spins, we in the pews see the broken floes and tilting bergs, the clogged, calm polar sea, and the variously lighted sky and water's rim, shift and revolve enormously behind the group standing around the baby. Once I think I see a yellowish polar bear spurting out of the water as smoothly as if climbing were falling. I see the bear splash and flow onto a distant floeberg which tilts out of sight.

Now the acolytes bring a pitcher, a basin, and a linen towel. The father tilts the rigid baby over the basin; the priest pours water from the pitcher over the baby's scalp; the mother sops the baby with the linen towel and wraps it over his head, so that he looks, proudly, as though he has just been made a swami.

To conclude, the priest brings out a candle, for the purpose, I think, of pledging everybody to Christian fellowship with Oswaldo. Actually, I do not know what it is for; I am not listening. I am watching the hands at the candlestick. Each of the principals wraps a hand around the brass candlestick: the two acolytes with their small, pale hands at its base, the two families—Oswaldo's and his godparents'—with their varicolored hands in a row, and the priest at the top, as though he has just won the bat toss at baseball. The baby rides high in his father's arms, pointing his heels in his tennis shoes, silent, wanting down. His father holds him firmly with one hand and holds the candlestick beside his wife's hand with the other. The priest and the seated members of Wildflowers start clapping then—a round of applause for everybody here on the ice!—so we clap.

II

Months have passed; years have passed. Whatever ground gained has slipped away. New obstacles arise, and faintness of heart, and dread.

The Land

Polar explorers commonly die of hypothermia, starvation, scurvy, or dysentery; less commonly they contract typhoid fever (as Stefansson did), vitamin A poisoning from polar bear liver, or carbon monoxide poisoning from incomplete combustion inside tents sealed by snow. Very commonly, as a prelude to these deaths, polar explorers lose the use of their feet; their frozen toes detach when they remove their socks.

Particularly vivid was the death of a certain Mr. Joseph Green, the astronomer on Sir James Cook's first voyage to high latitudes. He took sick aboard ship. One night "in a fit of the phrensy," as a contemporary newspaper reported, he rose from his bunk and "put his legs out of the portholes, which was the occasion of his death."

Vitus Bering, shipwrecked in 1740 on Bering Island, was found years later preserved in snow. An autopsy showed he had had many lice, he had scurvy, and had died of a "rectal fistula which forced gas gangrene into his tissues."

The bodies of various members of the Sir John Franklin expedition of 1845 were found over the course of twenty years, by thirty search expeditions, in assorted bizarre postures scattered over the ice of Victoria Strait, Beechey Island, and King William Island.

Sir Robert Falcon Scott reached the South Pole on January 17, 1912, only to discover a flag that Roald Amundsen had planted there a month earlier. Scott's body, and the bodies of two of his companions, turned up on the Ross Ice Shelf eleven miles south of one of their own supply depots. The bodies were in sleeping bags. His journals and farewell letters, found under his body, indicated that the other two had died first. Scott's torso was well out of his sleeping bag, and he had opened wide the collar of his parka, exposing his skin.

Never found were the bodies of Henry Hudson, his young son, and four men, whom mutineers in 1610 had lowered from their ship in a dinghy, in Hudson's Bay, without food or equipment. Never found were the bodies of Sir John Franklin himself, or of Amundsen and seventeen other men who set out for the Arctic in search of a disastrous Italian expedition, or the bodies of Scott's men Evans and Oates. Never found were most of the drowned crew of the United States ship *Polaris* or the body of her commander, who died sledging on the ice.

Of the United States Greely expedition to the North Pole, all men died but six. Greely himself, one of the six survivors, was found "on his hands and knees with long hair in pigtails." Of the United States De Long expedition to the North Pole in the *Jeannette*, all men died but two. Of the *Jeannette* herself and her equipment, nothing was found until three years after she sank, when, on a beach on the other side of the polar basin, a Greenlander discovered a pair of yellow oilskin breeches stamped *Jeannette*.

The People

Why do we people in churches seem like cheerful, brainless tourists on a packaged tour of the Absolute?

The tourists are having coffee and doughnuts on Deck C. Presumably someone is minding the ship, correcting the course, avoiding icebergs and shoals, fueling the engines, watching the radar screen, noting weather reports radioed in from shore. No one would dream of asking the tourists to do these things. Alas, among the tourists on Deck C, drinking coffee and eating doughnuts, we find the captain, and all the ship's officers, and all the ship's crew. The officers chat; they swear; they wink a bit at slightly raw jokes, just like regular people. The crew members have funny accents. The wind seems to be picking up.

On the whole, I do not find Christians, outside of the catacombs, sufficiently sensible of conditions. Does anyone have the foggiest idea what sort of power we so blithely invoke? Or, as I suspect, does no one believe a word of it? The churches are children playing on the floor with their chemistry sets, making up a batch of TNT to kill a Sunday morning. It is madness to wear ladies' straw hats and velvet hats to church; we should all be wearing crash helmets. Ushers should issue life preservers and signal flares; they should lash us to our pews. For the sleeping god may wake someday and take offense, or the waking god may draw us out to where we can never return.

The eighteenth-century Hasidic Jews had more sense, and more belief. One Hasidic slaughterer, whose work required invoking the Lord, bade a tearful farewell to his wife and children every morning before he set out for the slaughterhouse. He felt, every morning, that he would never see any of them again. For every day, as he himself stood with his knife in his hand, the words of his prayer carried him into danger. After he called on God, God might notice and destroy him before he had time to utter the rest, "Have mercy."

Another Hasid, a rabbi, refused to promise a friend to visit him the next day: "How can you ask me to make such a promise? This evening I must pray and recite 'Hear, O Israel.' When I say these words, my soul goes out to the utmost rim of life. . . . Perhaps I shall not die this time either, but how can I now promise to do something at a time after the prayer?"

Assorted Wildlife

INSECTS

I like insects for their stupidity. A paper wasp—*Polistes*—is fumbling at the stained-glass window on my right. I saw the same sight in the same spot last Sunday: Pssst! Idiot! Sweetheart! Go around by the door! I hope we seem as endearingly stupid to God—bumbling down into lamps, running half-wit across the floor, banging for days at the hinge of an opened door. I hope so. It does not seem likely.

PENGUINS

According to visitors, Antarctic penguins are . . . adorable. They are tame! They are funny!

Tourists in Antarctica are mostly women of a certain age. They step from the cruise ship's rubber Zodiacs wearing bright ship's-issue parkas; they stalk around on the gravel and squint into the ice glare; they exclaim over the penguins, whom they find tame, funny, and adorable; they take snapshots of each other with the penguins, and look around cheerfully for something else to look around at.

The penguins are adorable, and the wasp at the stained-glass window is adorable, because in each case their impersonations of human dignity so evidently fail. What are the chances that God finds our failed impersonation of human dignity adorable? Or is he fooled? What odds do you give me?

III

The Land

Several years ago I visited the high Arctic and saw it: the Arctic Ocean, the Beaufort Sea. The place was Barter Island, inside the Arctic Circle, in the Alaskan Arctic north of the North Slope. I stood on the island's ocean shore and saw what there was to see: a pile of colorless stripes. Through binoculars I could see a bigger pile of colorless stripes.

It seemed reasonable to call the colorless stripe overhead "sky," and reasonable to call the colorless stripe at my feet "ice," for I could see where it began. I could distinguish, that is, my shoes, and the black gravel shore, and the nearby frozen ice the wind had smashed ashore. It was this mess of ice—ice breccia, pressure ridges, and standing floes, ice sheets upright, tilted, frozen together and jammed—which extended out to the horizon. No matter how hard I blinked, I could not put a name to any of the other stripes. Which was the horizon? Was I seeing land, or water, or their reflections in low clouds? Was I seeing the famous "water sky," the "frost smoke," or the "ice blink"?

In his old age, James McNeill Whistler used to walk down to the Atlantic shore carrying a few thin planks and his paints. On the planks he painted, day after day, in broad, blurred washes representing sky, water, and shore, three blurry light-filled stripes. These are late Whistlers; I like them very much. In the high Arctic I thought of them, for I seemed to be standing in one of them. If I loosed my eyes from my shoes, the gravel at my feet, or the chaos of ice at the shore, I saw what newborn babies must see: nothing but senseless variations of light on the retinas. The world was a color-field painting wrapped round me at an unknown distance; I hesitated to take a step.

There was, in short, no recognizable three-dimensional space in the Arctic. There was also no time. The sun never set, but neither did it appear. The dim round-the-clock light changed haphazardly when the lid of cloud thickened or thinned. Circumstances made the eating of meals random or impossible. I slept when I was tired. When I woke I walked out into the colorless stripes and the revolving winds, where atmosphere mingled with distance, and where land, ice, and light blurred into a dreamy, freezing vapor which, lacking anything else to do with the stuff, I breathed. Now and then a white bird materialized out of the vapor and screamed. It was, in short, what one might, searching for words, call a beautiful land; it was more beautiful still when the sky cleared and the ice shone in the dark water.

The Technology

It is for the Pole of Relative Inaccessibility I am searching, and have been searching, in the mountains and along the seacoasts for years. The aim of this expedition is, as Pope Gregory put it in his time, "To attain to somewhat of the unencompassed light, by stealth, and scantily." How often have I mounted this same expedition, has my absurd barque set out half-caulked for the Pole?

The Land

"These incidents are *true*," I read in an 1880 British history of Arctic exploration. "These incidents are *true*,—the storm, the drifting ice-raft, the falling berg, the sinking ship, the breaking up of the great frozen floe: these scenes are *real*,—the vast plains of ice, the ridged hummocks, the bird-thronged cliff, the far-stretching glacier."

Polar exploration is no longer the fashion it was during the time of the Franklin expedition, when beachgoers at Brighton thronged to panoramas of Arctic wastes painted in shopwindows, and when many thousands of Londoners jammed the Vauxhall pleasure gardens to see a diorama of polar seas. Our attention is elsewhere now, but the light-soaked land still exists; I have seen it.

The Technology

In the nineteenth century, a man deduced Antarctica.

During that time, no one on earth knew for certain whether there was any austral land mass at all, although the American Charles Wilkes claimed to have seen it. Some geographers and explorers speculated that there was no land, only a frozen Antarctic Ocean; others posited two large islands in the vicinity of the Pole. That there is one continent was not in fact settled until 1935.

In 1893, one John Murray presented to the Royal Geographic Society a deduction of the Antarctic continent. His expedition's ship, the *Challenger*, had never come within sight of any such continent. His deduction proceeded entirely from dredgings and soundings. In his presentation he posited a large, single continent, a speculative map of which he furnished. He described accurately the unknown continent's topology: its central plateau with its permanent high-pressure system, its enormous glacier facing the Southern Ocean, its volcanic ranges at one coast, and at another coast, its lowland ranges and hills. He was correct.

Deduction, then, is possible—though no longer fashionable. There are many possible techniques for the exploration of high latitudes. There is, for example, such a thing as a drift expedition.

When that pair of yellow oilskin breeches belonging to the lost crew of the *Jeannette* turned up after three years in Greenland, having been lost north of central Russia, Norwegian explorer Fridtjof Nansen was interested. On the basis of these breeches' travels he plotted the probable direction of the current in the polar basin. Then he mounted a drift expedition: in 1893 he drove his ship, the *Fram*, deliberately into the pack ice and settled in to wait while the current moved north and, he hoped, across the Pole. For almost two years, he and a crew of twelve lived aboard ship as the frozen ocean carried them. Nansen wrote in his diary,

"I long to return to life . . . the years are passing here . . . Oh! at times this inactivity crushes one's very soul; one's life seems as dark as the winter night outside; there is sunlight upon no other part of it except the past and the far, far distant future. I feel as if I *must* break through this deadness."

The current did not carry them over the Pole, so Nansen and one companion set out one spring with dog sledges and kayaks to reach the Pole on foot. Conditions were too rough on the ice, however, so after reaching a record northern latitude, the two turned south toward land, wintering together finally in a stone hut on Franz Josef Land and living on polar bear meat. The following spring they returned, after almost three years, to civilization.

Nansen's was the first of several drift expeditions. During World War I, members of a Canadian Arctic expedition camped on an ice floe seven miles by fifteen miles; they drifted for six months over four hundred miles in the Beaufort Sea. In 1937, an airplane deposited a Soviet drift expedition on an ice floe near the North Pole. These four Soviet scientists drifted for nine months while their floe, colliding with grounded ice, repeatedly split into ever-smaller pieces.

The Land

I have, I say, set out again.

The days tumble with meanings. The corners heap up with poetry; whole unfilled systems litter the ice.

The Technology

A certain Lieutenant Maxwell, a member of Vitus Bering's second polar expedition, wrote, "You never feel safe when you have to navigate in waters which are completely blank."

Cartographers call blank spaces on a map "sleeping beauties."

On our charts I see the symbol for shoals and beside it the letters "P.D." My neighbor in the pew, a lug with a mustache who has experience of navigational charts and who knows how to take a celestial fix, tells me that the initials stand for "Position Doubtful."

The Land

To learn the precise location of a Pole, choose a clear, dark night to begin. Locate by ordinary navigation the Pole's position within an area of several square yards. Then arrange on the ice in that area a series of loaded cameras. Aim the cameras at the sky's zenith; leave their shutters open. Develop the film. The film from that camera located precisely at the Pole will show the night's revolving stars as perfectly circular concentric rings.

The Technology

I have a taste for solitude, and silence, and for what Plotinus called "the flight of the alone to the Alone." I have a taste for solitude. Sir John Franklin had, apparently, a taste for backgammon. Is either of these appropriate to conditions?

You quit your house and country, quit your ship, and quit your companions in the tent, saying, "I am just going outside and may be some time." The light on the far side of the blizzard lures you. You walk, and one day you enter the spread heart of silence, where lands dissolve and seas become vapor and ices sublime under unknown stars. This is the end of the Via Negativa, the lightless edge where the slopes of knowledge dwindle, and love for its own sake, lacking an object, begins.

The Land

I have put on silence and waiting. I have quit my ship and set out on foot over the polar ice. I carry chronometer and sextant, tent, stove and fuel, meat and fat. For water I melt the pack ice in hatchet-hacked chips; frozen salt water is fresh. I sleep when I can walk no longer. I walk on a compass bearing toward geographical north.

I walk in emptiness; I hear my breath. I see my hand and compass, see the ice so wide it arcs, see the planet's peak curving and its low atmosphere held fast on the dive. The years are passing here. I am walking, light as any handful of aurora; I am light as sails, a pile of colorless stripes; I cry "heaven and earth indistinguishable!" and the current underfoot carries me and I walk.

The blizzard is like a curtain; I enter it. The blown snow heaps in my eyes. There is nothing to see or to know. I wait in the tent, myself adrift and emptied, for weeks while the storm unwinds. One day it is over, and I pick up my tent and walk. The storm has scoured the air; the clouds have lifted; the sun rolls round the sky like a fish in a round bowl, like a pebble rolled in a tub, like a swimmer, or a melody flung and repeating, repeating enormously overhead on all sides.

My name is Silence. Silence is my bivouac, and my supper sipped from bowls. I robe myself mornings in loose strings of stones. My eyes are stones; a chip from the pack ice fills my mouth. My skull is a polar basin; my brain pan grows glaciers, and icebergs, and grease ice, and floes. The years are passing here.

Far ahead is open water. I do not know what season it is, know how long I have walked into the silence like a tunnel widening before me, into the horizon's spread arms which widen like water. I walk to the pack ice edge, to the rim which calves its floes into the black and green water; I stand at the edge and look ahead. A scurf of candle ice on the water's skin as far as I can see scratches the sea and crumbles whenever a lump of ice or snow bobs or floats through it. The floes are thick in the water, some of them large as lands. By my side is passing a flat pan of floe from which someone extends an oar. I hold the oar's blade and jump. I land on the long floe.

No one speaks. Here, at the bow of the floe, the bright clowns have staked themselves to the ice. With tent stakes and ropes they have lashed their wrists and ankles to the floe on which they lie stretched and silent, face up. Among the clowns, and similarly staked, are many boys and girls, some women, and a few men from various countries. One of the men is Nansen, the Norwegian explorer who drifted. One of the women repeatedly opens and closes her fists. One of the clowns has opened his neck ruffle, exposing his skin. For many hours I pass among these staked people, intending to return later and take my place.

Farther along I see that the tall priest is here, the priest who served grape juice communion at an ecumenical service many years ago, in another country. He is very old. Alone on a wind-streaked patch of snow he kneels, stands, and kneels, and stands, and kneels. Not far from him, at the floe's side, sitting on a packing crate, is the deducer John Murray. He lowers a plumb bob overboard and pays out the line. He is wearing the antique fur hat of a Doctor of Reason, such as Erasmus wears in his portrait; it is understood that were he ever to return and present his findings, he would be ridiculed, for his hat. Scott's Captain Oates is here; he has no feet. It is he who stepped outside his tent, to save his friends. Now on his dignity he stands and mans the sheet of a square linen sail; he has stepped the wooden mast on a hillock amidships.

From the floe's stern I think I hear music; I set out, but it takes me several sleeps to get there. I am no longer using the tent. Each time I wake, I study the floe and the ocean horizon for signs—signs of the pack ice which we left behind, or of open water, or land, or any weather. Nothing changes; there is only the green sea and the floating ice, and the black sea in the distance speckled by bergs, and a steady wind astern which smells of unknown mineral salts, some ocean floor.

At last I reach the floe's broad stern, its enormous trailing coast, its throngs, its many cooking fires. There are children carrying babies, and men and women painting their skins and trying to catch their reflections in the water to leeward. Near the water's edge there is a wooden upright piano, and a bench with a telephone book on it. A woman is sitting on the telephone book and banging out the Sanctus on the keys. The wind is picking up. I am singing at the top of my lungs, for a lark.

Many clowns are here; one of them is passing out Girl Scout cookies, all of which are stuck together. Recently, I learn, Sir John Franklin and crew have boarded this floe, and so have the crews of the lost *Polaris* and the *Jeannette.* The men, whose antique uniforms are causing envious glances, are hungry. Some of them start rough-housing with the rascally acolyte. One crewman carries the boy on his back along the edge to the piano, where he abandons him for a clump of cookies and a seat on the bench beside the short pianist, whose bare feet, perhaps on account of the telephone book, cannot reach the pedals. She starts playing "The Sound of Music." "You know any Bach?" I say to the lady at the piano, whose legs seem to be highly involved with those of the hungry crewman; "You know any Mozart? Or maybe 'How Great Thou Art'?" A skeletal officer wearing a black silk neckerchief has located Admiral Peary, recognizable from afar by the curious flag he holds. Peary and the officer together are planning a talent show and skits. When they approach me, I volunteer to sing "Antonio Spangonio, That Bum Toreador" and/or to read a piece of short fiction; they say they will let me know later.

Christ, under the illusion that we are all penguins, is crouched down posing for snapshots. He crouches, in his robe, between the lead singer of Wildflowers, who is joyfully trying to determine the best angle at which to hold his guitar for the camera, and the farmer's wife, who keeps her eyes on her painted toenails until the Filipino godfather with the camera says "Cheese." The country-and-western woman, singing, succeeds in pressing a cookie upon the baby Oswaldo. The baby Oswaldo is standing in his lace gown and blue tennis shoes in the center of a circle of explorers, confounding them.

In my hand I discover a tambourine. Ahead as far as the brittle horizon, I see icebergs among the floes. I see tabular bergs and floebergs and dark cracks in the water between them. Low overhead on the underside of the thickening cloud cover are dark colorless stripes reflecting pools of open water in the distance. I am banging on the tambourine, and singing whatever the piano player plays; now it is "On Top of Old Smoky." I am banging the tambourine and belting the song so loudly that people are edging away. But how can any of us tone it down? For we are nearing the Pole.

Joan Mikulka Albert

"*In* The Rose and the Ring, *a short novella for children, William Makepeace Thackeray has Fairy Blackstick wish her godson, the prince, 'a little misfortune' as a christening gift,*" Joan Mikulka Albert says. "*The key word here is 'little.' It is part of the heritage of western culture to trust that pain will make one better, more worthy. Our literature is full of such stories. We love to believe that there are rewards for such suffering. 'A little misfortune' might, as it did for the prince, make you grateful when it's gone, and nicer because of that. All people have 'a little misfortune' in their lives. But only hard work, and sometimes professional help, improve the character in the face of tremendous hardship. Crises have more often broken people than built them up; perhaps that's why we need the stories.*"

Counting on the Heart

"People don't live more than three years with a heart as damaged as yours," he says, looking right at me. He's handsome, Irish, reminds me of a boy I used to date from Notre Dame more than thirty years ago.

The doctor has a large head, lots of hair. His graying temples fooled me, but today in his small office I see he's young. Not much older than my sons. Was it the new drugs or was I too scared in the hospital to see clearly? I was there because my lungs were filled with fluid. I was exhausted and breathless. Drowning. I couldn't believe it was all caused by a damaged heart. I've always counted on my heart.

Now the doctor asks if I'm forty. "Fifty," I say, imagining that to him forty and fifty are both old. But it's not the years at all. It's not about numbers. I feel old because I'm weak, stiff, and nauseous. Cachexic is how one doctor described me. "Physical exam shows a dyspneic, somewhat cachexic woman." Dyspneic means "air hungry," and cachexic describes "a generally weakened emaciated condition of the body."

All I have to do here in the chair near his dust-free desk is process the pieces of information he's giving me that I don't want to hear. The piece about the damage to my heart, my projected life span, and the piece about the heart and lung transplant I could get, maybe, to give me a few more years. And the part about my size. "Well, most people, you know, are a bit bigger than you are. There aren't a lot of small hearts out there."

I could argue.

I've lost track of the days. Summer came and went so fast and slow. Sick people's time I call it. Very different, I contend, from healthy people's time. I've been unwell since last January.

Today is warm and humid. I managed to find a blue Indian

cotton skirt, a white short-sleeved blouse with large buttons I don't have to struggle with. I have bad hands, damaged during the surgery on my spine in 1991 and again last January. (Buttons take forever. I can do it, but the effort.)

For this trip to the doctor's office I wore my sunglasses and put on earrings. Tried to act as if the only really weird things about me were the tank of oxygen that I carry over my shoulder in the ugly brown vinyl case, and my bent neck.

Since the eighteen-hour surgery in January to remove the last of a benign spinal tumor, my head bends forward from the base of my neck. The original tumor extended from C1 to T2. That means all the vertebrae in the neck and the two thoracic vertebrae. A tumor wrapped around my cord, like a garter snake. A benign tumor compromising my spine, threatening paralysis.

In 1989 the neurosurgeon removed part of six vertebrae to make more room for the tumor. In 1991, my chronic pain turned into the more dangerous numbness. "We don't care about pain," the neurosurgeon said when I complained. "It's numbness and weakness that worries us." That time he took most of the tumor and a lot of my neck too.

But the bent neck, and the lung trouble which makes me "air hungry," and also, perhaps, the damage to my heart are caused by something else entirely—a fibrosis, which could be a rare side effect from a medicine prescribed for a pituitary tumor found on my brain. I had no symptoms but I took the small tablet once a day for two and a half years to avoid blindness, or more surgery. The fibrosis is so rare it isn't even on the endless list of the medicine's possible adverse reactions and contraindications.

I have not spoken to the miracle doctor, the neurosurgeon, since my heart started failing in February. The heart is not his territory.

My supervisor for my first social work internship, Anne, drove me to the heart doctor's office. I went back to school two years ago, in training to work with the elderly when the photography I'd been doing became painful, impossible, because of the tumor in my spine. Weddings had been my mainstay but I couldn't be fast enough with my damaged hands, and the equipment was heavy. Besides, I told myself, I was interested in a change. I also think I wanted some instructions for aging—I never doubted my four score and ten. I never doubted my sixties, seventies, and eighties.

Anne is forty-one, which seems an age of innocence to me now. At forty-one my tumor was only tiny twinges of pain in my arms and neck. I had energy, I tried to look sexy. I did. I thought about it. I was trying to keep my younger boyfriend interested. Except for the flu and an occasional headache I was never, ever sick. I took my health, my spine, my lung function, and my heart utterly for granted.

I'd been alone with my kids for twelve years when I was forty-one. My husband took off right after our third son was born. I was formed by the rejection. I never trusted men for the long term after that.

Anne is a good social worker. During our drive back to my house she is appropriately serious, as horrified as I am. She does not try to cheer me up or change the subject. She drops me off and drives home in shock and I go inside and think about the magic of numbers, the horror of knowing. My mother is eighty and healthy. She's likely to have ten to fifteen more years. With luck I'll have three, three years is too little. I want more, no, I want uncertainty. I want to not know. My heart is beating too fast. I want to slow it down, stretch out my time.

I climb up the stairs to my apartment exhausted, breathless, utterly depleted. As I collapse on the hospital bed I have been renting since the January surgery, I think of the boy the doctor reminds me of. I dated him in my junior year at St. Mary's, the girls' college next to Notre Dame. If we had married would he have stayed, like so many of my friends' husbands? Why did I choose a man who'd leave without warning? Who has now, just this year, left his second wife the same way he left me. Why am I asking myself these same questions again, now? Questions I've asked myself off and on for years. Is my suddenly shortened life causing this reverie? "Life review" we call it when the elderly do it—gather their life's pleasures, accomplishments, and heartaches and try to make sense of it.

It's September. It's been cold and rainy every day for a week. Today I see the cardiac specialist in the transplant team at General Hospital. His huge new office reminds me of a hotel lobby. He tells me that the fibrosis will make the transplant surgery impossible. "It's a complicated and very bloody surgery," he says. His gentle face makes a strange sneer as he talks. I wonder if he knows his face does that. It's as if his face suffers for the bad news he delivers.

"We'd have to open you up completely." He advises that the fibrosis, the mysterious scar tissue replacing all my connective tissue, complicates any surgery for me, making the usually predictable ways into the body labyrinthine, complex. The knife cuts and finds confusion. A surgeon couldn't proceed on my body with the requisite speed.

The surgery I had in January took eighteen hours because of the mess. "You are all full of fibrosis," said the thoracic doctor standing at the foot of my bed in the ICU two days after the surgery. He was not pleased. He was apologetic for damaging my vocal cord but mostly angry because I'd made things too hard. Doctors, like all of us, love success. I've learned not to expect sympathy or even a visit when I get worse or cause complications.

My sons are breaking up with girlfriends these days. My youngest, Nathan, does not hesitate to remind me that he is afraid he may lose this girl he has been with a long time partly because of my bad example. I have provided love but not the stability of a nuclear family or the example of working things out with a partner.

I want to tell Nathan that life tricks you, that I hadn't planned any of this. I want to tell him I maybe should have married someone else. But if I had I wouldn't have Nathan. So I just listen and let him tell me how hard this is for him, that he might lose his girlfriend, that he might lose me.

I also want to tell him I have liked my life, even without a husband. And that I consider myself blessed, even with all this physical trouble. Amazing things have happened along my way. He is one, and I tell him I'm here now, and I love him. Then, when I take his large hand in mine, and I can feel his pulse, and my own heart still beating.

Marjorie Gross

*According to her father, Jules Gross, Marjorie Gross
has always broken the rules and gone against the
grain and flow. A "lousy" student in a posh private
school, she refused to attend college, opting instead to
do stand-up comedy first in her hometown, Toronto,
then in Manhattan, where she pioneered as a
woman comedian at Catch a Rising Star, The
Comic Strip and the Improvisation. She appeared
on "Late Night with David Letterman," although
she broke into TV as a writer for Newhart and
Gary Shandling before joining an old friend, Jerry
Seinfeld, as writer and producer of "Seinfeld."*

*Less than two months after "Cancer Becomes
Me" appeared in The New Yorker, Marjorie
Gross died of ovarian cancer, the same disease that
killed her mother.*

Cancer Becomes Me

So I'm sitting in the doctor's office, he walks in, just tells me straight out, "I was right—it's ovarian cancer, so I win. Pay up." And I say, "Oh, no, you're not gonna hold me to that, are you?" And he says, "Hey, a bet's a bet." You don't know what it's like to leave a doctor's office knowing you've lost a hundred dollars: suddenly everything's changed.

Well, OK, I've exaggerated a little. What really happens is the doctor walks in and gives you the sympathetic head tilt that right away tells you, "Don't buy in bulk." The degree of tilt corresponds directly with the level of bad news. You know, a little tilt: "We've caught it in time"; sixty-degree angle: "Spread to the lymph nodes"; forty-five-degree angle: "Spread to your clothes." In her book about cancer, Betty Rollin wrote, "First, you cry." However, she didn't mention what you do second, which is "Spend, spend, spend." You're sort of freed up, in a weird way. Suddenly, everything has a lifetime guarantee.

So I had a hysterectomy, and they found a tumor that they said was the size of an orange. (See, for women they use the citrus-fruit comparison; for men it's sporting goods: "Oh, it's the size of a softball," or, in England, a cricket ball.) I languished in the hospital for ten days, on a floor where everybody had cancer, so the sympathy playing field was level. You can't say, "Hey, can you keep it down? I just had my operation." You might get, "So what? I'm on my fifth." "Poor thing" doesn't really come into play much on this floor. My mother, who also had this disease (yeah, I inherited the cancer gene; my older brother got the blue eyes, but I'm not bitter)—anyway, my mother told me that for some women a hospital stay is a welcome relief. You know, to have someone bringing you food, asking how you are, catering to your every vital sign. See, she wound up in a room with five other women, and they would sit around talking on one bed, and the minute the doctor walked in they would jump into their own beds and re-create the "incoming wounded" scene from "M*A*S*H," insuring that they would not be sent home early.

Which now leads us quixotically but inevitably to chemotherapy. What can I say about chemotherapy that hasn't already been said, in a million pop songs? I was prepared for the chemo side effects. I had my bald plans all in place. I decided to eschew wigs—all except the rainbow wig. Once in a while, I'd put that on when I didn't want to be stared at. Luckily, in my life-style (Lesbeterian) you can be bald and still remain sexually attractive. In fact, the word "sexy" has been thrown my way more times this year than ever before. I've had dreams where my hair grows back and I'm profoundly disappointed. The bald thing works on other levels as well. The shortened shower time—in and out in three minutes easy. Shampoo-free travel. Plus, I get to annoy my father for the first time in twenty years. He hates to see me flaunting my baldness. I thought I'd lost the power to disgust him, but it was right there under my follicles all along.

The other side effect is that I've lost twenty pounds, which has sent my women friends into spasms of jealousy. I think I even heard "Lucky stiff." I said, "I think I'm closer to being a stiff than lucky!" But it fell on deaf ears. I suppose it's a testament to the overall self-esteem of my fellow-women that, after hearing all about the operations, the chemo, and the nausea, the only thing that registers is "Wow, twenty pounds!" and "You look fabulous!" It's a really good weight-loss system for the terminally lazy. I mean, a StairMaster would have been preferable, but mine wound up as a pants tree.

Then, there are my other friends, who are bugging me to go alternative. So now I'm inundated with articles, books, and pamphlets on healers, nutritionists, and visualization (which I know doesn't work, because if it did, Uma Thurman would be running around my house naked asking me what I want for breakfast). I was also given a crystal by a friend who was going through a messy divorce. She was given the crystal by a guy who died of AIDS. As far as I was concerned, this crystal had a terrible résumé. As far as the healing power of crystals goes, let me just say that I grew up eating dinner under a crystal chandelier every night, and look what came of *that:* two cancers, a busted marriage, and an autistic little brother. There, the healing power of crystals. Enjoy.

This is not to say I'm completely devoid of spirituality. I mean, when you're faced with the dark spectre of death you formulate an afterlife theory in a hurry. I decided to go with reincarnation, mixed with some sort of Heaven-like holding area. Then, of course, we could also just turn to dust and that's it. I come from a family of dust believers. They believe in dust and money: the tangibles. The thing about death that bugs me the most is that I don't want to get there before all my friends. I don't even like to be the first one at the restaurant.

The hardest part of this whole thing is that it has completely ruined my loner lifestyle. I've never felt the need to have anyone around constantly. I mean, I never wear anything that zips up in the back, and I hate cowboy boots. And now I get ten times as many phone calls—people wanting to come over and see me. When I'm well, I can go months without seeing someone. Why the rush to see me nauseated? I especially don't believe in the hospital visit. People come in, you're lying there, you can't do anything, and they start talking about their plans for the night.

I hope with all this negative talk I haven't painted too bleak a picture and therefore discouraged you from getting cancer. I mean, there are some really good things about it. Like:

(1) You automatically get called courageous. The rest of you people have to save somebody from drowning. We just have to wake up.

(2) You are never called rude again. You can cancel appointments left and right, leave boring dinners after ten minutes, and still not become a social pariah.

(3) Everyone returns your calls immediately—having cancer is like being Mike Ovitz. And you're definitely not put on hold for long.

(4) People don't ask you to help them move.

(5) If you're really shameless, you never have to wait in line for anything again. Take off the hat and get whisked to the front.

So it hasn't been all bad. I've done things I never would have done before. I even got to go to Europe with a creamy-white pop star. I used to use the word "someday," but now I figure someday is for people with better gene pools.

Natalie Kusz

*You don't know at first — but at the same time you
sense from the very beginning — that something
terrible is going to happen to Natalie Kusz during
the bitter Alaskan winter which she vividly captures
and describes in this excerpt from her memoir,
Road Song. As the narrative progresses, you begin
to understand, instinctively, that whatever will
happen will somehow relate to the Horner family,
the nearest neighbors, to Hobo, her dog, and to the
bare isolation of their daily existence. But the reader
cannot fathom — refuses to even consider — the
inevitable moment when, in her innocence, the little
girl reaches out to lay her mitten upon the head of
the Horners' wild and hungry husky. That fateful
moment becomes a vivid, burning image which will
forever haunt anyone harboring the slightest fear or
trepidation toward animals and the frightening
frigidity of darkness.*

The Dogs of Winter

Our nearest neighbors through the trees were the Horners, two cabins of cousins whose sons went to my school. Paul was in my class, Kevin was a year ahead, and both their families had moved here, as we had, from California, escaping the city and everything frightening that lived there. Kevin had a grown brother in L.A. who was comatose now since he'd been hit on the freeway; his mother, Geri, had come with her brother-in-law's family to Alaska to get well, she hoped, from her own mental breakdown, and to keep herself as far as she could from automobiles.

Paul and Kevin Horner were my best friends then, and we played with our dogs in the cousins' houses, or in the wide snowy yard in between. On weekends or days off from school, my parents took us sledding and to the gravel pit with our skates. Sometimes, if the day was long enough, Paul and Kevin and I followed rabbit tracks through the woods, careful not to step right on the trails for fear of leaving our scent there—for fear, that is, that the rabbits would abandon them. We mapped all the new trails we could find, and my mother gave me orders about when to be home. Bears, she said, and we laughed, said didn't she know they were asleep, and we could all climb trees anyway. We were not afraid, either, when Mom warned of dog packs. Dogs got cabin fever, too, she said, especially in the cold. They ran through the woods, whole crowds of them, looking for someone to gang up on.

That's okay, I told her. We carried pepper in our pockets in case of dogs: sprinkle it on their noses, we thought, and the whole pack would run away.

In December, the day before my birthday, when the light was dim and the days shorter than we had known before, Dad got a break at the union hall, a job at Prudhoe Bay that would save us just in time, before the stove oil ran out and groceries were gone.

Mom convinced us children that he was off on a great adventure, that he would see foxes and icebergs, that we could write letters for Christmas and for New Year's, and afford new coats with feathers inside. In this last, I was not much interested, because I had my favorite already—a red wool coat that reversed to fake leopard—but I would be glad if this meant we could redeem from the pawnshop Dad's concertina, and his second violin, and mine, the half-size with a short bow, and the guitar and mandolin and rifles and pistol that had gone that way one by one. Whether I played each instrument or not, it had been good to have them around, smelling still of campfires and of songfests in the summer.

It was cold after Dad left, cold outside and cold in our house. Ice on the trailer windows grew thick and shaggy, and Leslie and I melted handprints on it and licked off our palms. There had been no insulation when the add-on went up, so frost crawled the walls there, too, and Mom had us wear long johns and shoes unless we were in our beds. Paul and Kevin came for my birthday, helped me wish over seven candles, gave me a comb and a mirror. They were good kids, my mother said, polite and with good sense, and she told me that if I came in from school and she was not home, I should take Hobo with me and walk to their house. You're a worrywart, Mommy, I said. I'm not a baby, you know.

I wish now I had been tolerant of her fears, and perhaps even shared them. Alaska was a young place when we moved to it, much larger than it seems now, with more trees and thicker ice fog, and with its few people more isolated in the midst of them. During the very deep cold, car exhaust came out in particles rather than as gas, and it hung low and thick in the air, obscuring everything, so that even traffic lights were invisible to the car which was stopped right beneath them. In the middle of ice fog, a person was isolated, muffled and enclosed apart from anyone else on the road. Radio stations ran air-quality bulletins, warning asthmatics and old people to stay indoors, and most folks stayed home anyway, knowing how easily a fan belt would shatter in the cold. To us California-bred children, the rolling dense fog that billowed in our open door was a new and thrilling thing; but to my mother, who siphoned stove oil into the fuel barrel five gallons at a time, and who scavenged deadwood and sticks from under snow, that fog must have seemed formidable, the visual symbol of all one must fight against in this place. She kept the lock fastened even when we were home, and she looked and listened with her head out the door for long seconds each time she had to go out to the ice box. I remember her steps outside, slow and controlled on the bottom stairs, hitting faster and harder toward the top, and I remember her gasp as she lurched inside, her glasses clouding up with frost, Baggies of frozen berries falling down from her arms.

The morning after my birthday, Mom woke up and couldn't stand. She shivered and sweated, and when I helped her sit up she said the room was tilting away from her, and could I mix Bethel up a bottle. It was her tonsils, she said. They were tight in her throat and she couldn't swallow around them. Her skin was hot and wet under my hand; the sweat sat on her forehead and soaked into hairs that fell into it when she tried to lift her neck. "Stay there and I'll make some Russian Tea," I said. "Okay, Mommy? Maybe you can drink some tea?" Mom moved her head. She made a grunting noise as she swallowed, and her lips drew far back from her teeth.

Bethel had been sucking air from an empty bottle, and now she started to cry, dangling the nipple from her teeth and pulling herself up onto Mom's bed. Mom's eyes stayed closed, but her hand lifted off the mattress and patted limply at Bethel's shoulder. I breathed hard, and my eyes stung inside their lids. I picked my sister up and carried her into the trailer room, telling her, "Come on in here, Bethel. Let's make some milk and tea."

Leslie and Ian had their treasure chests out on the floor, and Leslie looked up. "Mommy's really sick, isn't she," she asked. I said yes, she was really sick.

I stayed home all week from school, making macaroni from boxes and saying everyone's prayers at night. Mom moved from bed to honeybucket and back and had me read Psalms at bedtime until she was strong enough again to see the words. The honeybucket in the corner was a five-gallon plastic paint can with a toilet seat on top, and under its red cloth drape it filled up, for Mom was too weak to carry it to the outhouse pit. I poured in more Pine Sol than usual each time someone used it, and the cabin filled with the fecund smell of pine oil and waste, a scent we would still loathe years later when we got a real toilet and electricity and began to boycott pine cleaners. The days got shorter all the time, and with no windows in the wanigan, we seemed to move in twilight, squinting at one another between four dark walls. I felt snappish and breathless, and I bossed Leslie and Ian until they cried. Finally, my mother was better and I went back to school, and she met me at the bus stop afternoons, walking me home down the road, shining the flashlight ahead of us.

Christmas passed, and Mom went into town every day—for water, or to do laundry, or to get the mail—but no check arrived from my father. He wrote often, including short notes to each of us, and he said he had sent his first paycheck down just two weeks after he started work. It was good money, he wrote, enough for stove oil and groceries and for the instruments in hock. When he came home, we would finish my violin lessons, and we'd start on the younger kids, too, and we would play together the same songs we had sung on the way up the Alcan and then after that at the campgrounds all summer long.

That first check never did come. Mom wrote back that it must have been lost, and could he get them to print another. When was the next one due, she asked. She would try to stretch things out until it came.

The redemption time was running out on all our things at the pawnshop. We had one violin left to pawn, the one my grandfather had given to Dad before I was born, when Dad had driven from L.A. to New York and brought the old man home with him. In Polish, it was a *Benkarty*, a wide, barrel-chested French violin, aged reddish-brown under its lacquer. It was for a master, made to play fast and ring loudly, its neck rounded and thinner than most, the back of its body all a single piece of maple. The wood and varnish had aged and crystallized so smoothly that when my father tuned it and began to play, each string he stroked resonated acutely with the sounds of the others. To pay the interest on the other things in hock, my mother took the *Benkarty* in to the pawnbroker, telling him she would be back for it soon. "It's my husband's," she said, trusting this Russian man to keep the violin safe, if only for the sake of the old country and my father's Slavic tongue. She could not know then that the man would sell the

Benkarty before its redemption date, or that she and my father would never get it back. At the time, the clearest thing for her was the extra cash she got for it, and the powdered milk and the gas she was able to buy that afternoon.

Mom arranged her days carefully around the hours I was in school. Her glasses had broken across the bridge one morning when she had come inside and set them to thaw on the wood-stove, so she walked me to the bus stop wearing prescription sun-glasses and then fastened my sisters and brother into the truck and drove into town, scraping ice from the windshield as she steered. I know from her journal that she was afraid, that she pad-locked the cabin door against the vandalism recently come into town, that she counted her time out carefully so she would be home in time to meet my afternoon bus. She reminded me and made me promise that, should she be late one day, I would take Hobo to Paul and Kevin's and wait there until she came for me. "Okay, Mommy," I said then, and turned to pull Hobo's ears.

"No, listen to me, Natalie." Mom held my arm until I looked up. Behind the dark lenses her eyes were invisible, but her cheeks were white, and her lips very nearly the same color. "This is not a joke," she said. "Now don't forget what I'm saying. You must go to the boys' if I'm late. This is very important."

"It's okay," I repeated. I looked into her glasses. "I'll remember."

On January 10, only Hobo met me at the bus stop. In the glare from school-bus headlights, his blue eye shone brighter than his brown, and he watched until I took the last step to the ground before tackling me in the snow. Most days, Hobo hid in the shadow of the spruce until Mom took my bag, then he erupted from the dark to charge up behind me, run through my legs and on out the front. It was his favorite trick. I usually lost my balance and ended up sitting in the road with my feet thrown wide out front and steaming dog tongue all over my face.

Hobo ran ahead, then back, brushing snow crystals and fur against my leg. I put a hand on my skin to warm it and dragged nylon ski pants over the road behind me. Mom said to have them along in case the bus broke down, but she knew I would not wear them, could not bear the plastic sounds they made between my thighs.

No light was on in our house.

If Mom had been home, squares of yellow would have shown through the spruce and lit the fog of my breath, turning it bright as I passed through. What light there was now came from the whiteness of snow, and from the occasional embers drifting up from our stovepipe. I laid my lunchbox on the top step and pulled at the padlock, slapping a palm on the door and shouting. Hobo jumped away from the noise and ran off, losing himself in darkness and in the faint keening dog sounds going up from over near the Horners' house. I called, "Hobo. Come back here, boy," and took the path toward Paul's, tossing my ski pants to the storage tent as I passed.

At the property line, Hobo caught up with me and growled, and I fingered his ear, looking where he pointed, seeing nothing ahead there but the high curve and long sides of a Quonset hut, the work shed the Horners used also as a fence for one side of their yard. In the fall, Paul and Kevin and I had walked to the back of it, climbing over boxes and tools and parts of old furniture, and we had found in the corner a lemmings' nest made from chewed bits of cardboard and paper, packed under the curve of the wall so that shadows hid it from plain sight. We all bent close to hear the scratching, and while Paul held a flashlight I took two sticks and parted the rubbish until we saw the black eyes of a mother lemming and the pink naked bodies of five babies. The mother dashed deeper into the pile and we scooped the nesting back, careful not to touch the sucklings, for fear that their mama would eat them if they carried scent from our fingers.

It seemed that we had spent most of the fall looking out just like that for shrews and lemmings. Oscar and Vic had cats, and Paul and Kevin had three German shepherds, and one or another of them usually found a rodent to play with. Oscar's cats would catch a shrew in their teeth, holding tight to skin behind its neck until its eyes swelled out and it stopped breathing. The boys and I squeezed the cats' jaws, screaming, "You're not even *hungry*," until the teeth parted and the shrew dropped into our palms. If we were fast enough, it was still alive, and we pushed its eyes back in and let it go. The dogs worried a lemming in their mouths, dropping it out on occasion and catching it back into the air, over and over again until it couldn't move and was no longer any fun. When we caught the dogs doing this, we beat their ears with walking sticks, but usually we were too late and had to bury the thing under moss.

The dogs were loud now beyond the Quonset, fierce in their howls and sounding like many more than just three. Hobo crowded against my legs, and as I walked he hunched in front of me, making me stumble into a drift that filled my boots with snow. I called him a coward and said to quit it, but I held his neck against my thigh, turning the corner into the boys' yard and stopping on the edge. Paul's house was lit in all its windows, Kevin's was dark, and in the yard between them were dogs, new ones I had not seen before, each with its own house and tether. The dogs and their crying filled the yard, and when they saw me they grew wilder, hurling themselves to the ends of their chains, pulling their lips off their teeth. Hobo cowered and ran and I called him with my mouth, but my eyes did not move from in front of me.

There were seven. I knew they were huskies and meant to pull dogsleds, because earlier that winter Paul's grandfather had put on his glasses and shown us a book full of pictures. He had turned the pages with a wet thumb, speaking of trappers and racing people and the ways they taught these dogs to run. They don't feed them much, he said, or they get slow and lose their drive. This was how men traveled before they invented snowmobiles or gasoline.

There was no way to walk around the dogs to the lighted house. The snow had drifted and been piled around the yard in heaps taller than I was, and whatever aisle was left along the sides was narrow, and pitted with chain marks where the animals had wandered, dragging their tethers behind. No, I thought, Kevin's house was closest and out of biting range, and someone could, after all, be sitting home in the dark.

My legs were cold. The snow in my boots had packed itself around my ankles and begun to melt, soaking my socks and the felt liners under my heels. I turned toward Kevin's house, chafing my thighs together hard to warm them, and I called cheerfully at the dogs to shut up. Oscar said that if you met a wild animal, even a bear, you had to remember it was more scared than you were. Don't act afraid, he said, because they can smell fear. Just be loud—stomp your feet, wave your hands—and it will run away without even turning around. I yelled "Shut up" again as I climbed the steps to Kevin's front door, but even I could barely hear myself over the wailing. At the sides of my eyes, the huskies were pieces of smoke tumbling over one another in the dark.

The wood of the door was solid with cold, and even through deerskin mittens it bruised my hands like concrete. I cupped a hand to the window and looked in, but saw only black—black, and the reflection of a lamp in the other cabin behind me. I turned and took the three steps back to the ground; seven more and I was in the aisle between doghouses, stretching my chin far up above the frenzy, thinking hard on other things. This was how we walked in summertime, the boys and I, escaping from bad guys over logs thrown across ditches: step lightly and fast, steady on the hard parts of your soles, arms extended outward, palms down and toward the sound. That ditch, this aisle, was a river, a torrent full of silt that would fill your clothes and pull you down if you missed and fell in. I was halfway across. I pointed my chin toward the house and didn't look down.

On either side, dogs on chains hurled themselves upward, choking themselves to reach me, until their tethers jerked their throats back to earth. I'm not afraid of you, I whispered; this is dumb.

I stepped toward the end of the row and my arms began to drop slowly closer to my body. Inside the mittens, my thumbs were cold, as cold as my thighs, and I curled them in and out again. I was walking past the last dog and I felt brave, and I forgave him and bent to lay my mitten on his head. He surged forward on a chain much longer than I thought, leaping at my face, catching my hair in his mouth, shaking it in his teeth until the skin gave way with a jagged sound. My feet were too slow in my boots, and as I blundered backward they tangled in the chain, burning my legs on metal. I called out at Paul's window, expecting rescue, angry that it did not come, and I beat my arms in front of me, and the dog was back again, pulling me down.

A hole was worn into the snow, and I fit into it, arms and legs drawn up in front of me. The dog snatched and pulled at my mouth, eyes, hair; his breath clouded the air around us, but I did not feel its heat, or smell the blood sinking down between hairs of his muzzle. I watched my mitten come off in his teeth and sail upward, and it seemed unfair then and very sad that one hand should freeze all alone; I lifted the second mitten off and threw it away, then turned my face back again, overtaken suddenly by loneliness. A loud river ran in my ears, dragging me under.

My mother was singing. *Lu-lee, lu-lay, thou little tiny child,* the song to the Christ Child, the words she had sung, smoothing my hair, all my life before bed. Over a noise like rushing water I called to her and heard her answer back, Don't worry, just sleep, the ambulance is on its way. I drifted back out and couldn't know then what she prayed, that I would sleep on without waking, that I would die before morning.

She had counted her minutes carefully that afternoon, sure that she would get to town and back, hauling water and mail, with ten minutes to spare before my bus came. But she had forgotten to count one leg of the trip, had skidded up the drive fifteen minutes late, pounding a fist on the horn, calling me home. On the steps, my lunchbox had grown cold enough to burn her hands. She got the water, the groceries, and my brother and sisters inside, gave orders that no one touch the woodstove or open the door, and she left down the trail to Paul's, whistling Hobo in from the trees.

I know from her journal that Mom had been edgy all week about the crazed dog sounds next door. Now the new huskies leaped at her and Hobo rumbled warning from his chest. Through her sunglasses, the dogs were just shapes, indistinct in window-light. She tried the dark cabin first, knocking hard on the win-dows, then turned and moved down the path between doghouses, feeling her way with her feet, kicking out at open mouths. Dark lenses frosted over from her breath, and she moved toward the house and the lights on inside.

"She's not here." Paul's mother held the door open and air clouded inward in waves. Mom stammered out thoughts of bears, wolves, dogs. Geri grabbed on her coat. She had heard a noise out back earlier—they should check there and then the woods.

No luck behind the cabin and no signs under the trees. Wear-ing sunglasses and without any flashlight, Mom barely saw even the snow. She circled back and met Geri under the windowlight. Mom looked toward the yard and asked about the dogs. "They seem so hungry," she said.

Geri looked that way and then back at my mother. "No.

Paul's folks just got them last week, but the boys play with them all the time." All the same, she and Mom scanned their eyes over the kennels, looking through and then over their glasses. Nothing seemed different. "Are you sure she isn't home?" Geri asked. "Maybe she took a different trail."

Maybe. Running back with Geri behind her, Mom called my name until her lungs frosted inside and every breath was a cough. She whistled the family whistle my father had taught us, the secret one he and his family had used to call one another from the woods in Nazi Germany. *"Dodek, ty-gdzie,"* the tune went, "Dodek, where are you?" She blew it now, two syllables for my name, high then low, then a lower one, quick, and another high slide down to low. Her lips hardly worked in the cold, and the whistle was feeble, and she finished by shouting again, curling both hands around her mouth. "Come on," she said to Geri. "Let's get to my cabin." The three younger children were still the only ones home, and Mom handed them their treasure chests, telling them to play on the bed until she found Natalie. Don't go outside, she said. I'll be back real soon.

Back at the Horners', Geri walked one way around the Quon-set and Mom the other. Mom sucked air through a mitten, warming her lungs. While Geri climbed over deeper snow, she approached the sled dogs from a new angle. In the shadow of one, a splash of red—the lining of my coat thrown open. "I've found her," she shouted, and thought as she ran, Oh, thank God. Thank, thank God.

The husky stopped its howling as Mom bent to drag me out from the hole. Geri caught up and seemed to choke. "Is she alive?" she asked.

Mom said, "I think so, but I don't know how." She saw one side of my face gone, one red cavity with nerves hanging out, scraps of dead leaves stuck on to the mess. The other eye might be gone, too; it was hard to tell. Scalp had been torn away from my skull on that side, and the gashes reached to my forehead, my lips, had left my nose ripped wide at the nostrils. She tugged my body around her chest and carried me inside.

I had little knowledge of my mother's experience of the accident until many months afterward, and even then I heard her story only after I had told mine, after I had shown how clearly I remembered the dogs, and their chains, and my own blood on the snow—and had proven how little it bothered me to recall them. When I said I had heard her voice, and named for her the songs she had sung to me then, my mother searched my face, looking into me hard, murmuring, "I can't believe you remember." She had protected me all along, she said, from her point of view, not thinking that I might have kept my own, and that mine must be harder to bear. But after she knew all this, Mom felt she owed me a history, and she told it to me then, simply and often, in words that I would draw from long after she was gone.

She said that inside the Horners' cabin she had laid me on Geri's couch, careful not to jar the bleeding parts of me, expecting me to wake in an instant and scream. But when I did become conscious, it was only for moments, and I was not aware then of my wounds, or of the cabin's warmth, or even of pressure from the fingers of Paul's grandfather, who sat up close and stroked the frozen skin of my hands.

Geri ordered Paul and Kevin to their room, telling them to stay there until she called them, and then she stood at Mom's shoulder, staring down and swaying on her legs.

Mom looked up through her glasses and said, "Is there a phone to call an ambulance?"

Geri was shaking. "Only in the front house, kid, and it's locked." She held her arms straight toward the floor, as if to catch herself when she fell. "Karla should be home in a minute, but I'll try to break in." She tugged at the door twice before it opened, and then she went out, leaving my mother to sing German lullabies beside my ear. *When morning comes,* the words ran, *if God wills it, you will wake up once more.* My mother sang the words and breathed on me, hoping I would dream again of summertime, all those bright nights when the music played on outside, when she drew the curtains and sang us to sleep in the trailer. Long years after the accident, when she felt healed again and stronger, Mom described her thoughts to me, and when she did she closed her eyes and sat back, saying, "You can't know how it was to keep singing, to watch air bubble up where a nose should have been, and to pray that each of those breaths was the last one." Many times that night she thought of Job, who also had lived in a spacious, golden land, who had prospered in that place, yet had cried in the end, "The thing that I so greatly feared has come upon me." The words became a chant inside her, filling her head and bringing on black time.

The wait for the ambulance was a long one, and my mother filled the time with her voice, sitting on her heels and singing. She fingered my hair and patted my hands and spoke low words when I called out. Paul's grandfather wept and warmed my fingers in his, and Mom wondered where were my mittens, and how were her other children back home.

Geri came back and collapsed on a chair, and Karla, her sister-in-law, hurried in through the door. Geri began to choke, rocking forward over her knees, telling Karla the story. Her voice stretched into a wail that rose and fell like music. "It's happening again," she said. "No matter where you go, it's always there."

Karla brought out aspirin and gave it to Geri, then turned and touched my mother's arm. She whispered, "She's remembering her boy." She said that as soon as Geri was quiet, she would leave her here and fetch my siblings from the trailer.

"Thank you," Mom told her. "I'll send someone for them as soon as I can." She looked at Geri, wishing she had something to give her, some way to make her know that she was not to blame here; but for now Mom felt that Geri had spoken truth when she said that sorrow followed us everywhere, and there was little else she could add.

The ambulance came, and then everything was movement. I drifted awake for a moment as I was lifted to a stretcher and carried toward the door. I felt myself swaying in air, back and forth and back again. Paul's whisper carried over the other voices in the room, as if blown my way by strong wind. "Natalie's dying," he said; then his words were lost among other sounds, and I faded out again. A month later, when our first-grade class sent me a box full of valentines, Paul's was smaller that the rest, a thick, white heart folded in two. Inside, it read: "I love you, Nataly. Pleas dont die." When I saw him again, his eyes seemed very big, and I don't remember that he ever spoke to me anymore.

It was dark inside the ambulance, and seemed even darker to my mother, squinting through fog on her sunglasses. She badgered the medic, begging him to give me a shot for pain. The man kept working, taking my pulse, writing it down, and while he did,

he soothed my mother in low tones, explaining to her about physical shock, about the way the mind estranges itself from the body
and stands, unblinking and detached, on the outside. "If she does
wake up," he said, "she'll feel nothing. She won't even feel afraid."
When Mom wrote this in her journal, her tone was filled with
wonder, and she asked what greater gift there could be.

Judy Ruiz

Judy Ruiz's essays are startlingly honest and admirably daring.

She re-creates herself in a variety of situations from infancy to institutionalization, repeatedly losing and rediscovering herself in the process. She talks to the reader, confides to her son, addresses her lover, berates herself in a jarring symphony of lyrical voices. Manipulating her narrative, she takes incredible leaps back and forth across place and time.

Ruiz is one of those writers who has yet to be embraced by the mainstream literary community (New York); she has yet to publish a book. But her work is highly regarded among serious writers of nonfiction prose, primarily in the academic community, and by many woman who view her life as a metaphor of the feminist struggle. A draft of this essay originally appeared in Iowa Review, but it was substantially revised for this reader.

The Mother, the Daughter, and the Holy Horse: A Trilogy

Women Know Nothing

The worst feeling of lost I ever had was when I was eighteen. I'd left home, I think. Maybe not. Those times were so intensely sad that I lose track. One night, I drove around in a '55 Chevy all evening, knowing that the man who owned the car would want something in return for letting me drive it, not to go all the way, as we called it back then, but to do some kissing, maybe some petting. So I drove and drove and it never entered my mind to just abandon the car. I drank 3.2 beer and drove some more.

Finally, around midnight, I drove the car back to the owner's house. He was waiting for me on his porch. He came out to the car and got in and wanted to kiss me and he had a harelip, with a voice that seemed to come from a well inside his head. All I can remember is that I didn't want to kiss him, but I felt I owed him because he had let me drive his car around all night. Now I can't remember if I kissed him, but I think I did.

Then I walked to a friend's apartment in hopes of getting some sleep. He let me in and I asked if I could sleep there and he said sure. I had awakened him, but he went right back to bed, without turning any lights on. I took off my shoes and got into his bed in my clothes. We slept.

He woke me up kissing me and touching my breasts, and then he was on top of me and he didn't pull my panties off. He just pulled the crotch part over to one side and went inside me. It was over within about a blink. I got up and asked him if I could wash my clothes out in the sink and stay there until they were dry enough to wear. He said sure and gave me a shirt of his to wear. I washed my skirt and blouse and hung them by the space heater to dry. It was cold that autumn. Then his parents came over.

I was sitting on a chair by the heater with my legs hanging

out. He talked to his parents. They wanted to know who I was and he told them, "No one. She needed a place to sleep."

That was the worst feeling of lost I ever had. It's been thirty years since that night, but that feeling, the edge of it, or the curve of it, or the shade or space or dark of it, is still with me. Not that I think of it every day. But that it ever happened so that I would ever have to think of it, even now, is my empty house, or at least a part of it.

That a woman should be so tired at the age of eighteen that a man could enter her, that she would need sleep, just a bed, a place, a shelter, so desperately that she could feel him pull at her underwear and not have the idea to scream or move or say no, that she would help herself to become who she was to him that night—no one—that these things happened is beyond God, this earth, or ever.

When you get out of prison, my sweet son, I will go with you and we will find your father, and you will see his face. And perhaps, some day, you will forgive me all of this—my passion and his. This is how you were conceived: in a sudden heat.

It sounds too schmaltzy. I know. Forgive me that too. And forgive me all the other miserable fucking things I ever did because I couldn't love or do a thing softer than I did once I found fire. These requests for forgiveness are hereby entered into the world of people and the realm of tell me doctor, if she's sane enough to strike a proper bargain, how can we keep her in the confines of her skin? I was going to write "the world of people and the realm of God, this world, or ever." I was going to write "the realm of people and the world of God." I was going to write the word bastard and get it over with. But he was my baby. Mine.

This is where it always happens, this room where the light pours in and the walls are white. This is where the alpha and omega, the yin and yang, the past and present, the withdrawals—all of it happens right here and the room rears its ugly head and says who cares. Recipes get invented here, lists made, addresses entered and deleted. The cats can't come in anymore. They eat the plants and bathe on the keyboard and chew the corners of the disc covers and mainly do not understand that this is where it always happens and if I were young, I would birth a child in this room and gnaw the cord with my teeth and open the windows and let the elements freeze us in those first few hours, me, drunk from the perfect rush of birth, the baby nursing the death away.

Pretend there's some music in the background, music from the part of the movie when a famous literary figure from long ago time-travels into the present only to find herself at some local bar which is alive with purple faces and wheezing laughter. Camera pan to a person who leans into our literary figure's face, a person who says, "But to put it into perspective, Virginia, this room-of-one's-own thing, Virginia, or may we just call you Virgin, for short, but not for long." Sweep shot of laughter all around and a little bit of back-slapping. Close up of Virginia's face, how the corners of her mouth do not make a move in any direction. Close up of the inside of her brain, the left temporal region, where a sentence is just beginning to form. Watch carefully as the words appear on the screen. Follow along, if you will. The dot above the word, like in those old sing-along film clips, will tell you exactly where we are.

What do they make those dots from? Okay. Imagine that there is a darkness that is also dense. It presses in and in forever. In the exact center of the dark there is a perfect circle of light. It is about the size of this: o. No matter how dense or dark the pressing-in gets, the circle stays the same. Then one day it becomes a dot above a word. No one knows exactly how this happens. Anyhow, follow the dancing dot:

Some of life is inenarrable; however, there is language, and an organ that sits as a ceiling—the brain. Fantasmagorical in its reaches and realms, and physically an organ that is so closed in its nature that it convolutes into itself, the brain tucks into its folds tiny pictures until we, as human beings, are walking photo albums of ourselves—ourselves with others, ourselves alone. One interesting thing about these photographs, these brain ones, is that the "ourself" part is missing, just as gone as if we had taken scissors to the real photographs on the mantle at home and had carefully carved our faces away. The eye of the beholder is an odd eye. It goes to the beholden in the album of the mind. And the camera, which is also the eye of the beholder, but a different eye, an eye with ears and mouth and nose and skin and language, does not lie.

You have made for me this evening, ladies and gentlemen, a picture that may not be pressing in at me at all times, but one, nevertheless, that I shall hold dear from this moment forward, as I shall also revere your words to me spoken here in this public establishment. I will show this picture to the world and say, "This is something I want you all to see."

I lost my virginity before I was two. I don't remember much about that one—his penis floating in the water in the bathtub and me being taken into the warm water, how it was different than the pink bag that hung on the door under my mother's robe.

I suppose the other events between then and when I was sixteen and went out in deliberation to "do it" need to be mentioned, not so that anyone will say poor baby, but so what I'm talking about here will have a frame.

There were the usual laps with bulges for a little girl to sit on, there was the cousin in the root cellar, there was the uncle and a summer of dry-fucking, the orthodontist and his hard-on leaning into my shoulder, a lover's kiss from the drunken father in the hallway, and there's just not time for all the list. What there is time for is to say I liked it, I loved it, I craved it. I sat in group therapies later while we all showed our scars, and I never said, "Well, part of the deal here is that I liked it. It always scared the hell out of me and made me feel numb and on fire at the same time."

Maybe there was something about my face. Maybe it was my eyes. Maybe all it took was a glance at me and a person could tell I was so far away already that all it took to go the distance was a little time, a little space, a little privacy. Maybe my eyes said, "Go ahead. I will tell my mother. But she will not believe me. She will tell others not to believe me. She has done this before."

I'd like to yank them all up out of their sleep, even the dead ones, and bring their immortal souls right up to my face and say, "There. I went on and never lost my mind. Not even when my mother told me, when I was forty and she was sixty, how relieved she had been when I, at nineteen, became pregnant for the first time, how she had held her breath wondering if the infection I had when I was little would render me sterile, telling me this over mashed potatoes and gravy in the cafeteria of the hospital where my father lay two days post-operative, having had his testicles removed to ease some of the pain caused by his cancerous tumors, the tumors that fed on testosterone. I was in the hospital with a venereal disease before I was two, so what you did with me was some small fucking potatoes, and I don't even remember all of it, so kiss my perfect ass in your dreams, pal." Then I'd let go of them, and they'd all fall, forever and permanently, into the abyss of profound spirituality. They would turn into tiny round circles of light. They could become dancing dots. They could keep track of this:

> Tell everyone that I know nothing. Tell them I learned how. Tell them I told.

Remember My Horse

My friend and I sit attentive in a graduate-level creative writing workshop. We are wearing lapel buttons. Her button has these words on it: Come near me and I'll kill you. Mine reads: Just one of the boys.

When class is over, we'll go to a local restaurant, drink hot chocolate, and make lists on napkins—the names of all the people whose hats we'd like to shoot off. We know our anger is impotent, and we know the only revenge worth having is to outlive and outwrite everybody. Our motto is, "Who are these people, and why are they trying to kill us?"

This anger feeling is some strange thing that blasts through me like the suddenness of all the fierce glare of winter light, blinding light, all the blinding cold light. No. It's ice. It's hot ice and it covers the planet and it's a million miles thick. Wait. It's a hammer and I'm hitting myself between the eyes. My aim is true. I hit and it lands hard, not like in those dreams where I hit as hard as I can, and the impact of my blow is less than being touched by a feather, the recipient of my rage standing blank in the dream, as blank as I have stood in the reality.

· · ·

The first time I felt my own anger, I thought I was dying. That's how serious the reaction in my body was. It was November, 1983. I was almost forty. And I wouldn't remember the date so clearly, except I was in a treatment center when it happened. And it wouldn't have happened if I just could have managed to stay drunk and disorderly, or swacked out on Xanax for a little while longer. I mean, if I could have just drank and drugged a couple more weeks, I could have been all the way dead, and not merely wandering around in hospital garb feeling the first feeling I can remember having felt in my life, the first feeling other than depression, which is not a feeling at all, but an absence of feeling.

Because I thought I was having a heart attack or something, I sought out one of the nurses who reassured me that I wasn't dying and went on to explain what was happening in me: all the depressants (alcohol and drugs) I had ingested during the past twenty-seven years had depressed my nervous system so that my feelings had not surfaced in all those years. She told me I was angry, and that I could expect other surprises in my body as I detoxified. At that time, I thought, "Sure. Whatever." But I didn't know what I was angry with, or why I felt it so hard that it almost knocked me down in the hallway.

Back in the sixties and seventies, a person could attend anger workshops—maybe they still exist today, I don't know. But back then, you brought a tennis racket to workshop. The cushions were provided. The workshop leader talked with you until you got in touch—that's what it was called, in touch—with your anger. Then you stood, feet apart, brought the racket up over your head, and began to beat on a cushion. I have seen folks ruin tennis rackets this way, beating until all that was left was the handle part. The cushion represented anyone or anything you were angry at or with, from Mom to God to driving in rush-hour traffic.

Another tactic for the release of anger was to lie down on the floor or a mat or your bed at home and throw a tantrum by flailing your arms and legs while screaming. I participated in such workshops and exercises back then, and at the end of those sessions, I would be exhausted and feel embarrassed.

My mentor would tell me that embarrassment was not a feeling, but an intellectualization of feelings because embarrassment is a combination of hurt and anger, not a pure feeling taken care of as it occurred. He asserted that the body can handle only one feeling at a time, and if that feeling is not expressed *with the body* immediately then it goes directly to the mind where it is mulled over and sent back into the body for storage. He also maintained that the storage of these unexpressed feelings is what causes human beings to become sick and crazy, causes us to slouch our shoulders or stiffen our spines or lock ourselves up in the pelvis, tilting forward or backward out of alignment.

He was a language behavioralist, and his students studied until they could differentiate between sensing, imagining, feeling, wanting, and not wanting. His students learned the language of feelings—how to say I hurt, I'm angry, I feel disgust, I feel joy, I am sad—and how these feelings had different degrees of intensity, from mild irritation, for example, to white cold rage. I comprehend, now, that my embarrassment was just as he said—an intellectualization of feelings. When I took those workshops, I *thought* I was feeling; I took his courses over and over, earning, finally, thirty semester hours in a course called Practicum in Language Behavior. Prospective employers have been known to give considerable pause when viewing this part of my undergraduate transcript.

Who knows where any of it starts? There are beliefs. There are religions. There are theories. There are parents. Then, there are those delicate seconds when the cell divides. There are the intricacies of chromosomes. There are the miracles and mysteries of the brain.

Maybe some synapses in my brain have always been frayed or missing, so that I never got the joke of why the chicken crossed the road, or the jokes my father told, such as NAACP stands for Niggers Ain't Actin' Like Colored People. My father was an American hero. I was the colonel's daughter in my white floor-length formal going through the reception line, shaking hands with the generals and their wives, wanting desperately to say something like good evening, turds.

But in my family, that sort of talking was forbidden, as was that sort of thinking. And, of course, all feelings were prohibited. We were emotional contortionists—if sad, we bucked up under it; if bored or bewildered, we put our noses to the grindstone; if hurt, we would grin and bear it; if depressed, we pulled ourselves up by our own bootstraps; if angry, well, we didn't get angry; if joyful, well, we didn't get that either.

When I was thirteen, I took my first diet pill. My mother gave it to me. It was Dexedrine. I was gone, instantly. The reason she gave me pills is that she had a problem with my body, only I didn't know that was the reason back then. I thought I was too fat because she *said* I was too fat, and I lived in such an odd isolation that I had no other sources to check with. I can remember looking into mirrors and wondering what there was about me that was so fat, and I looked into those mirrors long enough and hard enough, with my mother's voice in the background, so that I finally became convinced that I was indeed fat—and ugly, too.

The Dexedrine, however, gave me a tremendous sense of power—so it didn't matter whether or not I was or was not fat. I thought that these diet pills made it possible for me to think. As my drug use progressed to include Seconal, Nembutal, and Librium, I became more convinced of my ugliness, and I began thinking that the Dexedrine only gave me the illusion of thinking—the downers were *really* thought. By the time I was eighteen, I was in a mental hospital. I got even more drugs then—Thorazine and Stelazine. And I didn't feel a thing.

Once, when I was out on a pass from the mental institution, my parents took me to the Air Force Academy. We visited Arnold Hall, where we stopped to admire the Hughes trophies my father had won for being the commander of the most outstanding fighter squadron in the world. We watched the cadets march off in formation to the dining hall. As we left the academy grounds that afternoon, my mother turned around to face me as I sat staring out the back window of the Oldsmobile. She said, "You could have had all this." What she meant was I could have married a cadet. That was the farthest thing from what I wanted. I wanted to stop hurting, wanted the pain to go away, the thing that felt big in my throat, the choking—I had no clue as to how to go about it. I didn't even know what *it* was. The other thing I wanted that day was to not have to clean the oven for her.

Well, the next day I did have to clean the oven. And scrub and wax the floor in the entire basement, on my hands and knees. No Cinderella metaphors intended. I was not out on pass from the state hospital so a messenger from the prince could come by with slippers. I was out on pass to clean the oven and the floors. My parents and brothers were getting ready to move to another state two thousand miles away. I, of course, would stay in the institution. I don't recall being angry about it. I do recall sitting at my mother's kitchen table and putting oven cleaner on the flesh of my left forearm. Then I sat there quietly as the cleaner ate a huge hole into me. When I couldn't stand the pain any longer, I rinsed my arm off under cold running water until I couldn't stand that any more. Then I finished cleaning the oven.

When my parents got home that evening from their dinner at the officer's club, I greeted them with shining floors, a gleaming oven, and my most spectacular second- and third-degree burn. Of course, I received medical attention at the local Air Force base dispensary. Then Dad drove me back to the state hospital where later I got a staph infection and am lucky not to have lost my arm altogether.

I never told anyone that I had burned myself deliberately, but rather passed it off as if I had just barely touched my arm to the side of the oven and had been burned instantly, such delicate skin, before I could dash to the sink to wash the stuff off. Also, if I had told anyone the truth about how the burn had come about, I'd have been dealt some more psychological mumbo-jumbo, maybe lost my Saturday night dance privileges on the ward. What I did was self-mutilation. Such acts are not regarded highly in mental institutions, especially if one mutilates oneself while out on pass.

In retrospect, I understand why I branded myself. It marked a passage. It meant that I would never clean my mother's spatterings again. It meant I would never bend again to scrub the black heel marks from my father's shoes off of any floor. It meant I was out of a job, the only job I'd ever known. It meant my family was leaving me in a mental institution.

· · ·

I should mention now that in those days, I knew I wasn't right, somehow, but I knew that I wasn't crazy in the same way the folks around me were crazy. And I'm not just talking about other patients who were on the same wards I was on. I'm talking about everybody. Everybody I knew, anyhow. And I knew my parents, my brothers, my grandparents, aunts, uncles, and a few cousins. I knew my friends as closely as one can. I had many acquaintances and several teachers with whom I had brief contact. Without exception, I was a different kind of crazy. I was like that funny-looking pecan, culled from the rest of the nuts just after harvest.

The difficulties in me came, clearly, from the way I thought. I found it impossible to comprehend, for example, why my parents argued drunk in the middle of the night and then acted as if they had no middle-of-the-nights, washing us children up and taking us to church, both of them so strangely rumpled looking, singing "The Old Rugged Cross," watching to make sure we put our quarters and dimes in the collection plate—the change they'd handed us in the car on the way—money I got to hold and almost have. It seemed that my whole life was like that—one instance after another of something I got to almost have. And I knew then, just as I know now, that almost is close—and close, after all, only counts in horseshoes, hand grenades, and skunks. The loneliest child in the world is the one the dog almost bites.

When I was two years old, we lived in Germany. I ran away from home every time I got the chance. I ran to the home of a German family who had children a little older than I was, a family who had a typewriter. The children were actually allowed to play with it. I would go there knowing my mother would take a branch off a bush in our yard and switch the backs of my chubby little legs for running off again. The switching was annoying, and I could count on it happening, but it didn't matter. What mattered was going to that other house and using the typewriter, even though I never wrote anything other than "pklmck dnh ieopdm" stuff. It was, to me, magic. The other writing I did at that time consisted of drawings I'd make on any blank space in my children's books— mainly figures of people and breasts, lots and lots of breasts. My mother was not amused.

In August of 1984, many years, pages, and drawings later, I entered a graduate writing program as a sober woman. I had no money. I asked my father if he would buy me a typewriter and let me make payments to him until it was paid off. At the time, he was retired from the Air Force and living in Florida in a beautiful home, complete with a swimming pool and fountain and grape-fruit trees in the back yard. He couldn't help me, he said, because he was still paying the bill for my youngest brother's education—a bill, he said, that was more than fifty thousand dollars. When he told me no, I thought I would explode. I am not exaggerating. I felt *the* anger. I felt it from years of this sort of sexism. The edu-cation of my brothers was important. My education was some sort of scheme that wouldn't amount to anything.

I was told this sort of thing by many members of my family who thought my obsession with words was a nice little hobby, and inexpensive—how much can pencils cost?—but that I needed to study something, if I was determined to study, that would help me get a job doing something I was suited for, such as taking care of children, you know, in a day care center, or working with the elderly in a nursing home, or sitting with the dying in a hospi-tal—families pay good money to people who will do that sort of thing—on and on, while I was banging out poems on borrowed machines and putting them on car windshields, holding them there with the wiper blades.

See, it doesn't matter what sorts of things are happening on the freedom front or which women are winning Nobel Prizes if you're living with lunatics who think art is something other, something disgusting, something so frivolous that it need not even be considered, especially by women or girls. I'm angry that my family didn't encourage me, and for years I've beat this horse, expecting some sort of miracle, a whinny and a snort and a fine ride on the beach. I suppose I want that horse to sing some Dylan, sing "she's got everything she needs, she's an artist, she don't look back, She can take the dark out of the nighttime and paint the daytime black."

But the horse is dead. I suppose I'll be singing a song about how it's so lonely in the saddle since my horse died. Or how it's not. But I'll be singing. And I suppose that what I wanted to say here is how it's the singing that's important, surviving long enough to find your voice.

After locating the primary anger in my self—that I was unknown to and virtually abandoned by my own parents—I tried to trivialize that rage, saying that there are many more terrible things in life than *that*—millions of people who'd had it rough, millions of children who never made it out. For a while, I was convinced that I was a self-pitying whiney sniveler. But then a gesture or phrase from an anonymous someone, a certain tilt of someone's head or a glance of disapproval, the way afternoon sun came through a gauze curtain, a yowling alley cat—something would trigger me, send me time-travelling backwards to the racist, sexist, anti-common pile of shit I was born into—a place where there was no room for the beauty I have come to call life, no time for embracing all that is tender, no reason or need for wonder.

And I told myself I *should* be angry at all the other things I've endured out of ignorance—a husband who emptied a nine-shot automatic at my running-away back, a target he couldn't hit because he was too drunk to aim straight; a man who put a gun to my head, pulled the hammer back, then told me I wasn't worth a bullet; the molesting and offenses some of the esteemed male members of my family heaped upon my girl's body; my father's kisses; my mother's games. Those occurrences, God help us all, are in me somehow forever. Sometimes it's enough to have lived through it. It's when the creation of art is threatened that I become furious and begin writing lists with headings such as "Why I Don't Own a Gun."

All those years of my early life, when I thought I was crazy, or when my mother thought I was crazy and told anyone who'd listen, all those years of an absolute abject poverty of spirit, there was in me a tiny, tiny thing that was soft and pure, that wanted nothing more than to sleep clean and sound and unafraid, a tiny thing that talked to me in a soothing way, that told me it will be all right, don't cry now, it's going to be OK, a tiny warm something that was inside me when I hugged myself because the tears were not stopping and I had no words to say for the sorrow of my heart. That small thing is somehow the adult I am growing into—that grown woman who comforts, having comforted herself all those other years, that woman who is finding the words.

Today I worked for a while on a jigsaw puzzle—one of those with lots of blue and green that reduces me to sorting puzzle pieces into shape categories, then trying each piece in one category in an appropriately shaped space—maybe only puzzle folks will understand what I'm trying to say. Anyhow, when this puzzle is completed, I'll laminate it with some of that puzzle glue and hang it on the wall. Then I'll go buy a new puzzle and go through the motions again. I find puzzles help because of the concentration they demand. Back in my state hospital days, we had only one puzzle on our ward. We put it together over and over and over. When we wanted variety—a challenge—we would put it together gray side up. The past. What a hoot.

It is because of my experiences as a human being on this planet that my interests have always been sanity and language. It doesn't surprise me that my undergraduate degree is a double major: Mental Health and English. I went on to graduate study in Guidance and Counseling, dropping out of that program six hours short of a degree when one of my counseling program professors wrote on a paper of mine that my writing was so entertaining that he was certain it was a defense mechanism and that it would behoove me to "quit horsing around." My mother had used that word toward me when I was little—behoove—and I thought it meant to cut the feet off horses. "It might behoove you to clean your room."

It may be ironic that when I was first admitted to a mental hospital at eighteen, I was diagnosed, in part, on the basis of what I'd written in diaries and in a suicide note—these writings given by my mother to the psychiatrist at his coercion because I wouldn't talk to him. I would go into his office, stare at my bandaged wrists, and cry. I thought he was profoundly weird. He moved too quickly and tapped his pen on his shoe sole, his right foot resting on top of his left knee, his office walls boasting horse heads—painted well and framed—and horse figurines, some ceramic, some bronze, some stopped cold in brass. He acted impatient with me, increased my medication, and sent me to occupational therapy where I laced a wallet. When the ward nurse found the diary I'd written while on the ward that included notes about the smell of the place, the food, the doctor—notes that were not kind, but true—she gave them to the doctor. I lost television privileges and got some more Librium. But it didn't stop me. Pretty soon, I was running an underground writing coalition with the other patients.

The hospital I was first in was a private one and the primary treatment was electroshock therapy. We called it the fry. The electroshock caused horrible memory problems. So we made lists of things we didn't want to forget. I wrote those lists. After the initial six-hour recovery, I'd get whoever's list and we'd read it over and over so we could get ourselves back a little. I taped these lists to my feet, putting a finger inside my sock from time to time as if scratching my ankle or arch, feeling for a corner of paper so I'd know we were safe. Socks were the only thing they didn't take off of you for the shock-rack, the table with the straps. Sometimes they'd give some pentathol before the jolt. Sometimes not.

Another interesting thing occurred when I entered a treatment center at age forty. (I want to mention that my early hospitalizations—three months in a private hospital and a year in a state hospital—taught me how to stay out of mental hospitals as a patient. I became an employee.) I took with me to treatment a carton of cigarettes, a purple chenille robe, three poems, and my expired driver's license. When the treatment staff read the poems, they decided to contact an English professor at a local college so that he could help them discern if I was a member of a Devil Cult. The professor told them not to worry, that I was just a writer.

The reason I know this story is that one of the staff members told me. She liked to remind me about my first days of sobriety, how I marched up to her desk, in between delirium tremens, and demanded I be allowed to write in pen because I was a writer, telling her that pencils were for people who weren't on purpose. She told me I would use a pencil just like everyone else, because in the next few days I'd need to erase a lot.

All of us in treatment had to write our drug and alcohol history before we could be transferred out of detox. And everybody wanted out of detox because we wanted our clothes back. You had to wear hospital gowns in detox, but you also had to go places, such as the cafeteria, and sit in the breeze. I wrote in pencil. I erased. I wrote in pencil some more. It took me nine days to write my history of alcohol and drug use. After revising, it was one sentence: "My name is Judy, and I'm an alcoholic." My notes for that sentence were fifty pages long. But I was new. And since that day, I have been present and able to attend to my continuous newness. I am the parents of this creation. I am the one who loves me.

My friend and I graduated from the writing program, both of us earning degrees in creative writing. We visit each other a couple times a year. She practices Siddha Yoga these days and says it helps with the rage. We both know that part of the impotency of our anger is historical in nature—women are expected to be a little crazed, it's hormonal, etc.—and that part of it is that we really don't know what to *do* with anger, so we polish the toaster or busy ourselves with cloth, we take walks that get longer and longer, we keep bees. And we make art.

Many of us make in-between art, and I don't mean an art that is less-than. I mean art that is sandwiched in between everything else in those few moments we must make for ourselves. Sometimes there is irritation at being called away from a poem or painting or piano or bowl or song, but there is also a reverence for those call-aways. After all, we get our voices and hone them, we compose from our experiences, our call-aways. We are on hold, sort of, on both sides.

These days, I live in the country—a village with a population of 114. I feel my feelings—all of them—and seldom do they get saved in my body for longer than a day. I'm still learning. I keep a very low profile. Now, it's enough to live and write. I have a garden in the summer—tomatoes, peppers, beans, melons, and potatoes. As I've been working on this writing, the female white German Shepherd has given birth to eleven puppies in the bathroom closet. The second pup to come was stillborn and is buried in the yard. The other ten will open their eyes soon. I can hardly wait for them to see the world.

My neighbor to the southwest has beautiful horses, white ones. Some mornings I watch them from our back porch and they look like ghost horses when the fog's just right. I say these could be the horses of the Apocalypse. I say I've got a good seat for the show.

Out in the Middle of Somewhere

I'd like to say I don't know how I got here, but that would be a lie. I broke the law. I got caught. I'm here. This is the law I broke: "Love humanity, but do not love any particular human." It's one of my own laws. Humans do that, make up laws for themselves— rules to live by. Such as never eat anything with mayonnaise in it at a restaurant. That was one of my mother's rules. If I could trace that rule to its origins, maybe I'd discover that at some point in history a person had become ill after eating a tuna salad sandwich in a cafe. Maybe the person died from the illness. Maybe it was even caused by the tuna salad. And the story caught on— poor old Henry ate that sandwich and folded out in the street . . . it was the mayonnaise . . . it can kill you if they don't keep it cold. Like that.

The reason I made up the law about loving humanity but not any one human in particular is that people are such jerks. There's something almost endearing about billions of bozotrons on one planet, something distantly dangerous in the infinite possibilities a billion egos can create, whereas there's a more immediate danger when being real and being in a room with just one lunatic other than yourself.

And I'm not talking about the lunatics who murder their children, although I've known two women who did just that; and I'm not talking about the crazed teenager who takes an ax to her mother in the cellar, although I've known one girl who did exactly that; and I'm not talking about having Easter dinner in the same house with a couple who are already having trouble and by Halloween he will have put five bullets into her at point-blank range until she quits crawling away from him and dies on her living-room rug, but I knew them too.

Just today I came out of a restaurant in a small town in the cold rain and saw a man in thermal wear carrying deer antlers that were so fresh that the blood was still red and wet on the skull between. At the curb was a pickup truck with an entire dead deer in it. Three men were standing at the tailgate. One of them said something and laughed and slapped the dead deer's front shoulder as if they were pals of some sort.

When I was eight, I killed a snake. At least I think I did. I don't remember doing the actual killing. I remember the snake was dead. I remember remorse, and that I had an elaborate funeral for the snake, complete with a shoe box casket and a grave. I read from the Bible. I think the snake was in pieces. Everything is a no-win situation when you're eight and the snake is dead, a situation that only gains in speed and gravity as you begin to understand words such as Creature. Create. Creation.

I mean, pretty soon, if you're lucky, you'll be fifty and still promising yourself fire, casting off on the way all things of diminishment so that you may—at last—sit down some morning in sunlight and write all those notes you've been composing in your head for years, starting with the ones of love for a change because there's just not enough time, even if you live another fifty years, to file those formal complaints about how the biscuits at Hardee's just aren't as good today as they were ten years ago. And when it comes to biscuits, I know what I'm talking about. I'm talking about people, like me.

I'm sure it would all have turned out a lot different if I hadn't spent five years of my life trying to pass myself off as a lesbian. And now I've got to deal with all the consequences of *that*. I don't know if it was love for women that took me to their beds or simply the desire to be the best lover any of them had ever had. And then to let them crave me. From afar, since I'd be long gone by dawn, even if dawn was a year in arriving. Certainly there was some swooning around in the gentle forbidden. There was an odd pride in being a part of the "alternative" lifestyle—a pride that felt *almost* like power. There was also a voice in my head that would, from time to time, say quiet things to me, such as, "This is fucking crazy." And although what the voice in my head said is a twentieth-century idiom, it became—for me—an absolute. I stress the "for me" because I do not presume the consciousness or the correctness, politically or otherwise, of any other person.

I told one of my friends about my lesbianism, and he wrote me a long letter about how he thought it was a shame that I'd gotten all svelte for girls. In what I thought was an attempt to accept my decision, he ended his letter by writing, "It doesn't really matter. Fucking is fucking." I want to call attention to the fact that lesbianism was a decision for me—a conscious decision. It may not be so with other women. And my friend was wrong. It does matter.

I'm trying to tell the story of how I came to love a man, a man I met while professing to be a lesbian, and how I came to live in a small hovel in extremely rural Missouri with him. But trying to tell this story is like trying to get my mind around some philosophy of life that is larger and lighter and darker than life is, a philosophy that is both dense and filament, the train and the dream of it. Part of the problem is motherhood. I suppose I need to identify the problem now since I've written the word *motherhood*. I wanted to write "part of the problem is my mother." In fact, that's what I did write and then change because of one of those minor epiphanies that occurs when I am certain I've just written the unmitigated truth, but then a can of paint hits me in the head, just like in the movies, swinging from a rope.

So. My mother, let me be the first to extend my round, middle-aged woman's body to her after a two-hour ride through Florida in mid-July in an old Chevrolet in which the air conditioner no longer works, during which time I smoked at least ten cigarettes. Let me arrive with a sweat-soaked blouse to the front door of her new house, let her show me around, the new car they got yesterday, let me take photographs of her and her new husband, let her sit me down in her kitchen where there's a huge chocolate cake on a plate under a glass dome. Let me be cooling off from the hot ride there, let me be thirsty, let her husband come from his office into her kitchen and get himself a refill from the cold bottled water, let him say something about the road construction, the miles and miles of it to get to where they live, let me hear myself talking about the heat and how we made the ride with the windows down, let my mother tell her four-sixty air-conditioning joke—four windows down, sixty miles an hour—let her bring me up to date, let me be stubborn or stupefied or bewildered, let me just see my mother's face, not this face, let me not have to ask for water, oh please, please see me and give me water, cake.

That's close to how it went. She didn't offer me anything to eat or drink, not even a glass of water; and I didn't ask for anything, not even a glass of water. I've left out pages of conversation, but it was the same conversation we have had for at least thirty years and is actually a play I'm writing called *Tickle Tokie*. I've named it that to commemorate a childhood game my mother taught me, a game I played with her, a game I went on to play with others, a game I got in trouble for playing without her. "Tickle Tokie" is what my mother called masturbation, and her name for it is actually more musical. Maybe it doesn't make a difference what it's called. I mean, the drum in the head keeps the beat regardless. Anyhow, it was in her kitchen that the memories came back as clear and cold as the bottled water her husband poured, scenes from under or beyond the bourne of consciousness. I kept an empty, smiling countenance even though I felt as if my face was sliding off onto the floor.

Here comes that can of paint: all of this is from my point of view. What about how she saw it? What story did she tell her friends, her husband, herself? After all, we had not seen each other in ten years and I call her from Orlando and say I'm in the neighborhood, that I'd like to take her out for lunch and she says come over, but she can't go out to lunch because she's in too much pain. Then I show up all hot and sweaty and big-breasted and blonde, the sort of woman she can't stand anyhow. There I go again with my point of view. She talked about being vain, about not wanting to have to use a cane. I told her she could get a designer cane, maybe something diva-like with jewels. She said she wanted one with a button she could press and a stiletto would come out the end. She was joking. And I suppose therein lies the rub. Our humors.

What this has to do with this man I live with and love gets complicated here, or maybe not. Maybe this is where it gets figured out. His mother loves him, and she is the sort of woman who either knows love instinctively or has learned it so well and deep that it appears instinctive. She knows that it is most important to keep the rituals of common living out in front with her family—on Thanksgiving, there *will* be turkey with all the trimmings and pie and cake; at Christmas, the tree *will* be a living one to plant in the yard later, the gifts *will* be ready for the children, Santa *will* come with bicycles and doll houses, and everyone *will* eat too much homemade candy; for Easter, we'll blow the egg part out of the duck eggs and paint the shells with beautiful enamel colors; there *will* be birthday parties for every birthday of every child, with a big cake and candles and lots of presents. And to hell with the rest of it, the rest of it being what the neighbors might think or what anyone in the world might think, and to hell with thinking. We've got to go pick up a trampoline for the side yard. There will be time for thinking later. Right now, we've got things to do.

And the man I love also loves his mother. He is the sort of man who will go on vacation and buy jewelry for all his women relatives back home—and he'll buy that jewelry from a woman at a rest stop in Arizona, a woman who has displayed her work on a blanket she's spread out on the concrete. He's the sort of man who has made a tampon run on behalf of his niece during an ice storm. He's a man who knows how to love and does it so completely I just cry. He's the man my mother never told me about.

Here are a couple of the ones my mother did tell me about: her brother, only she didn't tell me the part about how he'd be my lover when I was fifteen and he was thirty and then how he'd never speak another word to me for the rest of our lives; her husband (my father), only she didn't tell me the part about how he would drink and kiss me in the dark when I was thirteen, a kiss that made the world swirl, or how he was probably in a blackout when he changed my life forever. The information she omitted are experiences she could not have predicted, certainly; however, after she was informed, and she was informed (I told her), she launched a campaign to discredit what I had told her, an activity she continues to this day just as I continue to speak the experiences. Somehow, it keeps us both alive. That may be part of the problem. And if that's too hard for me to swallow, I'll call it something else.

I'll say part of the problem is silverware and cloth napkins. I like real silver, sterling, the older and more ornate the better. I like the weight of a silver fork in my hand, the balance of it, the way it says *real*. I like cloth napkins, the feel of linen against my lips. I have never been the sort to keep the silver in a drawer somewhere or a silver chest, silver to be taken out and cleaned and used for special occasions. I like a silver soup spoon even if it's bean soup for lunch. But I wasn't born into spoons, and most likely I will not inherit my mother's silver. I am blessed with the silver we use by way of *his* mother who gave it to his sister who lets me keep it at our house, who lets me use it because I love it so much. If she wanted it back to use or to sell or to give to someone else, I would miss it but not so much I'd go buy any of it, not even if I were rich. If I were rich, I'd take us all to a Moroccan restaurant and we'd sit on pillows and eat with our hands. Or we'd go on a picnic and eat potato salad with plastic spoons. Or we'd order a pizza.

Eating at my mother's house was always such a nightmare, all the time I was growing up, and since then when I've gone to visit. She absolutely controls the food. She makes enough so that everyone gets one dietetic portion. There are no seconds. There are no leftovers. She decides what the portions are and that's that. Imagine my joy when Terry's mother, May Lou, asked if I'd like more. "You mean there *is* more?" That's my joy. But that never happened in my mother's house. Never. I don't remember ever getting into the refrigerator. Ever.

So I'm not very good in the kitchen, except for doing dishes and taking out the garbage—those were two of my chores at my mother's house. I know how to scrub pans and clean the copper bottoms. I know how to clean the broiler pan. I know to wash the glasses first. Then the plates. Then the utensils. Then the pans. Last thing in the water is the ashtrays. I know how to clean the bathroom. I know how to scrub and wax the floors. I know how to iron. I know how to do the laundry. The thing I don't know how to do very well is love. And cook.

And of course, I passed all of my ignorance on to my children. We do not get to go back and make it better. We do not get to undo anything. The slaps stay that way. The empty cupboards are always the empty cupboards. The ratty clothes and funny haircuts follow me. My children hound me, and I am the guiltiest of all, guilty until there is no ground for me to prostrate myself upon, no dirt for me to eat, no dull razors for me to use when I shave my head.

Anyhow, I met his mother and she loved me so much that when I called from Florida to say I'd been to see my mother and she hadn't even offered me water, his mother told me to come home because she loved me. She adopted me when I was fifty years old. It wasn't a legal thing. It was a heart thing. She was proud to have me around and she brought me presents for no reason, stopping by our place on her way home from someplace else.

It was the day after my fifty-first birthday that she was diagnosed with lung cancer. Terry or I took her every day for radiation treatments, and God, she tried to keep everything working, tried to keep herself together for the grandson she had raised, for the great-granddaughter she was raising, for Linda—her autistic daughter who lived in a mobile home next to the big house, who was sweet and terrified of the night, who painted her face and screamed at us all, who finally used her mother's wig for toilet paper, who told us all over and over she wanted to go to a nursing home, a nice place where she could have friends and go see some shows in Branson.

Terry and I moved into the big house a little at a time, taking turns staying overnight at first. Then May Lou one day got out of the car at the radiation center and started walking sideways. The doctor found the brain tumor an hour later, and *that* radiation began. We moved out of our little place into May Lou's farm house. Jed, her grandson, and a friend of his moved into our little house. Linda went into a thirty-day psychiatric facility. May Lou ordered baby chicks and baby ducks and a pair of baby Chinese geese. May Lou ordered a new rototiller. May Lou ordered trees. Terry and I kept the baby chicks in boxes under lamps upstairs in the room we lived in. Then the pups were born. Then it was almost warm enough to put the chicks out in the chicken house, so we did that and they all died or were killed by the neighbor's dogs. Terry put the rototiller together. Terry planted trees.

Then one night, way up in our room, I heard a sound from downstairs. I went immediately to May Lou's room. She was on the floor and she was tapping her water glass on the floorboards. She had fallen. She told me not to move her, so I didn't move her. We called for the ambulance, and they came and took her into town to the hospital. The next morning the hospital called for us to come and pick her up. We got her home and into bed, but the hospital wouldn't tell us anything. When the hospice nurse came the next day, she told us about compression fractures. May Lou had broken her back. She broke her back and they just sent her home. And that's what happened. She never got out of bed again.

I think she was up that night to get her gun. The .45 she kept in the top drawer of her dresser. Only she fell because the brain tumor took away her balance. Finally, the tumor took away everything and the night she went to meet the saints, Terry and I were doing her evening care. When the hemorrhaging started, she tried to leave the bed. Terry was at her side and I was trying to get hospice on the phone. He called to me, and I looked at his face and saw angels. There was so much blood coming from her little body. Terry was shaking his hands as if there was something on them he was trying to get off. Shaking and shaking his hands. He said, "I can't do this." I was getting a recording that said the number I was dialing was either blah-blah-blah or blah. So we traded places.

I watched her jugular vein until it stopped pulsing and I cradled her head and whispered right into her ear. I whispered over and over, "I love you so much. You're safe now." And I told Terry that she was safe now. Later, after the hospice nurse had come to prepare her body for the undertaker and to dispose of the medications, I had to hold Terry's face in my hands. We were in the kitchen. He was still in some terrified state of shock, and his hands still moved as if their motion could make everything go away. I held his face and made him look at me and told him again and again, "You are all right. You will be fine. It's over." The hospice nurse asked me if he was reacting this way because his mother had died or if he was reacting this way because it had been so violent. Both, I told her. And I told her he would be OK. I knew he would. I was there to see to it. Later, he will tell me how the body prepares the mind, how caring for May Lou had confirmed that thought. I had never thought of dying that way. I thought the mind prepared the body, or that it was a combined effort of the body/mind, that there came a time when the two joined with the spirit somehow to ease the flesh into its demise, the brain pumping its best chemicals into the body as the final distraction.

She was my best friend. I chose her. And she chose me. Out of everyone else in the world, I was the one she trusted with her body. She was the most beautiful and most private woman I have ever known. She went to the other side with skin like a newborn. All during the time we had together, I never felt compelled to tell her anything. It was as if I had no past. It was heaven. And she never expected anything from me, so I was free to give just my own self. Not a day goes by that I don't miss her.

But before I ever met her, I met her son. And before I ever met him, I met his writing. He wrote a sestina about his mother, how she was magic and could levitate objects, objects such as oranges. He sent the poem to me via a friend of his. I wrote a note of sincere encouragement and praise, and sent the poem back to him. I was impressed, very impressed, with his writing and with the fact that he had composed a sestina. I was impressed that he had read my book of poetry and had understood what I was doing with my own sestinas, had understood it so well that he integrated the form and the meaning and then departed from that point to a creation of his own. After he got my note, he came to meet me in my office at the university where he was a graduate student and I was an instructor. And there I was, Ms. Lesbian this, Ms. Lesbian that, involved with a woman who was insane enough to threaten the life of one of my colleagues, a woman on Prozac who fluctuated between wanting to iron her face and wanting to drive her car on the wrong side of the road, there I was telling Terry, "I'm a lesbian." And there was Terry, not going away. Pretty soon, we were on our way—a road trip to northern California during Christmas break in my youngest daughter's car, a trip to the west coast where I met his lifelong friend, saw his hometown, saw the redwood trees breathing—a road trip when we had never spent a night together.

I became obsessed with him. When I wasn't with him, I was writing to him and thinking up ways to get his clothes off. I felt thirteen.

I told all my acquaintances not to knock on my door if his truck was parked in my driveway. Well, everybody got mad when I wanted to be with him and not them. Everybody got mad in those first days of solidarity. Even my children got mad. It was as if no one could access me anymore. No one got to know what I was thinking or what I was writing. Except Terry.

Not that there haven't been times when I've wanted to leave, times when I've actually begun packing. I think I have to leave because I cannot stay another moment with him because I've gone off my hormones again and decided he's the anti-Christ. I forget who he is. I forget who I am. I forget he's on my side. I even forget we are writers. Times like that, I want to leave a note for him to find, you know, the note that says I have gone to find myself in the elsewhere, that says my head feels like it's going to explode, that says we got way too close and now I have to bail out because I've never been here before and I'm scared. Times like that, he has to isolate me. So, he tells me to get into the truck and then he drives me to the trees and he tells me to get out and he tells me to come on and I follow him through the forest until we find the river. He will bend and pick up the most perfect stone, put it into my palm, and say, "Here's a treasure for you." And I will begin the journey back to him, back to all the warmth and comfort my heart can hold.

I got here via obsession, but I stay here because I am learning love. What I have here is his excellent company, someone who wants to know where I am and what I'm fixing for dinner, someone with whom I will gladly assume *any* position, a man I have loved since the day I met him, a human being who is simply the best person I have ever known, who makes me promise not to go crazy this time, who promises to hold me when I die, who *will* hold me, who doesn't want to come home to a note on the table, a note he will recognize at once as the one he will have to hunt me down over, hunt me down and spit on me for writing, the only note that I can't write from this place, this place where love only means one thing.

Joel Agee

Joel Agee's roots were anchored in the creative nonfiction form long before he was born. His father, James Agee, is the author of the classic Let Us Now Praise Famous Men. But Agee was separated from his father as an infant and raised in East Germany by his mother, leaving East Germany shortly before the construction of the Berlin Wall. Soon after coming to America, the incident described in "Killing a Turtle" took place.

In "Killing a Turtle" Agee tells a simple, straightforward story, but his extraordinary powers of observation, his vivid memory for every nuance of detail burst forth on the printed page. Agee muses about his fickle memory. He wonders why "a relatively banal moment like this one continues to burn as clear as yesterday while the entire month I spent in Kentucky, in circumstances as strange to me and as interesting as any I have encountered since, lies largely submerged in oblivion, with just a few details rising from the mist, like fragments from a dream."

Killing a Turtle

In the spring of 1962, a friend of my mother's introduced me to the folksinger and photographer John Cohen, who was planning to make a documentary film about Kentucky country musicians and needed an assistant. I said I wanted the job; he said, "You got it." I said I had no experience with a movie camera; he said, "I don't either." In fact he didn't have a camera.

We borrowed a 16mm camera from a friend of his. He showed us how to mount it on the tripod, load it, wind it, use it. We should give the machine a trial run, though, he said, just to make sure it was in working order. The trial run took place on top of a second friend's house. We were going to film the roofs of the Village, the sky, the pigeons, each other. But a third friend of John's dropped by, a folksinger named Bob Dylan who was all excited about some new songs he had written, and we ended up making a fifteen-minute film of him. I recognized him immediately: "I saw you at the Gas-Light Cafe," I said.

"I saw you, too," he said. "You walked out on me. You and your girl."

"It wasn't because of you," I said.

"I didn't think so," he said.

John Cohen was the filmmaker and I was the assistant. Throughout our work in Kentucky, he rarely let me use the camera. But on that roof, he let me do the shooting. After all, it was just a trial run.

Because we didn't have any sound equipment, Bob Dylan could pretend to do virtuoso runs up and down the neck of his guitar. Then he sang one of his new songs, something involving a request for a pillow from the woman who had locked him out of her room.

"It's rock 'n' roll!" John said.

"Yeh. Do you like it?"

"You've got something there. Keep it up."

"I will."

Memory is fickle, and maybe snobbish, and fame is a glue that makes time stick fast for a while. Why else would a relatively banal moment like this one continue to burn as clear as yesterday while the entire month I spent in Kentucky, in circumstances as strange to me and as interesting as any I have encountered since, lies largely submerged in oblivion, with just a few details rising through the mist like fragments of a dream? But as I jot down these fragments, I see others coming up with them: the tiny village of Daisy, some twenty wooden houses scattered in a valley among rugged hills, and the long, haggard face of one of its denizens, Roscoe Holcomb, looking old in his early sixties, with thin sad lips and creased cheeks, deep-set puzzled pale blue eyes shaded by a wide-brimmed hat, bony hands plucking the banjo strings, singing with a high reedy voice:

Uhcross the Rocky Maa-oon-taaaaaaaaaains . . .
Awaaaan-drinahdid-gooooo . . .

An alien sound interferes; it's Chubby Checker on the radio, Roscoe's daughter is dancing the twist and maybe protesting against the folkways we're here to record. Roscoe quietly puts down the banjo and looks out over the hills, as he often does, sometimes for hours. There is time in those hills, he told us that: "Waaay back inna ole Pro-high-bishun days you could hear the sound of banjers comin' down clangity-clang from all over dem hee-ills." And now I see the spirit moving like a whirlwind through a dark pinewood church, moving the women especially, "Jesus!," "Oh Jesus!," one of them driven up and off her bench so suddenly she drops her one-year-old—clunk!—head first on the wooden floor: "Waaaaa!," to be picked up by another woman, because the mother is hopping up and down with flat feet tight together raising her face and stretching her arms to heaven and letting out strangely sexual yelps and squeals and then dropping to her knees in a puddle of sunlight, with her arms thrown out to her sides, her head thrown back, her long blond hair spread over her shoulders, and immediately several women swoop in to stroke her hair, stroke, stroke, urging her deeper into ecstasy, while in front of the altar one of the five musicians, the guitarist, goes into a different kind of seizure, he's strumming away with his eyes rolled up and his whole body vibrating vertically, very fast, so that his shoes rattle against the floor like a jackhammer, and then I notice he's slowly sliding across the platform until he's facing the altar and has his back turned on the congregation. I see Roscoe again, in his garden, stalking one of his chickens with a rifle and shooting it inexpertly in the side and then whacking its head on a rock a few times while John Cohen and Roscoe's wife and a neighbor watch, laughing and clapping their hands. And now I realize why John urged me to read Isaac Babel's short stories and especially the one called "My First Goose," in which a bookish young Jew conscripted to a Red Army detachment of cossacks proves his mettle by brutalizing a blind old woman and crushing a goose's head with his heel, and why John told me a couple of times that "we'll make a man of action out of you." That was his fantasy for himself, going South with a banjo and telling the folks there his name was Cone ("No, definitely not Coon, no sir, it's Cone as in pine-cone, yup") was as close an equivalent as could be found, in American terms, to Isaac Babel's riding with the cossacks, and if I flinched at the sight of our dinner still half alive, mangled and fluttering in the bushes, it was because I was still, like the young Babel, content to live with "winter in the heart," ignorant of the inseparable beauty and cruelty of life. Of course John didn't say this outright, but for several days after the chicken episode all our talk took place in the nimbus of some such meaning. For example, I had brought with me a book of poems by Yeats and read out loud to John one evening that tremendous poem, "The Second Coming." There was one phrase in particular that struck me: "and everywhere/The ceremony of innocence is drowned." I said I imagined the image had come to Yeats from the common practice, among country people, of drowning kittens in a sack weighted with stones. John shrugged and said, "Maybe. But the poem isn't about pity. The point of view is cosmic, not human. It's the icy lake, not the kittens. And that's something country people know in their bones." It was the shrug that bothered me. I finally told him that I didn't believe in the virtue of blood and cathartic violence. I was quivering with anger, but I spoke with an air of philosophic dispassion. Consequently, the heat of our disagreement simmered on, unacknowledged and un-abated, until it manifested, not as an argument but in a ghastly and, as it were, illustrative event.

We went to visit the Carsons, a family of musicians. Mr. Carson, a miner, was late coming home from work. We waited for him. John chatted with Mrs. Carson while she peeled potatoes. A five-year-old girl stood half hidden behind her, hugging one of her arms, staring alternately at me and at John, the expression on her face constantly shifting from a look of wide-open astonishment to a faint and quickly suppressed tickle of amusement, which, I noticed, overcame her especially at moments when I spoke, I suppose because of my unfamiliar accent. Another daughter, approximately my age, sat shucking corn and partaking in her mother's conversation with smiles and nods of her head. A third girl, fourteen or fifteen years old, tall and slender, with carrot red hair reaching down to her waist, appeared briefly at the edge of the kitchen from behind the doorpost and watched me as I loaded the camera. When I looked at her, she withdrew—slowly, as if to hide the very movement of her disappearance. After a while, half her body and face emerged again, and this time I avoided looking at her. With Mrs. Carson's permission, I took a few preliminary shots of the house and the garden, the chickens, the tethered goat with its legs splayed, the better to tear up dry clumps of grass at the foot of the porch, and an old dog twisted in furious battle with the fleas at the root of his tail. Presently Mr. Carson could be heard roaring up the hill and with a bump through the creek we had stopped at on our drive up, and then we saw him in a battered jeep, waving his hat as he pulled up. He was still in his work clothes and his face and hands were streaked with soot, he hadn't washed up too good, he said, so he couldn't shake hands just yet, but he'd be right out, and while he went into the kitchen his wife said, smiling, that sometimes her husband came home looking just like a nigger. Then, by the time he'd come out washed and combed wearing a clean cotton shirt and a fresh pair of frayed overalls and had shaken our hands and admired the camera and chatted with John and played on John's banjo and listened to John playing, the light had gotten too dark for shooting and John asked if we could come back, maybe Sunday after church, and make pictures of all of them singing, and Mr. Carson said that would be just fine, and for now, he hoped we could stay for dinner because he'd brought something special, a big surprise for the kids, but it would take some work to prepare it and then a good long time of cooking. John said he was sorry but we were expected for dinner at the Holcombs', but he'd sure like to see what the big surprise was. I started packing up the gear while Mr. Carson went down to his jeep and lifted a pile of rags off the back seat and, with an effortful, squatting heave, lifted a large object and turned and walked toward us with bent knees pressing it against his waist, a giant snapping turtle, upside down, legs walking the air in slow motion, the gray serpentine head swiveling slowly from side to side. He put the turtle on its back on a table next to the porch and said to his youngest daughter, who was still hiding behind her mother, "Emily, go tell America to come on out." And while Emily went inside, he went into a shed in the back of the house and came out with a hammer and a handful of nails and laid them next to the turtle, which was still steadily moving its feet, and pulled out a jackknife and opened it and put it next to the hammer and nails, and said, looking at John, that he hoped we didn't mind if he just got to work on the turtle, and John said that was no problem at all, we'd be leaving soon anyhow, and picked up his banjo, and started playing a cheerful, here-we-sit-on-the-porch sort of tune. Emily came out with her older sister. All I remember now of her appearance is that her skin was of that creamiest white that makes the lips look painted, and that her eyes were wide-set and of gentle expression and ferociously blue, but what I thought then was: I can see why she hides herself, she's dangerous to look at.

"Girl," Mr. Carson said, "it ain't polite, hidin' back there when folks come and visit."

She bowed her head.

"You remember Mr. Cone?"

"I sure do," she said, smiling at John and nodding hello. John nodded and smiled back, still playing his tune. Then she came over to me, and as we shook hands, she made a slight dipping movement, a remnant or intimation of a curtsy, and in that moment I heard Mr. Carson pounding in his first nail. I pressed the girl's hand and held her eyes with mine, and then my chest began to ache as if some sharp thing was being driven into me, and there was no telling, later, when I thought back on it, whether it was the sight of her or the thought of the mute agony on the table that made me feel that way, or some unimaginable amalgam of these, but the frightening notion was there right away, that if I had to stay here another day, I would fall in love with this girl. "Joel," I said, "my name's Joel." "My name's America," she said, and "Pleased to meet you," she added, and began to blush. I released her hand, I'd held it much too long, and for a moment the only sounds were those of John's quiet playing and of the corn dropping softly into the pot between the oldest girl's feet, and of Mrs. Carson's knife carving the peel off the potatoes, but then came the pounding of the hammer again, and I decided to turn and look.

Emily was standing by the table, next to her father. The turtle was still upside down, its hind legs steadily walking—or who knows, in a turtle's measure, maybe scampering, racing. Mr. Carson was pressing one hand against the gray undershell and with the other pulling the turtle's left front leg out of its socket and over the rim of the shell and forcing it all the way down to the table. Then he set a nail against the foot and took the hammer and drove the nail through the foot into the table. The other front foot was already nailed down and grotesquely elongated. The neck, too, was pulled long and taut like a rubber rope and held fast by a nail just below the jaw, which was mouthing the air in a sideward scissoring motion. Mr. Carson picked up the knife and stepped around the table and bent over the turtle, blocking my sight. What I saw was the child, who was standing opposite. I looked at John, who was still plunking away at his ditty, and realized he couldn't see what Mr. Carson was doing, though he might well have imagined it, if he wished to. What he couldn't imagine, what I could not imagine either, though I was looking into her face, was what was happening to Emily. But it froze the blood in my veins to see the signs of it: her shoulders hunched almost up to her ears, her mouth open, the corners of her lips pulled way down, her arms cramped to her sides, her fingers splayed. She didn't look human. A demon? No. If I were to paint a soul at the gate of hell, that is how I would picture it. Right on the threshold, looking down, with nothing to hold her. Ten feet away, her two sisters, her mother, and John, like the rustic extras in a Bruegel landscape. But there is another figure in this tableau. It is me. I am just looking. Everything in me has turned cold, and in that coldness, there is no pity, no pain, only the prayer for an end.

Scott Murphy

"'Cold Sweat' is a string of soldier's nightmares,"
says Scott Murphy, a novelist and an attorney from
Decatur, Illinois. "The kind you have trying to
survive a war, and most importantly, the kind an
aging veteran like me has years later — the kind that
is supposed to lead to the ending and support it. All
the dreams are dreams, if you'll allow daydreams
and worries to be included. All the dreams are
true . . .

"The original title was 'Vietnam Dreams.' I
changed the title to 'Cold Sweat' to let the last words
resonate back to the title. If some readers feel a little
of the yin/yang attraction/repulsion that I feel, a
little chill at the words '. . . I want to go,' then 'Cold
Sweat' works."

Cold Sweat

These are the dreams I dream.

I dropped out of college, or flunked out, depending on whose story you believe, mine or the college's. The army wants me. I'm not ready to be a soldier. I decide to reclaim my student deferment. My application to the easiest college in the country is in my hand when the mailman arrives with a message from Uncle Sam, greetings, report to the army on your birthday.

When I'm sworn in, I hear the lieutenant tell the sergeant to count these sorry civilians off, every fifth one is going to the Marines. I'm number five. I have a coughing fit, get out of line and get in again at a different place. The sergeant counts us off. Now I'm number six. The lieutenant announces that every fifth man is now a Marine and will be a stateside clerk for his entire enlistment. The rest of us are going to the army's Advanced Infantry Training at Fort Polk and then straight to Vietnam.

Despite what the lieutenant said, at Fort Polk everybody in my company gets orders for Germany except me. My orders are to report to Khe Sanh. But the Marines are at Khe Sanh, I object. I'm in the army. The orders are a mistake, everybody agrees, but nobody can fix them. I go to Khe Sanh. The Marines don't know what to do with me so they make me permanent point man on permanent patrol.

I got my orders fixed, and I'm not going to Khe Sanh, but I'm still going to Vietnam to the 25th Infantry Division. The plane that takes me and two hundred others from Oakland, California, to Vietnam lands at Ton Son Nhut air base near Saigon.

As the door opens and I step out into incredibly bright sunlight, Viet Cong sappers assault the plane, killing everyone. Or as I step onto the first step, a rocket hits the next step down, blowing me into too many pieces to count, too small to collect. My family receives a casket marked "Do Not Open."

Sometimes I make it through that first day, through a week of last-minute training that ought to teach me how to survive, but doesn't, and then they load me and the other new guys onto a Chinook helicopter going to the field, to Hoc Mon. Halfway there, the Chinook crashes, killing us all.

Or the Chinook doesn't crash, and we arrive safely at the fire base where my company is located. The first night they send me out on Listening Post (LP). On LP four men and a radio go outside the perimeter at night to be sure to be the first to hear (or see) approaching enemy, and alert the company. The problem with an LP is that once you can hear (or see) them they can hear (or see) you, and so getting back inside the perimeter without them, or your own company, shooting at you is a low-odds proposition. Nobody volunteers for LP. They send new guys.

In the worst dreams they invent a one-man LP and I get to be the first to try it out. The Viet Cong are waiting for me. They drag me off as a prisoner, they torture me, they slit my throat.

There are a hundred variations on this one, and in each one I end up dead the first day.

I make it through the first day. The second day we're patrolling in the jungle. I've attached my hand grenades to the straps of my pack. As I brush by a bush a twig pulls the pin out of one of the grenades. As I was trained to do when the pin on a grenade is pulled, I count: One (I struggle with the grenade, I can't get it off the strap); Two (I can't get the pack off; everybody else is two counties away or behind a rubber tree); Three (it's off—); BLAM, too late.

I'm a little guy. They make me a tunnel rat. I don't know any better. I'll squirm around in tunnels all day long if they want me to. One day we find a big tunnel complex. I go down, then left for a few feet, then right, your left, your right, your left, then straight for about three miles. The tunnel gets narrower and narrower but I keep nudging through the tight places until one spot catches me. I can't go forward and I can't go back. I'm stuck. Nobody else is small enough or dumb enough to go where I've gone. They can't reach me; they can't even find me. I took one too many turns, like Tom Sawyer in the cave. They search for hours, then they go away. And I'm still stuck.

And a big rat the size of a raccoon shimmies up and gnaws on my nose.

Or a coral snake slithers onto my shoulder and bites my ear.

Or a V.C. with a big grin and a carving knife looms out of the dark at the end of the tunnel.

Or I make it out of that one somehow like Flash Gordon, and the next day we go up in Huey slicks, the small helicopters with open bays on both sides that carry six soldiers each, plus the crew and two door gunners. As usual, I sit on the knobby metal floor, hang my legs out the open bay and lose myself in the silver and black loops of the rivers and the squares of the rice paddies below. Some new guy behind me, too terrified to get near the open bay, shifts position, lurches and falls against my back just hard enough to push me out. I do quite a number of elegant front flips before I land in the Saigon River. Or on a water buffalo. Or in a punji pit. Any way you dream it, I'm DEE EE A DEE dead.

It's three in the morning. I'm asleep, safe inside the perimeter of Fire Support Base Keane. Mortars start exploding all around me and it sounds like a thousand AK-47s are firing into the perimeter. I roll off the slats I've been sleeping on into six inches of water (it's the rainy season). I grope for my M-16. My 16 is always next to me, I clutch my 16 in my sleep. But now I can't find it. Two thousand AKs are inside the wire, and now I remember, something was wrong with Rudy Taylor's 16, he had to go out on LP, and I loaned him mine. Three thousand V.C. assault me personally, and my only weapon is a steel pot.

My R & R comes through for Penang, in Malaysia. I get to leave the field today. Or I can kiss Penang off and hold out for Bangkok next month. I'm tough. I'm hardcore. I hold out for Bangkok. The North Vietnamese army overruns our position the night I would have landed in Penang.

• • •

A sham job in the rear is coming open in a month when Garcia goes home. I'm tight with Top, he says I'll get the job. But Garcia extends his tour and the job never opens up. Or Garcia goes home, but so does Top. The new first sergeant hates me. In three days I'm in so much trouble I can choose between six years in LBJ (Long Binh Jail) or a transfer to the Special Forces. I choose LBJ. The night I arrive the V.C. mortar LBJ for the first time in the war and disintegrate my hootch. Sometimes I choose the Special Forces and I get to infiltrate North Vietnam with my new buddies.

With only sixty days left in Vietnam, I pass out on patrol four days in a row. I feel foolish. They want me to go to Cu Chi to see a doctor. I don't want to go. That should be a clue how sick I am. They make me go in.

The doctors discover that I have a rare disease that would have kept me out of the army if it had been discovered before I got drafted. Now, however, they've found a cure. Sixty daily rabies-like shots with a needle the diameter of a baseball bat. In the solar plexus. Luckily the medic can give me the shots if six GIs hold me down, so I can stay in the field.

A jet lands on the dinky little road to Duc Hoa. It's my freedom bird to take me back to the world. But before I can get on, three hundred rear echelon troops arrive in an air-conditioned bus and board my freedom bird. The stewardess comes down and explains that grunts are not allowed. Her smile never leaves her face, but as she looks at my torn and crusty jungle fatigues, which like me have not been washed in over a month, her whole body quivers like an aspen tree. "So dirty," she says. In some of the dreams I shoot her, but she doesn't seem to mind. She goes back up the stairs smiling and the plane takes off without me. I shoot at it until it is out of sight.

I'm out of the field. I'm at Ton Son Nhut one year to the day after I arrived. I'm at the hangar and I can see my plane out there shimmering in the heat waves rising off the runway. They announce that it's time to board. We start to walk to the plane. A rocket hits the ground at my feet. The farm is mine, I bought it.

Sometimes the rocket's a dud; nobody's hurt and we board the plane. It takes off. We cheer. As the cheer fades, a rocket sneaks up from a village near the airport. No American passenger jet has ever been shot down in Vietnam. This is the first.

Sometimes the plane makes it to the coast; we see the water; we are finally, finally short—and the rocket gets us just as we fly over the ocean, splash. You're never short till you land in Oakland.

We land in Oakland. The President is waiting for us. He wants us to go back. We laugh. A regiment of MPs armed with fifty-caliber machine guns convince us to go back.

Or after showering in the empty terminal, we who have survived go out for a good time. We get so drunk we enlist in the Marines on the condition that they send us to the DMZ. They are willing to oblige us. When we sober up we're on a jet to Danang.

I come home. A woman spits on me and calls me murderer. My friends ask me where I've been, they haven't seen me in a while. The second morning my dad yanks me out of bed and says get a job. I don't have to take this crap. I re-up. Next day I'm on a jet to Vietnam.

Or I come home, go back to college, graduate, get a job, work, marry, have kids, develop a wee bit of a beer belly, enjoy life. Wars break out in Lebanon, Nicaragua, Afghanistan, Grenada, Panama, Iraq, and, of course, Vietnam again. We're in them all. The President calls back everybody with infantry training who is under forty-six. I make the cut by five days. It's only for six months to train new troops, he says. In the fifth month he makes my stay indefinite, for the duration, and I get orders to Vietnam.

Some of these dreams aren't dreams, they're memories. Some are old friends. But this one is the worst, the most dangerous.

Because I want to go.

I've forgotten the fear, the torn flesh, the counting of days, hours and minutes until I could get out of that place. All I remember is how my adrenaline raced at the speed of light, how I was free, young and fierce.

Those other dreams are bad. When I dream this one, I wake up in a cold sweat.

Lisa Hay

Lisa Hay's profile of this young and spirited stripper is raw and dramatic. Dominique is not at first a particularly likeable or charismatic character, but even in the beginning, the reader senses the inherent desperation of her actions. As the narrative proceeds, we see the emergence of a different Dominique, a young woman captivated by the universal desire for love and security. The fact that her hopes are dashed by an act of brutality from the source of her happiness — her lover — and that she reverts back to her past life is not a surprise. But the crack in her facade and the emergence of a fragile vulnerability are quite affecting.

Lisa Hay writes with a tone of immediacy and with the intimacy of an "insider's" perspective, but without egocentricity. Understanding that the compelling character in her story is Dominique (even though she too works at the strip club), Hay walks the line carefully, allowing herself to become part of the narrative rather than the objective of the narrative — a vital creative distinction.

Dominique

Dominique, in baby-blue spiked heels and lavender fabric wrapped around her like a ribbon, gets a two-handed hoist from another dancer. She grabs the pole that rises from the center of the stage and climbs using her inner thighs and arms, lifting herself to the top where the pole meets the black ceiling. As soon as the birthday boy looks up she lazily slides down, making a squeegee sound as her thighs are pinched by the pole. When she is right above him she unwinds her legs and sets them on his shoulders with her crotch at his chin, butt facing the crowd. We can't tell if the guy's happy about this because he can't move and we can't see his face. This is one of Dominique's specialties. She sets the standard. The other dancers have to match up. Every birthday boy or newlywed who comes to this strip bar from now on gets a crotch in the face.

Dominique has other surprises that make her money. It's her birthday now, and she's stuffing balloons into the top and back of her costume, a pink Spandex piece of cloth. It stretches the fabric so thin that it almost rips the fibers. The DJ speaks into the mike. "Is Dominique looking for a boob job?"

She yells back, "I don't need a boob job. I need to get laid." The all-male audience cheers. Their noise drowns out the music and the dancer on the main stage. Two of the men who are entranced by her leave and come back with a birthday cake and a 9mm to lay down at her feet. She always has one or two men waiting on her. She picks these guys out when she dances at the edge of the main stage, a square, black platform that is encircled by red flashing Christmas lights. A disco ball throws colored light all over the room and her body. Her music, usually something by George Thorogood, reaches everyone through its bass that explodes out of the speakers and ends up in everyone's stomach. She has her walnut-brown hair teased into a bird's nest at her forehead and the sides lacquered around her ears. She catches the eye of some men who are sitting close to the stage and dances only for them, putting her hands to the side of her head and rolling her pelvis towards them, then licking her finger and putting it between her legs, into her vagina, then pulling it out and licking it, all the while keeping eye contact. They will pay her ten dollars for table dances for the rest of the night. One night she plays to bikers. Another night it's someone in a wheelchair. Still another it's just some guys sitting at a table near the stage. She doesn't care who it is as long as they pay up. She is worth the money. I watch her get on her knees before one customer and take each of his fingers into her mouth and suck like she is scraping off the remaining meat from a spare rib. You'd like her. When we first met, I found her intimidating. But if you look directly into her eyes, past her tough tension, you can see that she is sad and scared.

A few nights later she stretches her body into various positions so the man who has asked her for a table dance has an unobstructed view of anything he wants to see. She starts by sitting between his legs. She looks him in the eyes and puts her hand under his balls. He stares at her. She moves her hand and begins to dance for him. She stands with her back to him and hikes her leg up onto his shoulder. Then she bends over using her hands to spread her butt cheeks and then bends further so everything is in view. The man with the beard smiles. Soon after that night she disappears. Bob, who sells pull-tabs, says she left to marry a man she met at the bar. He introduced them. It is a month before she comes back to show us her ring.

Her makeup is lighter when she comes back. Her lipstick is frosted pink instead of blood red. She sits on her stool with a straight back. "Where've you been?" I ask.

"I met the man of my dreams." The East Coast accented words sprint off her tongue. "Bob introduced us. And I'm getting married. See my ring?" She pushes one hand toward me while the other fiddles inside her purse for something. She moves her hand back and forth to make the ring catch light above us.

"It's nice," I tell her. A silver heel from one of her shoes taps the toes of her other foot. She smiles and waits for more praise. It doesn't come, and I notice her lipstick is bleeding. I say good luck to her and go back to waitressing.

I don't see her again for another month. This time it is at my day job at the local museum. She comes in with a class of third graders. My stomach dives as I see her walk in the door, but then she sees me and we both start laughing nervously knowing that we might blow each other's cover. The teachers look at us, curious as to how we know each other. We hug. We are allies here. The museum won't approve of my night job and neither the teachers nor her kids would be happy about her taking off her clothes for a living. She whispers into my ear that her real name is Debbie. I ask why she came and she points to a young boy who is in line with the class. "That's my son now."

"Oh," I say. We are surrounded by kids and teachers, and we can't say anything else. Today she looks like a mom. Instead of spiked heels and a strip of leotard, she's dressed in a red sweater and black pants. Her shoes are low black pumps, and she is wearing flesh-colored nylons. I can see them bunching at her heel. Even her Brooklyn accent has less of an edge.

During the program we get a chance to talk. She asks me if I have a cigarette, and tells me, "I'm still dancing to make ends meet, but I work days at the school where my adopted kids attend." She stops and gets down on her hands and knees to help her new son in the activity. His eyes are on her. When he is fine on his own she stands up and comes back to her chair. She tells me she is happy. Her accent is just a whisper in her words. She asks if we could get together on the weekend, and I say yes.

Several weeks go by before we see each other again. Neither of us calls the other. I see her again at the strip bar after I've been fired. I'm playing pool with a friend when she comes up and says, "Who's playin' the winna?" The accent is back and her eyes are lined with black kohl and pain. Her smile is weak. She is weighed down with hair spray, makeup and something else. Both of her eyes look unusually dark but I can't tell if it's just the makeup or fatigue. She moves around the table slowly, stiffly. After she picks a pool cue she smacks it hard against the side of the table as if calling court into session, and it grabs the attention of everyone within earshot. Then not changing her expression, she takes her shot. I don't know what to say, if anything. Her friend, a guy in his thirties, leans against a bar stool watching.

"Are you working?" she asks.

"No, I got fired. And they didn't give me a reason," I say, taking a drink of cranberry juice.

"Well, here's what I think of that," she says, going over to the bar and picking up her cigarette. She drags the lit end down the length of the bar leaving a burnt trail of ash. Her black sequined miniskirt moves like an upside-down umbrella bobbing back and forth and her black bra cuts into the skin of her back.

"What's going on with you?" I ask, taking my shot.

"I got raped and beat up last night," she says. I stop playing. "Was it last night?" she asks Bill. He nods. She puts her forearms out in front of her to prove it to me. "I have two fractured forearms, black eyes and a broken rib."

I put my hands on hers and look at the long brown bruises running from elbows to wrists. She tells me her fiancée knocked her out after she accidentally called him the name of an old boyfriend. Her voice begins shaking like the ice cubes in my glass. "I went to the women's shelter, but they wouldn't let me stay 'cause I had no ID. I didn't have no money so I had to walk home." She downs a shot of Jack. "While I was walking I got jumped by some nigger. He hit me in the face, and raped me. My wrists got fractured as he slammed me down, so did my rib. I got the cops and they took me to the hospital. I tried to press charges but they arrested me instead for being drunk." I don't ask any more. All emotion leaves her voice. Something sounds tilted in her story, but the terror in her actions keeps me quiet. She leans against Bill, and he puts his arms around her. The music blares out a Donna Summer song and I watch as men come in the front door and walk by us. Right now I hate each one.

"I'm working tonight for my plane fare so I can get out of here tomorrow," she says. "Remember when I told you about my old boyfriend?" I don't but I nod my head anyway. "He proposed on the phone, so I'm going back to Brooklyn to get married and be a secretary." She grabs the pool stick and begins playing pool with my friend. "Do you play dirty pool?" she asks.

"What's dirty pool?" He stands facing her. She grabs his crotch and looks into his eyes. "No," he says. His expression doesn't change. "Okay then, we'll play clean pool." While Dominique is losing her game to Stan, I lean against a table and watch. Her gait is unsteady in her black and silver heels. Each time she takes a step, the heel threatens to give. Her face is serious and some of the toughness has been taken from her. Her way of moving, now insecure and tired, makes her look more like a fifteen-year-old runaway than a twenty-one-year-old woman. I offer her a ride to the airport the next day. She accepts. A few hours later I leave her at the bar so she can get back to work. I hug her tight and tell her to be careful. Her body is so small. I feel like I am almost breaking her arms with my hug. She already has two fractured arms from the rape. I don't want to cause her any more pain. She looks at me like a hurt child, and she holds on to my arms as I start to let go. I put my arms back around her. I want to protect her from whatever else is lined up to hurt her. Even though she's tough enough to kick the ass of any dancer who steals her money, and tough enough to go up to a man she is attracted to and say, "I want to fuck you," this last thing has broken her.

The next day I pull my truck up to the back of the club and enter the side door. "Where's Dominique?" I ask the handyman. I can barely see him because he's dressed completely in black.

"She's in back," he says and turns and leaves me in the storeroom alone except for empty kegs and extra chairs. I walk through the dark bar. The tables look innocent without the drinks and men. A guy is trying new lighting sequences on the empty stage. The smell of cigarettes and beer is still in the air and pulls on me as I move to the back. I find her in the dressing room drying her hair. The bright show biz lights make it easier to see the black eyes she got from her fiancée two nights before, and the bruises on her wrists from the rapist's hands as he held her down. "Hi, Lisa," she says. I am surprised that she remembers my name. She hasn't ever said it that I can remember. It makes me feel closer to her, as though we are friends for real, instead of the transparent friendship I thought we were pretending to have.

I sit next to her on the white bench and look at her in the mirror. "Where is your stuff?" I ask. She points to the back of the dressing room, not looking me in the eye. I get up and walk past beat-up lockers with dancers' names on them and a washing machine, and into a room with three mock tapestry giant suitcases and five television-sized boxes. I yell back to her. "Are all these yours?"

"Yes," she says.

I check my watch. Her plane leaves in two hours. Connie, the manager, comes and sits down on the other side of Dominique. "Honey, do you have enough money to take all that stuff?" she asks.

"Yeah, from dancing last night," she says. She looks down when she says yes and swallows hard, holding the curling iron to her hair until it starts to smoke.

"I think you can only take three bags, Dominique," says Connie.

"Oh, then I don't." She looks down at some crumpled dollar bills that she pulls out of her purse. "Let's call," she says, turning to me. Connie and I walk back to the office. The Mark Air guy confirms that she can only take three bags and one carry-on. I go back to tell her, but she is on a pay phone crouched in the corner, crying, wiping her eyeliner off her cheeks as fast as it runs. "But I can't," is all I hear her say. I go and sit by the boxes. Fifteen minutes later I go to ask her what we're going to do. She's gone. I find her in the manager's office on the phone again, crying. The manager and the handyman are sitting there watching her as if they are watching an animal die. I leave. I feel uncomfortable being there as she crumbles in the brown vinyl chair that holds her like a child. When she's finished she walks past me, not meeting my eyes.

I catch up to her. "Do you want me to load up everything?" I ask.

"Yes," she says. "Bill will give me some money for the stuff." She makes more phone calls.

The handyman and I load up the things. She comes out just as Bill pulls up in a gray four-by-four. She hands me her plane ticket and a blue-flowered duffel bag. "Do you mind if I ride with Bill?" she says. When I say no she says for me to meet them at the airport. Her lavender lycra pants are tucked into white Sorrel boots. She's wearing a white jacket with streaks of dirt all over it. She looks so young.

I take off first and make it to the airport a few minutes before they do. The gray pickup pulls up behind me and Bill gets out to get a luggage cart. I walk in with Dominique to check in. We go to the Delta desk.

"I can't help you right now," the flight attendant says. "I'm booking a group, it'll be a few minutes." Her face is cramped underneath her red-rimmed glasses. We sit down. We stare at each other then I ask her if I can interview her for my thesis. She has ignored all of my other requests, but this time she smiles and grabs the small tape recorder out of my backpack, and says into the mike, "Do I just speak into here?" As she plays with the arms of a stuffed animal she tells me how long she's been dancing.

"I have been dancing for four years now. I've been dancing here for four months. There is no money here. The money is in New York," she says and her voice speeds up. "There I average $1,500 a week. With the money you make here you average, like, $200. Sometimes you can make more than that but you really have to work and you really have to know the customers."

She takes a deep breath, looks at me for a clue or a comment as to what I think about that, or what to go on to next. We both look at the customer service representative and she is still busy. I ask her if her first night was difficult. She smiles the smile of an older woman, one of her many faces, and starts again. "Every time you start dancing in a new club you get pretty nervous . . ." I'm looking at Bill. He's leaning over the suitcases looking around the airport, almost falling asleep. I wonder how long they've known each other. I watch Dominique's mouth moving. Her expressions and voice are surreal, coming from a far-away place. I'm wondering who raped her and if we could find him and make him pay for it.

The woman calls us up to the counter. She's ready to take Dominique's stuff. Dominique has four forty-five-pound boxes to take with her, and she doesn't have the money to pay for them. "I'll do it somehow," she says. The lady gives us the I-don't-have-time-for-this look. It makes me bitchy and I snap at her dumb questions about seating arrangements and destinations. I'm impatient with the way she's treating us. Dominique takes a different approach. She becomes calm, wide-eyed, and almost innocent. She asks if she can take the boxes on, and the lady says it will be thirty dollars a box. Dominique says she has no money, and that this is an emergency.

"I was raped last night and I just want to go home." The lady softens. She looks at me, then at Dominique. Her eyes focus on all the evidence, black eyes, and bruised wrists that Dominique has spread out palms up on the counter for inspection. The lady looks behind us. And she says "OK," but only if they are less than seventy pounds. Dominique doesn't even smile. The moment is too serious for that. I say, "Thank you," and feel like I did something wrong. Bill and I start filling out name tags before the lady changes her mind. The people behind us watch our movements with sympathy. Her voice was loud enough for everyone in line to hear what is going on. Dominique ignores them and starts shifting boxes. There is one white box that is really light. I ask her if the things in here can be put into her duffel bag. I expect to see clothes, but after Dominique says yes, and starts to re-pack, I see that there are eight different teddy bears, the kind little girls lean up against their pillows on their beds. I look at her and in her tough accent she says, "So I collect teddy bears, OK?" I say, "OK," and pull out a sparkly polar bear for her to hold on the plane. She'll need it. She smiles and tucks it under her arm. The customer service representative is a goner. Dominique wraps us all around her finger. I stuff the bears into her flowered bag. She checks in and we take the bags upstairs. I promised to buy her lunch so we go to the cafeteria and order soup, and two plates of French fries. We sit in the smoking section of the cafeteria so Dominique can have a Marlboro. While she eats she talks some more about her physical pain and about money.

"Stripping is hard on your body," she says. "I have to go to a chiropractor three times a week, and I have tendonitis in both ankles now. I fell off the pole and fractured my shoulder so now I have to go and get cortisone shots. You can't dance for very long. But you can make a lot of money. Like in New York, I made $150,000 a year. I own two houses, a condo, and two apartments." All of this is raising questions in my mind. Why didn't she leave a long time ago? Why didn't she pay for her own ticket? Her face is all confidence as she gives me her motherly advice.

"You have to have the right frame of mind to do this. You have to treat it as a business, that it is just a job like any other job. Nine to five. It will get to you at first, but once you learn to treat it as a business, you'll do really good at it." It sounds too easy, I tell her. I'm thinking of the men reaching for the women, wanting to take a piece for themselves.

"Oh yes," she says. "You have guys grabbing. You'll have incidents when a guy orgasms in his pants. They try to touch you. It can get really rough, but you just have to believe it's a nine to five job. The roughest night I had was when another dancer stole my money and a guy came on me. So I ended up fighting the dancer—punched a hole in the wall, broke my hand, got arrested for having a gun, got totally shitfaced, came back, got arrested again, and that was about it. One night a guy gave me a nine-millimeter. It wasn't loaded, though. I was putting it in my locker, and a chick saw it and freaked out, and said I was shooting at the bouncer and all this shit. Then the cops came. I told the cops, 'Listen, if I had a gun and wanted to shoot someone I would. I don't have a problem with shooting someone. I've shot someone before.' I didn't shoot her, I didn't have any bullets in the gun."

"Has anyone ever gotten violent with you after or during dancing?" I ask.

"No, I try to stop them before they do. I carry a gun in New York. I had a guy grab me before, but I don't put up with shit. I'll kick his ass for something like that." She is no longer vulnerable. Her black eyes almost disappear as she talks.

"Have you always been this tough? Did dancing change you at all?" I ask.

"Naw, I've been on my own since I was fourteen so I grew up this way . . . well, one change, I am more flexible," she says, laughing.

"What would you say to a woman whose husband or boyfriend goes into strip bars?" I'm wondering how she feels about those women. She is so in control with the men.

"Get a life. Nothing happens in there. I mean it's a nine to five job. We take off our clothes for a living. That's it. Some people say some of us sleep around for money, but most of us are legitimate. We go home by ourselves."

"So women have no reason to find it threatening."

"I wouldn't. As a matter of fact if I had a guy, I'd send him to a bar. I'd say get out there and tip somebody. I don't see why someone should be threatened about it. If they are threatened by their man going into a strip joint, then there is something else wrong with their relationship because nothing is going to happen."

"Why do men go in these places?"

"I have no idea. I have always wanted to know that. I guess maybe they want to see what they ain't got . . . They can't get."

We ask Bill the same question.

"Why," he says. "Let me see, why do men go in there? To get away . . ."

"No, some men come in for conversation," says Dominique. "Their wives don't give it to them, they are having problems at home, they just need someone to talk to that they don't know, and why not go talk to a beautiful woman? You know, I could be a psychiatrist, a licensed psychiatrist, because I've been doing this for four years, and because they tell you things that you would not believe. But I like it. I'm in it to meet people. I mean I've modeled, I've done *Playboy*, I've done porno, I've done *Cheri* magazine, *Club* magazine. I have. It's money. It's excitement. I mean how many people can say that *Playboy*, *Penthouse*, *Club* and *Cheri* wanted you to be in their magazine? You know?"

There is something very powerful about Dominique. Within her vulnerability and toughness is the power to get what she wants. Maybe I'm naive, but I don't know how she does it. Maybe by being childlike and inspiring protectiveness. Or maybe she does it by seeing and hitting everyone's weak spot.

"I give a money-back guarantee for my table dances. If you don't get a hard-on you get your money back. They get what they are paying for."

"What do you do to insure they get a hard-on?"

"Ask Bill," she says. Bill looks like he's being violated by our conversation. He doesn't say anything so she continues. "I use my eyes a lot. I have what people call fuck-me eyes. I use my knees a lot. A lot of knee contact in their crotch. You blow in their ears, play with their hair, a lot of butt action. It works every time. With every man."

It seems as if we've spent the whole day together. I'm tired and my yawn makes her yawn. "I retired last night," she says. "It was my last night. Now I'm going to go back and use my college degrees for something." Again her voice speeds up. "This time it's for good. I am retiring. You know, I have degrees in business man- agement, and medical secretary/transcriptionist. I know a lot of important people in New York. I can do something with that . . ." She lays it all on the table like a bluff poker hand, hoping that saying all those words will give her some of the security they imply. "The money ain't worth it . . . I have anything I'll ever need, you know? All I need now is a family, and you can't have a relationship when you are a stripper. Guys can't handle it. I mean could you handle your girlfriend showing her pussy to strange men who are trying to grab her and tip her for that? Giving her phone numbers. I do get lots of dates, though."

"Good dates or bad dates?" I ask.

She laughs. "Some good, some bad. My date last night was incredible." Bill is blushing. "You're blushing, Bill." She looks at Bill's red face and then at me. "We got thrown out of a hotel last night." They eye each other and smile.

"If I was thinking about dancing, what would you warn me about?"

"Everyone," she says. "The customers. Who you work for. The ones you work with. It's a money business, and a big money business, and it's run by the Mafia. I don't care what they say. You can get hurt really easily if you say the wrong thing and you can get ripped off. I mean, you can think that a girl is your best friend and the next thing you know you're missing five hundred bucks out of your wallet."

Dominique's expression changes from comfortable confidence to anguish as she focuses on something behind me. She tells me to hold on a second as she gets up and makes her way towards a man and two boys who just entered the cafeteria. One of the boys is the one I met at the museum. The man is her fiancée. His shoulders are hanging low and he has pulled the collar of his jacket up to his chin for protection from whatever he's feeling. He looks over at me and Bill and a flash of resentment passes over him. He grabs Dominique by her arm and leads her to a bar stool behind some plants.

The boys hang around me and Bill sitting in a booth behind us. I don't know why. They look sad and afraid. I start asking how Bill met Dominique and it isn't the kind of thing two young boys should hear. I lean back and give them her fries. The two boys munch on her French fries, and I look over at her and see that she has put her head in her hands. Despite that she looks strong. Her back is straight and she is looking at him straight in the eyes. I know he is asking her to come back by the way he puts his hand on her arm. I look over at the boys and the one I recognize says,

"Hi." I turn and talk to Bill while keeping my eyes on Dominique in case she needs some help.

"How long have you known her?" I ask. He tells me since last night. "How did you meet?"

"She watched me while she was dancing, then came up to me and told me she wanted to fuck me. I thought she was hustling me so I started to move, but she said, 'No, I'm serious, I want to fuck you.' So I bought a couple of table dances, then we left." I knew there was money involved because dancers cannot just leave early. There are fines involved. I asked him how much he spent on her. "Nothing," he says.

"Well," he says. "Let's see, $10 a table dance, three dances, some dollar bills, her fine, the hotel bill, and I gave her some money today because she needed it. . . ."

I look over to see what is going on. She is holding on to her bear, as black tears tattoo her face. The two boys leave the table and put their arms around her waist. I don't want to go over to them until he leaves. He is the one who hit her the night before. He stares at her as she cries, blinking a lot. Then he looks at me as if asking for help. I'm not going to help him. I think she will come over to us and tell us that she is going back with him. I know she really wants a family. A family would save her. Give her something solid. Finally I do go over to her and hug her. She holds on to me tight. I ask her if she is OK and she tells me that she is leaving her family, how can she be OK? I am proud of her for being strong. She has fifteen minutes before she can board her plane. I leave her with the kids and the man so she can say a final good-bye. He looks at me with tears in his eyes and I feel sorry for him. I don't know why. After they go, she comes to the table where Bill and I are talking. "I need a drink," she says. We circle back through airport security and sit down at the small bar. There are about six others sitting around. Dominique lays out a twenty and asks for as many shots of Cuervo as it can buy. The bartender, an Asian woman, insists on an ID and after a few "Oh, fucks" Dominique finds it in the bottom of her duffel bag, under her deodorant, makeup and bras of different colors. She gets down six shots before the flight attendant calls for early boarders. She is one of these because she is unable to carry her duffel bag with her fractured wrists. We lead her to the airplane, and she starts crying again. We hug and she holds on to me tight and thanks me for being her friend. She hugs Bill and says good-bye. As she starts boarding she calls back to us to call her. We say, "OK," not realizing that she hasn't given either of us her phone number or address. I watch as a flight attendant carries her duffel down the ramp, and Dominique follows with her head down and her polar bear in her arms.

Richard Rodriguez

In "Proofs," Richard Rodriguez demonstrates how
writers vary voices, points-of-view, personae and
characters while maintaining control and building
momentum in a narrative. Rodriguez, an essayist
on the NewsHour with Jim Lehrer (PBS)
and the author of an autobiography, Hunger of
Memory: The Education of Richard
Rodriguez, begins "Proofs" in the second person,
but in his father's image. The voice abruptly changes,
almost immediately; Rodriguez questions his father,
addresses the reader and then captures the history of
his ancestors. This is the jangled, staccato rhythm
that prevails from start to finish. Yet the narrative
has momentum and direction; Rodriguez never loses
control, but creates a tightly knit, explosive package
of dramatic, bittersweet emotion.

You stand around. You smoke. You spit. You are wearing your two shirts, two pants, two underpants. Jesús says, if they chase you throw that bag down. Your plastic bag is your mama, all you have left; the yellow cheese she wrapped has formed a translucent rind; the laminated scapular of the Sacred Heart nestles flame in its cleft. Put it in your pocket. The last hour of Mexico is twilight, the shuffling of feet. A fog is beginning to cover the ground. Jesús says they are able to see in the dark. They have X-rays and helicopters and searchlights. Jesús says wait, just wait, till he says. You can feel the hand of Jesús clamp your shoulder, fingers cold as ice. *Venga, corre.* You run. All the rest happens without words. Your feet are tearing dry grass, your heart is lashed like a mare. You trip, you fall. You are now in the United States of America. You are a boy from a Mexican village. You have come into the country on your knees with your head down. You are a man.

Papa, what was it like?

I am his second son, his favorite child, his confidant. After we have polished the DeSoto, we sit in the car and talk. I am sixteen years old. I fiddle with the knobs of the radio. He is fifty.

He will never say. He was an orphan there. He had no mother, he remembered none. He lived in a village by the ocean. He wanted books and he had none.

You are lucky, boy.

In the nineteenth century, American contractors reached down into Mexico for cheap labor. Men were needed to build America: to lay track, to mine, to dredge, to harvest. It was a man's journey. And as a year's contract was extended, as economic dependence was established, sons followed their fathers north. When American jobs turned scarce—during the Depression, as today—Mexicans were rounded up and thrown back over the border. But for generations it has been the rite of passage for the poor Mexican male.

I will send for you or I will come home rich.

In the fifties, Mexican men were contracted to work in America as *braceros,* farm workers. I saw them downtown in Sacramento. I saw men my age drunk in Plaza Park on Sundays, on their backs on the grass. I was a boy at sixteen, but I was an American. At sixteen, I wrote a gossip column, "The Watchful Eye," for my school paper.

Or they would come into town on Monday nights for the wrestling matches or on Tuesdays for boxing. They worked over in Yolo county. They were men without women. They were Mexicans without Mexico.

On Saturdays, they came into town to the Western Union office where they sent money—money turned into humming wire and then turned back into money—all the way down into Mexico. They were husbands, fathers, sons. They kept themselves poor for Mexico.

Much that I would come to think, the best I would think about male Mexico, came as much from those chaste, lonely men as from my own father who made false teeth and who—after thirty years in America—owned a yellow stucco house on the east side of town.

The male is responsible. The male is serious. A man remembers.

The migration of Mexico is not only international, South to North. The epic migration of Mexico and throughout Latin America is from the village to the city. And throughout Latin America, the city has ripened, swollen with the century. Lima. Caracas. Mexico City. So the journey to Los Angeles is much more than a journey from Spanish to English. It is the journey from *tu*—the familiar, the erotic, the intimate pronoun—to the repellent *usted* of strangers' eyes.

Most immigrants to America came from villages. The America that Mexicans find today, at the decline of the century, is a closed-circuit city of ramps and dark towers, a city without God.

The city is evil. Turn. Turn.

Mexico is poor. But my mama says there are no love songs like the love songs of Mexico. She hums a song she can't remember. The ice cream there is creamier than here. Someday we will see. The people are kinder—poor, but kinder to each other.

Men sing in Mexico. Men are strong and silent. But in song the Mexican male is granted license he is otherwise denied. The male can admit longing, pain, desire.

HAIII—EEEE—a cry like a comet rises over the song. A cry like mock-weeping tickles the refrain of Mexican love songs. The cry is meant to encourage the balladeer—it is the raw edge of his sentiment. HAIII—EEEE. It is the man's sound. A ticklish arch-ing of semen, a node wrung up a guitar string, until it bursts in a descending cascade of mockery. HAI. HAI. HAI. The cry of a jackal under the moon, the whistle of the phallus, the maniacal song of the skull.

Tell me, Papa.

What?

About Mexico.

I lived with the family of my uncle. I was the orphan in the village. I used to ring the church bells in the morning, many steps up in the dark. When I'd get up to the tower I could see the ocean.

The village, Papa, the houses too . . .

The ocean. He studies the polished hood of our beautiful blue DeSoto.

Mexico was not the past. People went back and forth. People came up for work. People went back home, to mama or wife or village. The poor had mobility. Men who were too poor to take a bus walked from Sonora to Sacramento.

Relatives invited relatives. Entire Mexican villages got re-created in three stories of a single house. In the fall, after the har-vest in the Valley, families of Mexican adults and their American children would load up their cars and head back to Mexico in car-avans, for weeks, for months. The school teacher said to my mother what a shame it was the Mexicans did that—took their children out of school.

Like wandering Jews. They carried their home with them, back and forth: they had no true home but the tabernacle of memory.

. . .

Each year the American kitchen takes on a new appliance. The children are fed and grow tall. They go off to school with children from Vietnam, from Korea, from Hong Kong. They get into fights. They come home and they say dirty words.

The city will win. The city will give the children all the village could not—VCRs, hairstyles, drum beat. The city sings mean songs, dirty songs. But the city will sing the children a great Protestant hymn.

You can be anything you want to be.

We are parked. The patrolman turns off the lights of the truck— "back in a minute"—a branch scrapes the door as he rolls out of the van to take a piss. The brush crackles beneath his receding steps. It is dark. Who? Who is out there? The faces I have seen in San Diego—dishwashers, janitors, gardeners. They come all the time, no big deal. There are other Mexicans who tell me the crossing is dangerous.

The patrolman returns. We drive again. I am thinking of epic migrations in history books—pan shots of orderly columns of paleolithic peoples, determined as ants, heeding some trumpet of history, traversing miles and miles . . . of paragraph.

The patrolman has turned off the headlights. He can't have to piss again? Suddenly the truck accelerates, pitches off the rutted road, banging, slamming a rock, faster, ignition is off, the truck is soft-pedalled to a stop in the dust; the patrolman is out like a shot. The cab light is on. I sit exposed for a minute. I can't hear anything. Cautiously, I decide to follow—I leave my door open as the patrolman has done. There is a boulder in the field. Is that it? The patrolman is barking in Spanish. His flashlight is trained on the boulder like a laser, he weaves it along the grain as though he is untying a knot. He is: Three men and a woman stand up. The men are young—sixteen, seventeen. The youngest is shivering. He makes a fist. He looks down. The woman is young too. Or she could be the mother? Her legs are very thin. She wears a man's digital wristwatch. They come from somewhere. And somewhere—San Diego, Sacramento—somebody is waiting for them.

The patrolman tells them to take off their coats and their shoes, throw them in a pile. Another truck rolls up.

As a journalist, I am allowed to come close. I can even ask questions.

There are no questions.

You can take pictures, the patrolman tells me.

I stare at the faces. They stare at me. To them I am not bearing witness; I am part of the process of being arrested. I hold up my camera. Their eyes swallow the flash, a long tunnel, leading back.

Your coming of age. It is early. From your bed you watch your Mama moving back and forth under the light. The bells of the church ring in the dark. Mama crosses herself. From your bed you watch her back as she wraps the things you will take.

You are sixteen. Your father has sent for you. That's what it means: He has sent an address in Nevada. He is there with your uncle. You remember your uncle remembering snow with his beer.

You dress in the shadows. Then you move toward the table, the circle of light. You sit down. You force yourself to eat. Mama stands over you to make the sign of the cross on your forehead with her thumb. You are a man. You smile. She puts a bag of food in your hands. She says she has told *La Virgin.*

Then you are gone. It is gray. You hear a little breeze. It is the rustle of your old black *Dueña*, the dog, taking her shortcuts through the weeds, crazy *Dueña*, her pads on the dust. She is following you.

You pass the houses of the village; each window is a proper name. You pass the store. The bar. The lighted window of the clinic where the pale medical student from Monterey lives alone and reads his book full of sores late into the night.

You want to be a man. You have the directions in your pocket: an address in Tijuana, and a map with a yellow line that leads from the highway to an "X" on a street in Reno. You are afraid, but you have never seen snow.

You are just beyond the cemetery. The breeze has died. You turn and throw a rock back at *La Dueña*, where you know she is—where you will always know where she is. She will not go past the cemetery, not even for him. She will turn in circles like a *loca* and bite herself.

The dust takes no gravel, the path becomes a rutted road which leads to the highway. You walk north. The sky has turned white overhead. Insects click in the fields. In time, there will be a bus.

I will send for you or I will come home rich.

Florence Epstein

*The subtle humor — and stark understated
honesty — of "Sixty" are impressive and compelling.
Rather than dramatizing a sad, unfulfilled life,
Florence Epstein thrusts readers into an unfamiliar
but intriguing milieu which both informs and
entertains — the basic objectives of the best writing
and reporting. In "Sixty" Epstein is not simply
writing a story or describing an incident in
which she participated, but exposing herself to
humiliation — or admiration. Either way, Epstein
says: "I have always had the feeling that whatever
happened to me was inevitable. I could not have
lived my life any differently."*

Sixty

When I woke up that morning I sat bolt upright in bed staring straight ahead. *Kiddo, you're sixty,* I said to myself. It was hard to believe. I could believe my age up until forty-five. Then doubt began to creep in. I don't feel a day older, I'd think, looking around at my surroundings wherever I happened to be: forty-five in New York; fifty in London; sixty in Spain—i.e. here in Mallorca, in the mountains.

Be that as it may. Sixty. At about ten in the morning I went down to the village cafe and ordered a *cafe con leche.* Here's looking at you, kid, I said, in memory of Humphrey Bogart, and sipped the coffee. Too hot as usual. I took it over to a table. But certainly I looked older. A long time since I looked thirty; too long even to worry me.

When I was thirty I was writing about the death of Marilyn Monroe for *Motion Picture* and other popular movie magazines. There was a lot of speculation about her death but she was not yet a legend. Why would she have been? The world was full of women just like her. Granted they didn't have the charisma, the looks, the fame or even, necessarily, the horrible childhood. What they had was the same wounded psyche, similar ways of loving and hating themselves. Now and then someone tells me I look like her. Of course I don't but I know why they say it: it's that wounded doe in the eyes and maybe the smile—not really phony but easy and habitual—*feminine.*

I've been living with Antonio for about five years. A couple of years ago we moved in with his father. That wasn't my original plan. The plan was just to live with Antonio, write another book—this time something that would not only be published but widely acclaimed—and buy a house with a garden. Instead. I can't believe it. After living in a rented house of our own Antonio, insisting he loved me, gave me this ultimatum: either we move in with his father or I'm free to leave. He would understand fully if I decided to leave. I thought that living with his father would just destroy me. I would stop writing and turn into a "local" with a flowered housedress and rubber-soled slippers. The house itself would destroy me. Basically it was a disaster area in a state of decay. I can't do it, I thought. "All right," I said.

And in no time I was sixty.

Another One

I have a friend named Calypso (Calypso? Cali for short) who is only six months older than I but seems to think I'm much younger. I don't disillusion her. Sometimes I even forget my age. It comes back to me as a shock.

In the past, say thirty or more years ago, Calypso was one of the most famous high-fashion models in the profession. A Richard Avedon favorite. Often on the cover of *Vogue, Harper's Bazaar,* etc. She was a great beauty. You can still see it in the bones.

She lives down in the valley which is to say a couple of miles away in the next village, really a town, of about ten thousand. She owns a big if somewhat empty house which is all she managed to salvage out of her fabulous career and the couple of husbands and the children who are eyeing their inheritance from a distance. Some people think she's a drug addict but she isn't. She just tends to surround herself with young men who take drugs on the theory that a) she likes young men and b) she might save them from themselves. So far b) has never happened. It is true that she drinks too much and acts crazy from time to time.

Cali's Birthday Party

A sunny afternoon for sixty. Cali is sitting at her big round table near the courtyard window. She's in blue jeans, a white cotton shirt with ruffled front, blue espadrilles.

"*Salud,*" I say, tapping my glass of wine against hers. "*Muchos Años.*"

"Now I'm old," she says. I suppress a shudder. Mustn't let on.

Antonio, who is more than ten years younger than I, is sitting across the room laughing and chatting with two other Spanish men. Antonio is not only English-free, he's also a mere laborer. We live a slightly marginalized life. Other foreigners don't usually invite us to parties. The guests here are the local boys Cali befriends and a few local girls—and us.

Everyone looks up and away when José makes his entrance. On aluminum crutches, I'm sure he wasn't invited. He stands quietly surveying the guests. It's hard to tell if he's drunk. His chin is raised as if he's trying to see from under closed lids. A man in his fifties, he has black hair, a still handsome Gypsy face; bantamweight with, as I remember, a lightfooted cocky walk. Now he has one foot in a cast, a cowboy boot with rundown heel on the other.

Cali and José used to live together. She cooked him two hot meals a day. Occasionally she would hide the wine bottles from both of them. Then she would find them. The relationship lasted for about two years with Cali giving as good as she got. But after José broke her beautiful nose and split open her scalp she made him leave. Now he lives with a couple of drinking buddies. He has a reputation for working hard when he works (usually outdoors on roads and tunnels) but no one's offered him a job in a long time.

"Hey Flora," he calls out, *"Como va?"*

"I'm fine," I call back, smiling but nervous. I hate abusive relationships. I don't even like Cali when she gets going but I know she's manic-depressive and I try to remember that.

"Look who's here," Cali says to me. José is across the room talking to Antonio.

"He won't do anything," I say, hoping she won't.

"I want him out of here," she says, emphasis on the out. Until now I've been denying the fact that I'm sorry we came. It's boring. There's no one I want to talk to. Cali and I are both so far away from our former lives in New York that it's a bond between us. But I really only enjoy talking to her when she's depressed. At those times she seems full of wisdom and compassion. The more manic she gets, the crazier. Sometimes a look comes into her eyes that scares me.

"Goddamn it, he isn't wanted here. I'll kill that bastard! Did you hear me?" she calls out in Spanish—a language neither one of us has mastered.

SURVIVING CRISIS

I want to go home. I suppose I mean New York but I sold my CPW co-op years ago and I really have nothing to go back to. I left New York of my own free will (although I didn't think it would be forever) and I want my life to work. That's what I can't figure out. Is it working? Was I foolish to cast in my lot with Antonio?

"Listen, we won't leave until he's gone," I tell Cali.

"He may try to come back." Her party mood is over. Pretty soon the party is over such as it is. When Antonio and I leave, Cali is still sitting at the big round table with a Spanish lad on either side of her. I have the sinking sensation that they don't like her just for herself. If José comes back—well, Cali will have the advantage: no crutches; also she's skinny, fast and, in her own words, doesn't take shit from anyone.

Six Months Later

So it's nearly seven p.m. and here I am sitting in my trainers (all the new words I've had to learn since P.S. 94 in the Bronx) wondering if Antonio is going to remember it's my birthday. I know he's not going to remember so in case he doesn't I'm trying to compose myself in advance. It would be foolish to get angry just because he doesn't remember. Not being middle class he doesn't adhere to conventional middle-class customs. Besides, the Spanish have different customs. What they remember is the day of their namesake—their Saint's Day. If you happen to be in the cafe on your Saint's Day you buy everyone a drink. If you're a man. I've rarely seen a woman do it.

I'm wearing a quilted ski jacket because this four-hundred-year-old house, in addition to having no kitchen or bathroom and no hot water, is cold, colder inside than outside in this month of December.

I watch half of the big double door, a few steps below me and on the far side of the *entrada*, swing open. In comes our little silky black dog holding aloft his white plume of a tail. Right behind him is Antonio looking exhausted in his work clothes—secondhand jeans, beat-up sweater, earth-caked work boots. He doesn't remember. I wonder if I should leave him. Should I leave him? Why does he work so hard? And earn so little money? (And give half of it to his father?) Is it him or Spain? What kind of world is this where people kill themselves just earning a living? If they're lucky enough to have a job. I can't bear it. It has nothing to do with me. This is my birthday.

He comes up the few steps to where I'm sitting and gives me an absentminded kiss. I can't stand how tired he looks. I hate myself for having gotten involved with him, with this whole Third World mentality. I'm just an ordinary person and it's pulling me down. How can I ever leave him? I can't ever leave him. It would kill him. Not so much because it's me but because whoever it was (me) has left him.

"It's my birthday," I say. No response. "I knew you wouldn't remember."

"Flora, I forgot," he says.

"I know. That's what I'm saying. You forgot. You remembered last week. You said you would take me to a restaurant."

"I'm just telling you I forgot." I realize that that is his excuse. Or his apology. Have it my own way.

"Is there any hot water?" he says.

"It's on the stove." The stove is actually a two-ring gas burner in the next room. Two steps up don't bump your head. Windowless. More of a cave than a room. Long and narrow with unspeakable stone walls. It bears some resemblance to an ancient dungeon, not to get too dramatic about it. His father is up there overseeing the water.

"There's football at seven o'clock," I hear Antonio telling his father. Of course. It's Saturday night. What else is there?

"Football?" says his father, playing dumb. His father cooks the supper for himself and Antonio. They've had that arrangement for twenty years—before I ever met them and it has not been my intention to change it, awful as the menu is: spare ribs fried in oil every night. Nothing else. Well, bread. And on Friday nights fresh sardines fried in oil. The same oil.

Antonio comes back past me bearing a round aluminum pan filled with hot water. "Would you give my father his drops?" he says. "I have to shave."

"I notice you remember the football game," I say, not able to stop myself. "My birthday no."

"I told you I forgot." He's getting angry. I would like to get him so angry that it comes to blows. But he would never hit me. He has an inner discipline. I admire him for it.

I follow him down the sloping floor of the *entrada* into the washroom. Watch him pour the water into a blue plastic bowl set on a low stone shelf below a small shaving mirror. Various thoughts come flying at me. Why isn't there a larger mirror, hot running water, a *shower?* Why is he so dumb? Is he really very intelligent? A true gentleman. Lean and muscular. Not an ounce of fat on him. Scrubbing himself inch by inch every single day. He never complains.

His Father's Drops

What makes it hard for me is that I've had a privileged life. I didn't realize it at the time. I thought it was natural. Now it's gone to the other extreme: underprivileged. It would be useful if I wanted to learn something from it, but I don't really. I have hopes of getting out and taking Antonio with me. He could do with a change.

I go back into the *entrada* and look around. This is it. There's a certain amount of charm. If it were a painting in a museum it would be charming: life of the *peesants.* Earth tones, decrepit surroundings. All of it seems to be decomposing. Up there is his father. That *is* a picture because, for one thing, he is already in a frame, thanks to the window set in the wall. In the black fedora he wears day and night. Face like bleached stone. Once he was a swineherd in the south of Spain. He and his family lived in poverty like medieval serfs. Maybe he's never gotten over it. And he compensates with that startling combination of ignorance and arrogance.

"Do you want your drops?" I call out.

He doesn't answer. No doubt he thought that when I moved in I'd take care of him and the house. Maybe he even hates me. Coming between him and his nearly fifty-year-old son.

"Do you want your drops?" I ask louder.

"Drops," he says, stamping down the stairs and marching across the *entrada.* Little fellow, perfectly straight back, eighty years old. Watching him stomp up the stairs to his bedroom.

"He'll be right back," Antonio calls out from the washroom.

Oh, thanks. "He's coming," he says, leaning back to catch sight of me through the washroom door.

"The drops," his father announces, marching back across the *entrada*, little white box in hand. I follow him up to the room with the inner window and watch him slam the box down on the table. I don't really care. I am unmoved.

I slip the rubber band off the box and take out a little bottle. Just as I might have expected: it's upside down and the little white plastic spoon has crumbs on it.

"Don't talk," I say, letting the drops fall one by one onto the spoon. Thirty drops. Can this be real medicine or was the doctor kidding? I hand him the spoon. Don't say thank you, I think as he swallows the drops and hands it back; never say please, never smile just because. Some people when they get older cry easily. Not me; not yet.

Antonio is still in the washroom. Still shaving.

"Antonio, I'm going out for a walk."

"All right," he says. All right? Doesn't he care whether I eat or not? Whether I starve to death? I feel like slamming the big outer door behind me. Oh don't be an idiot, I think, just keep moving.

My Comparison

The next morning, Sunday, the cafe is full of village people and a few of us live-in foreigners (there are never many). Cali is there, downing brandy with her coffee. I wave at her but stay where I am. I wonder if I'm a prig. An American named Lester who is about my age and unmarried comes over to wish me happy birthday and hands me a package. I am flabbergasted but stay cool. I'm beginning to understand why Lester once called my relationship with Antonio The Great Romance, emphasis on the sarcasm. Profuse thanks to Lester. When he leaves I take the gift over to Antonio and show it to him. It's a lovely round mirror in a dark wood frame set on a wooden stand.

"Flora, do you know, I would have bought you that mirror myself if only I had remembered," Antonio says. This takes my breath away. Rarely have I heard such a bare-faced lie. It is the way a child might lie, one who is not so much out of touch with reality as able to slip contentedly into his own fantasy world.

"That's not true," I say, smiling at him.

"Yes it is, Flora. I promise you I would have bought it."

"Antonio," I say, "cut it out. It doesn't matter." I feel like punishing him a little for lying to me. "It probably cost three or four thousand *pesetas*," I say. (Thirty dollars, more or less; in other words, a small fortune.)

"Five thousand," Antonio says.

"No, not that much." I realize he's proud that some man he hardly knows has spent so much money on me. It's not a typical male reaction; or maybe—at what I refer to delicately as my age—it is.

"I want you to notice Lester's interest in you," Cali says after coming over to examine the gift. "Are you noticing?"

"I've been giving it some thought," I say. But why would I want to live with Lester? It would be like two middle-class tourists thinking they were going native away from home.

"Just you do that because I want you to know that I care what happens to you."

"And I care what happens to you," I say before embarrassment prevents me.

"Because we cannot live without *calefacción* in our declining years. So you just pay some attention to Lester there. He is a man with money."

I leave the mirror with Antonio and walk Cali out to her beat-up Seat parked in the No Parking area of the village plaza. It has been a rainy morning and her broken umbrella is lying on the wet ground near the car.

"You know what I'm going to do with that umbrella?" she says. I can guess. "I'm going to leave it right where it is. What do you think?"

"Good idea."

I watch her sway toward the car in her long skirt and scruffy boots. Head high. She still has that throwaway self-assurance. Or looks as if she has. She scoops up the umbrella and turns around to give me a big wink.

"Don't wait for me to back up," she says. "It could be dangerous."

I feel thoughtful, slightly moody going back to the cafe. The problem is we're getting old. No one ever told us about that.

What could they have told us? Fear. The need to laugh in the face of oblivion or at least not to whimper. Not to whimper too much: nobody's perfect.

Question and Answer

Why do I live with Antonio?

One bright day I was struck by the thought that not only everyone else but I myself was getting old and would surely die. I suddenly realized that I had never loved anyone. An astonishing thought. I decided to do something about it. So I said, "All right."

I was sorry—if not immediately then soon. I mean—look at how I'm living. The squalor. The vast cultural difference between us. Antonio can just about read and write. Nevertheless he's an intelligent perceptive man.

No, wait a minute. I keep forgetting that my whole life has been motivated (distorted?) by this one obsession: to prove I'm a writer. I never really wanted to get married or have children (even though being of my generation I took for granted that I'd do both. But I didn't and I never really missed it). And I had this father whom I always looked up to until I got old enough for him to tell me that a woman should "merge" with a man, and what have I ever written? Maybe I was fifteen at the time or younger.

So why? So I was always attracted to men who wanted to be Number One no question. But I always found it hard, impossible, to be Number Two.

Maybe that's why.

Some Time Later

Without Cali José had no one. He never did have anyone. Certain childhoods are probably too severe for any kind of love—self or other—to come out of them. Too much violence, sometimes even murder. José's father had actually killed someone because he disagreed with his politics or had been humiliated, disappointed in his own ambitions. José was very young at the time, living in a small poor southern village on the Spanish mainland.

By now it was very far away—that time and place.

José was very far away. He was nowhere. It could be said that Cali should never have taken up with him. It could even be said that Cali's own father should never have deserted her when she was ten years old. But that wasn't his intention: his intention was to desert Cali's mother which he did.

Christmas Eve came along and José and his buddies went out to celebrate. José got drunk and staggered home alone. I should mention that he smoked a lot. Apparently he lit a cigarette and went to bed. He was found dead a couple of days later although it took some time before he could be properly identified.

Without José Cali had herself. Her manic-depression seemed to become more pronounced. Certainly her feet got dirtier. When the mania was on her she threw off her shoes. (She had long since thrown away her lithium tablets.) True, it wasn't New York but the streets were paved or cobbled and pollution from automobiles was increasing by leaps and bounds.

So there she was in her dirty naked feet giving the finger to anyone who looked at her sideways. One day she attended Mass in the big beautiful church they have down there in her village. She didn't exactly attend. What she did was walk down the center aisle in the middle of Mass holding a live dove in her hands—outstretched. Peace, she said, or a word to that effect, and let the bird fly free.

The next day a couple of Guardia Civil showed up at her door ready to escort her to the airport. They put her on a plane to New York and warned her not to come back for at least five years. She is still there. I sent her a letter and it was returned, as I might have expected, with "addressee unknown" stamped on it.

By Comparison (cont'd.)

I take the mirror up to my bedroom and realize it deserves a much nicer setting. On the other hand, living here I never feel guilty about not cleaning the house. It would be like cleaning a trench.

I have the key to a friend's unoccupied house and permission to use it. I go over there to take a hot bath. Lying in the bathtub is so relaxing I almost forget where I am and I forget the time. Antonio and his father always have their meals on time. If Antonio notices I'm missing he won't let on. His father will probably sigh in relief while not letting on.

When I get back to the house I can see them sitting up there at the table eating lunch. Munching away on their chunks of bread and Sunday *tortilla*—an omelet filled with potatoes—banging down the wine bottle. No, only Antonio's father does that. And he never offers any of the wine to his son. After every meal he stores the bottle up in his room.

I go up the few steps and sit down facing Antonio at the warped wooden table. I smile at him. He acknowledges my presence with a friendly look.

"You don't seem to realize that you're living with me," I hear myself saying calmly. "That must be it. I mean you're living with your father and I just happen to be here. That's the way it is."

"I don't know that I'm living with you?" Antonio asks. He seems slightly surprised, even interested.

"That's right. Maybe you really don't know," I say thoughtfully. Do I know? The thought occurs to me that maybe I don't know, either. Typing away up there in the bedroom, baffling his father.

"That's possible if you say so," Antonio says. Sweet man. He is a sweet man.

"At one o'clock you come up here and sit down and eat what your father prepares. It's all the same to you if I'm here or not, if I eat or not." I wonder what to say next or even if I know what I'm talking about, but I have an audience hanging on my every word. I can't let him down.

"Maybe that's the way it is in Spain," I say, stalling for inspiration. "It's different in my country." Oh God. "In my country a man and woman who live together are very close." I realize I can say anything I want to about America. These two boys often as not confuse it with London. "A man and woman who live together do everything together. But maybe it's different here. Well, that must be the way it is."

I get up and cross over to the white mini-refrigerator, the only intact piece of furniture in the house, and open it to take out a couple of eggs.

"But I love this woman," Antonio says getting up from the

table. "A woman like this. This woman is a treasure." I can feel him right at my back. "I love this woman more—more—more than . . ." Words fail him. He catches me up in a bear hug (maybe that's why) and I giggle squirming to get free.

Anyway my little scolding relieves the atmosphere. Or so it seems. It relieves me.

"Good," I say, smiling down at the eggs. "I'm going back to my friend's house to eat."

"Whatever you want. My *mujer* can do whatever she wants. And next week I'm taking her to a restaurant."

"It doesn't matter," I say.

"Yes, it matters very much."

I kiss him on the cheek. Good-looking man.

I don't remember if we went to a restaurant. But by the week after that I was already accustomed to being sixty.

Andre Dubus

In his Introduction to Broken Vessels, *the collection of essays from which "Lights of the Long Night" is taken, Tobias Wolff captures the physicality of his friend, the novelist, essayist, short-story writer Andre Dubus. "I remember only too well the robust, swaggering pleasure he took in his own, dense, physical being — his body, like his mind, always itching for something strenuous to do with itself."*

Then came the early summer morning when Dubus, driving home from Boston, came upon a car blocking the highway after an accident and pulled over to see what he could do to help. The moments following that act of kindness are vividly described in "Lights of the Long Night." Dubus, having lost one leg above the knee and the effective use of the other, spent months in the hospital. He went home as what he insists on calling a "cripple," according to Wolff. "It's an important word, not a flourish of self-pity but an insistence on facing his situation honestly." In "Lights of the Long Night" Dubus captures a definitive and horrific moment in time, with clarity, distance and remarkable detail.

Lights of the Long Night

I remember the headlights, but I do not remember the car hitting Luis Santiago and me, and I do not remember the sounds our bodies made. Luis died, either in the ambulance, or later that night in the hospital. He was twenty-three years old. I do not remember leaving the ground my two legs stood on for the last instant in my life, then moving through the air, over the car's hood and windshield and roof, and falling on its trunk. I remember lying on my back on that trunk and asking someone: *What happened?*

I did not lose consciousness. The car did not injure my head or my neck or my spine. It broke my right hand and scraped both arms near my wrists, so my wife believes I covered my face with my arms as I fell. I lay for a while on the trunk, talking to a young man, then to a woman who is a state trooper, then I was in an ambulance, stopped on the highway, talking to a state trooper, a man, while he cut my trousers and my right western boot. That morning my wife saw the left boot on the side of the highway, while she was driving home from the hospital in Boston. The car had knocked it off my foot. The state troopers got the boot for my wife, but I did not leave the hospital with a left foot or, below the middle of my knee, a left leg.

While the state trooper was cutting and we were talking, I saw Luis Santiago on a stretcher. People were putting him into an ambulance. Lying in the ambulance and watching Luis I knew something terrible had happened and I said to the trooper: *Did that guy die?* I do not remember what the trooper said, but I knew then that Luis was either dead or soon would be. Then I went by ambulance to a clinic in Wilmington where Dr. Wayne Sharaf saved my life, and my wife Peggy and my son Jeb were there, then an ambulance took me to Massachusetts General Hospital in Boston, where they operated on me for twelve hours.

Luis Santiago said what were probably his last words on earth to me: *Por favor, señor, please help, no hablo Ingles.* This was around one o'clock in the morning of 23 July 1986. I was driving north on Route 93, going from Boston to my home in Haverhill, Massachusetts. The highway has four lanes and I was driving in the third. That stretch of road is straight and the visibility on 23 July was very good, so when I saw the Santiagos' car I did not have to apply the brakes or make any other sudden motions. It was ahead of me, stopped in the third lane, its taillights darkened. I slowed my car. To the right of the Santiagos' car, in the breakdown lane, a car was parked and, behind it, a woman stood talking into the emergency call box. Her back was to me. I was driving a standard shift Subaru, and I shifted down to third, then second, and drove to the left, into the speed lane, so I could pass the left side of the Santiagos' car and look into it for a driver, and see whether or not the driver was hurt. There were no cars behind me. Luz Santiago stood beside the car, at the door to the driver's side, and her forehead was bleeding and she was crying. I drove to the left side of the road and parked near the guard rail and turned on my emergency blinker lights. Because of the guard rail, part of my car was still in the speed lane. I left the car and walked back to Luz Santiago. She was still crying and bleeding and she asked me to help her. She said: *There's a motorcycle under my car.*

I looked down. Dark liquid flowed from under her engine and formed a pool on the highway, and I imagined a motorcycle under there and a man dead and crushed between the motorcycle and the engine and I knew I would have to look at him. Then, for the first time, I saw Luis Santiago. He came from the passenger's side, circling the rear of the car, and walked up to me and Luz, standing beside the driver's door and the pool of what I believed was blood on the pavement. Later I learned that it was oil from the crankcase and the abandoned motorcycle Luz had run over was no longer under her car. Luis was Luz's brother and he was young and I believe his chest and shoulders were broad. He stopped short of Luz, so that she stood between us. That is when he spoke to me, mostly in his native tongue, learned in Puerto Rico.

I do not remember what I said to him, or to Luz. But I know what I was feeling, thinking: first I had to get Luz off the highway and lie her down and raise her legs and cover her with my jacket, for I believed she was in danger of shock. Then I would leave Luis with Luz and return to her car and look under its engine at the crushed man. We left her car and walked across the speed lane to the left side of the highway. We did not have to hurry. No cars were coming. We walked in column: I was in front, Luz was behind me, and Luis was in the rear. At the side of the road we stopped. I saw headlights coming north, toward us. We were not in danger then. If we had known the car was going to swerve toward us, we could have stepped over the guard rail. I waved at the headlights, the driver, my raised arms crossing in front of my face. I wanted the driver to stop and help us. I wanted the driver to be with me when I looked under Luz's car. We were standing abreast, looking at the car. I was on the right, near the guard rail; Luz was in the middle, and Luis stood on her left. I was still waving at the car when it came too fast to Luz's car and the driver swerved left, into the speed lane, toward my Subaru's blinking emergency lights, and toward us. Then I was lying on the car's trunk and asking someone: *What happened?*

Only Luis Santiago knows. While I was in Massachusetts General Hospital my wife told me that Luz Santiago told our lawyer I had pushed her away from the car. I knew it was true. Maybe because my left thigh was the only part of my two legs that did not break, and because the car broke my right hip. When the car hit us, Luis was facing its passenger side, Luz was between its headlights, and I was facing the driver. In the hospital I assumed that I had grabbed Luz with my left hand and jerked and threw her behind me and to my right, onto the side of the highway. That motion would have turned my body enough to the left to protect my left thigh, and expose my right hip to the car. But I do not think the patterns of my wounds told me I had pushed Luz. I knew, from the first moments in the stationary ambulance, that a car struck me because I was standing where I should have been; and, some time later, in the hospital, I knew I had chosen to stand there, rather than leap toward the guard rail.

On 17 September 1986 I left the hospital and came home. In December, Dr. Wayne Sharaf talked to me on the phone. He is young, and he told me I was the first person whose life he had saved, when he worked on me at the clinic in Wilmington. Then he said that, after working on me, he worked on Luz Santiago, and she told him I had pushed her away from the car. I thanked him for saving my life and telling me what Luz had told him. I said: *Now I can never be angry at myself for stopping that night.* He said: *Don't ever be. You saved that woman's life.* Perhaps not. She may have survived, as I have. I am forever a cripple, but I am alive, and I am a father and a husband, and in 1987 I am sitting in the sunlight of June and writing this.

Cynthia Ozick

Most everyone has fantasized about separating
themselves from their past mistakes and the physical
and intellectual flaws that have made them who and
what they are while simultaneously learning from
life's bitter lessons. But in "The Break," an essay
from her highly praised book Fame and Folly,
Cynthia Ozick has actually done it through a
daring, metaphorical procedure: a symbolic,
irreversible psychic surgery. In this short essay, she
discusses the person she is (but often refers to herself
as a person who once was) and the person she wants
to be (by referring to a person she long ago left
behind). A triumph in this essay is the seriousness
with which she confronts her own flaws and the
subtle humor which renders her self-deprecation
simultaneously caustic and compelling.

The Break

I write these words at least a decade after the terrifying operation that separated us. Unfortunately, no then-current anesthesia, and no then-accessible surgical technique, was potent enough to suppress consciousness of the knife as it made its critical blood-slice through the area of our two warring psyches. It is the usual case in medicine that twins joined at birth are severed within the first months of life. Given the intransigence of my partner (who until this moment remains recalcitrant and continues to wish to convert me to her loathsome outlook), I had to wait many years until I could obtain her graceless and notoriously rancorous consent to our divergence.

The truth is I have not spoken to her since the day we were wheeled, side by side as usual, on the same stretcher, into the operating room. Afterward it was at once observed (especially by me) that the surgery had not altered her character in any respect, and I felt triumphantly justified in having dragged her into it. I had done her no injury—she was as intractable as ever. As for myself, I was freed from her proximity and her influence. The physical break was of course the end, not the beginning, of our rupture; psychologically, I had broken with her a long time ago. I disliked her then, and though shut of her daily presence and unavoidable attachment, I dislike her even now. Any hint or symptom of her discourages me; I have always avoided reading her. Her style is clotted, parenthetical, self-indulgent, long-winded, periphrastic, in every way excessive—hard going altogether. One day it came to me: why bother to keep up this fruitless connection? We have nothing in common, she and I. Not even a name. Since our earliest school years she has masqueraded as Cynthia, a Latin fancifulness entirely foreign to me. To my intimates I am Shoshana, the name given me at birth: Hebrew for Lily (anciently mistransliterated as Susanna).

To begin with, I am honest; she is not. Or, to spare her a moral lecture (but why should I? what has she ever spared *me*?), let me put it that she is a fantasist and I am not. Never mind that her own term for her condition is, not surprisingly, realism. It is precisely her "realism" that I hate. It is precisely her "facts" that I despise.

Her facts are not my facts. For instance, you will never catch me lying about my age, which is somewhere between seventeen and twenty-two. She, on the other hand, claims to be over sixty. A preposterous declaration, to be sure—but see how she gets herself up to look the part! She is all dye, putty, greasepaint. She resembles nothing so much as Gravel Gertie in the old Dick Tracy strip. There she is, done up as a white-haired, dewlapped, thick-waisted, thick-lensed hag, seriously myopic. A phenomenal fake. (Except for the nearsightedness, which, to be charitable, I don't hold against her, being seriously myopic myself.)

Aging is certainly not her only pretense. She imagines herself to be predictable; fixed; irrecoverable. She reflects frequently—tediously—on the trajectory of her life, and supposes that its arc and direction are immutable. What she has done she has done. She believes she no longer has decades to squander. I know better than to subscribe to such fatalism. Here the radical difference in our ages (which began to prove itself out at the moment of surgery) is probably crucial. It is her understanding that she is right to accept her status. She is little known or not known at all, relegated to marginality, absent from the authoritative anthologies that dictate which writers matter.

She knows she does not matter. She argues that she has been in rooms with the famous and felt the humiliation of her lesser-ness, her invisibility, her lack of writerly weight or topical cachet. In gilded chambers she has seen journalists and cultural consuls cluster around and trail after the stars; at conferences she has been shunted away by the bureaucratic valets of the stars. She is aware that she has not written enough. She is certainly not read. She sees with a perilous clarity that she will not survive even as "minor."

I will have none of this. There was a time—a tenuous membrane still hung between us, a remnant of sentiment or nostalgia on my part—when she was fanatically driven to coerce me into a similar view of myself. The blessed surgery, thank God, put an end to all that. My own ambition is fresh and intact. I can gaze at her fearfulness, her bloodless perfectionism and the secret crisis of confidence that dogs it, without a drop of concern. You may ask, Why am I so pitiless? Don't I know (I know to the lees) her indiscipline, her long periods of catatonic paralysis, her idleness, her sleepiness? Again you ask, Do you never pity her? Never. Hasn't she enough self-pity for the two of us? It is not that I am any more confident or less fearful; here I am, standing at the threshold still, untried, a thousand times more diffident, tremulous, shy. My heart is vulnerable to the world's distaste and dismissiveness. But oh, the difference between us! I have the power to scheme and to construct—a power that time has eroded in her, a power that she regards as superseded, useless. Null and void. Whatever shreds remain of her own ambitiousness embarrass her now. She is resigned to her failures. She is shamed by them. To be old and unachieved: ah.

Yes, ah! Ah! This diminution of hunger in her disgusts me; I detest it. She is a scandal of sorts, a superannuated mourner: her Promethean wounds (but perhaps they are only Procrustean?) leak on her bed when she wakes, on the pavement when she walks. She considers herself no more than an ant in an anthill. I have heard her say of the round earth, viewed on films sent back from this or that space shuttle, that Isaiah and Shakespeare are droplets molten into that tiny ball, and as given to evaporation as the pointlessly rotating ball itself. Good God, what have I to do with any of that? I would not trade places with her for all the china in Teaneck.

Look, there is so much ahead! Forms of undiminished luminescence: specifically, novels. A whole row of novels. All right, let her protest if it pleases her—when *she* set out, the written word was revered; reputations were rooted in the literariness of poets, novelists. Stories are electronic nowadays, and turn up in pictures: the victory, technologically upgraded, of the comic book. The writer is at last delectably alone, dependent on no acclaim. It is all for the sake of the making, the finding, the doing: the *Ding-an-Sich*. The wild *interestingness* of it! I will be a novelist yet! I feel myself becoming a voluptuary of human nature, a devourer, a spewer, a seer, an ironist. A hermit-toiler. I dream of nights without sleep.

She, like so many of her generation, once sought work and recognition. Perhaps she labored for the sake of fame, who knows? Five or six of her contemporaries, no more, accomplished that ubiquitous desire. But here in the gyre of my eighteenth year, my goatish and unbridled twentieth, my muscular and intemperate and gluttonous prime, it is fruitfulness I am after: despite the unwantedness of it—and especially despite *her*—I mean to begin a life of novel-writing. A jagged heap of interferences beclouds the year ahead, but what do I care? I have decades to squander.

As for her: I deny her, I denounce her, I let her go. Whining, wizened, hoary fake, with her cowardice, her fake name!

Sandell Morse

In "Canning Jars," Sandell Morse freezes a bare
moment of time — an ordinary incident made extraordinary by a passing comment. It is masterfully
and narrowly focused — a vital and difficult literary objective. There are no diversions or descriptions,
no twisting tangents to distract a reader from the
quiet yet explosive incident in the thrift store, near
Crabtree Falls in rural Virginia. "Canning Jars"
offers a welcome simplicity along with an intriguing
ambivalence that will long sustain the lingering
questions the essay presents.

Canning Jars

The old blue-green canning jars, opaque and bubbled, are the only things of beauty in this place. I lift them carefully and place them on a cardboard box where the light can shine through. The lids are that old silvery metal, dull and flaking. One of the jars is large, more than a quart. The others are pints, perfect for storing dried beans or lentils. Hanukkah gifts for my sons.

I approach an older man and an older woman sitting on wooden folding chairs in back of the shop—a thrift shop on a country road in rural Virginia.

I'm not the only person in this shop. I've come with a friend, an artist, and the stop is impulsive, a veering off on our way to Crabtree Falls. It's Sunday afternoon, late in November, and we know the sun will not shine with such intensity much longer. It's been an unusually warm and sunny fall, and we intend to drive to the falls and bask in the sun's last warm rays.

Another customer talks with the owners, their voices rambling over and around counters and boxes, all stacked and overflowing with baseball caps, glass dishes, ceramic dishes, tottering in towers, glasses stored inside of glasses, old sneakers, old shoes (men's and women's), cotton skirts, woolen skirts, shirts and blouses, dresses and coats, hanging on and off of hangers, plastic bowls, all of it coated with dust or spotted with mildew and smelling musty. The accent I hear is thick and Southern. The speech is rhythmic, soft and slow, and I'm taken with its lilting sounds. I catch words about sons and guns. "They ain't gonna take mine."

His sons or his guns, I wonder. "I'll take all four of those canning jars, if you give me a good price," I say to the woman.

"You go take a look," she says to the man. "I already marked them down, though. They come in with eight dollars each. More for the big one."

I follow behind the slight, small-boned man, weaving through the aisles. "You make me an offer. Go ahead, put a price on."

I look at the jars, their imperfect bubbles as tiny as pinpricks, as large as beads, all of them trapped inside those blue glass walls. I calculate. Not too low. Not too high. The man waits. It's a game we play. The stakes aren't high. I want the jars, not for myself, but to give as gifts. The total price is $25. I figure a twenty percent discount and offer eighteen, $2 less. I don't know why. Maybe it's the man's eyes, cold, gray and watching me.

He counters with twenty. I shake my head.

Instinctively, I know he'll cave. Won't lose a sale for $2. Now we wait. I walk away, lift a plate, turn it over, check for chips. In the center, pink roses fade and crack. I trace one with my finger feeling grit. My friend feigns an interest in a mixing bowl. I set the dish back on the stack. "Ready?" I say.

Her head tilts toward the blue-green jars, still sitting on the cardboard box. "Aren't you going to buy them?" she says.

"Guess not."

Before I leave, I make my $18 offer one last time.

The man lifts his chin and looks at his wife who no longer sits in back of the store. She stands now, behind a counter, leaning an elbow on an old cash register. "Up to you," she says to her husband. "A bird in the hand . . ."

"What's the tax?" the man says.

The woman holds a small calculator and punches numbers. "Eighty-one cents," she says.

"Make it nineteen," the man says.

I smile. "Nineteen."

He looks at me, and I expect that he'll smile, too. After all, he's saved face. Nineteen. Less than twenty, but more than the eighteen I'd offered, originally, so I'm not prepared for what he says, can't believe I'm hearing correctly. I lean in. His words slur. Understanding seeps, slowly, so slowly that he must repeat. "I hate a woman Jew," he says.

The blow is swift, rushing quickly into my stomach where revulsion and fear swirl in a vortex. I'm stunned; my friend is too, and in that instant when our glances meet, I see her wince. She feels the blow as keenly as I do, for we are women; we are Jews. We know the same icy fear, bred into us for centuries—flee, but not too swiftly. She walks slowly toward the door, moving backwards. I want to move, but I can't. I feel rooted, rooted and mute, and I wonder: Does he see a telltale sign? Smell an odor?

Absently, I run my thumb over worn leather and look down to see my brown wallet in my hand, and I know I'll never open it, never take out the bills, never give those beautiful bubbled jars to my sons, and I wonder if I've done something wrong—played the game incorrectly, been too cheap, should've gone up. And so I take whatever it is that is happening here in this room into my gut where it opens up old wounds—taunts on the playground, "dirty Jew," "Christ killer." And later, "Jew you down," "Cheap Jew," words that make me into "the other."

I look the man in the eye. "You've just lost a sale, Mister."

In the car, my friend looks for ways to close the wound and scab it over one more time. "He'll look at those jars, and he'll know. They'll sit there. They'll haunt him," she says.

But, it's we who are haunted. All we can talk about is that man, the soft lilt of his speech, his deadpan face, and the way he drew us in. Was he joking? Didn't we get it? Would he have said those words if he knew? His words echo inside the car, woman, Jew, hate, as we try to figure out what went wrong.

We stop talking and drive along without words, lost for these moments in private thoughts. Perhaps like me, my friend looks out at the countryside and tries to recapture the pleasantness of the afternoon—blue sky, rolling hills, a long green valley where cows graze, and seeing those cows, my mind leaps back in time to a ranch in Wyoming. One morning, I awoke to the sorrowful mooing of a herd of cows. It wasn't a sound I'd heard before. Then I heard a series of pops. I knew the sound of rifle shot, and I'd been warned that the ranch hands would be killing the herd. Too many head to winter over. Still, all that morning and after-noon, I felt sick. Couldn't eat. It was the cows and their awful mooing. I thought of their bulk, and the way they moved, lum-bering almost side to side. I thought of their eyes and their moist pink muzzles. I thought of their bones holding up their hairy coats. Nobody else seemed to notice those missing cows.

At supper that night, a Jewish friend and I talked about those missing cows, and what I saw in my mind's eye was a long line of black-coated men walking slowly into a forest. I saw women in dresses clutching children. I saw the shiny boots of the S.S. These are images I carry like bubbles trapped inside of blue-green glass.

"They told them they were going to another pasture," my friend joked about those cows.

I smiled. It is what Jews do; we laugh instead of cry.

The road narrows. It twists and curves, climbing the mountains, approaching the turn-off to the falls. Beside the road, a stream skims rocks and rushes past. Hawks circle and spiral up into the clear blue sky. Sunlight glitters and dapples the pavement as I drive, and I think I must be nuts, linking a man in a thrift shop in rural Virginia to slaughtered cows on a ranch in Wyoming to dead Jews in a Polish forest, all so distant in place and time. But in my heart, I know I'm not. In fertile soil, misunderstanding takes root, grows and flowers into hate. Best to dig up those roots and dry them out in the glittering sunlight of a nearly perfect autumn day.

John Edgar Wideman

In this seven-thousand word excerpt of his memoir,
Brothers & Keepers, *John Edgar Wideman describes a frozen fifteen minutes that most writers
would have dispensed with in a sentence or space
break. Wideman discovers substance and significance
in his family's journey from the parking lot of the
prison to their first moments with his younger
brother, Robert, whose life as a petty thief led to
murder and, eventually, life imprisonment. Wideman re-creates those minutes and, in the process,
captures the spirit and the turmoil within the
African-American male psyche, while simultaneously illustrating his conflicting emotions of alien-
ation and his love for Robert. Note that Wideman
is able to continue to engage the reader while periodically departing the narrative to address his
brother directly.*

At the Penitentiary

⁓

Western Penitentiary sprouts like a giant wart from the bare, flat stretches of concrete surrounding it. The prison should be dark and forbidding, but either its stone walls have been sand-blasted or they've somehow escaped the decades of industrial soot raining from the sky.

Western is a direct descendant of the world's first penitentiary, Philadelphia's Quaker-inspired Walnut Street Jail, chartered in 1773. The good intentions built into the Walnut Street Jail—the attempt to substitute an enforced regime of solitary confinement, labor, and moral rehabilitation, for the whipping post, pillory, fines, and executions of the British penal code—did not exempt that humane experiment from the ills that beset all societies of caged men. Walnut Street Jail became a cesspool, overcrowded, impossible to maintain, wracked by violence, disease, and corruption. By the second decade of the nineteenth century it was clear that the reforms instituted in the jail had not procured the results its zealous supporters had envisioned, and two new prisons, one for the east, one for the western half of the state, were mandated by the Commonwealth of Pennsylvania. From the ashes of the Walnut Street experiment rose the first Western penitentiary. The architect, a William Strickland known for revivals of classic Greek models and his engineering skill, created a classic of a different sort on a plain just west of Allegheny City. With massive, forbidding bulwarks, crenellated parapets, watchtowers buttressing the corners of the walls, his notion of a prison recapitulated the forms of medieval fear and paranoia.

The immediate successor of Strickland's Norman castle was constructed sporadically over a period of seventeen years. This new Western, grandson of the world's first penitentiary, received its first contingent of prisoners in 1886, and predictably black men made up a disproportionate percentage of these pioneers, who were marched in singing. Today, nearly a hundred years later, having survived floods, riots, scandals, fires, and blue-ribboned panels of inquiry, Western remains in working order.

Approaching the prison from Ohio River Boulevard, you can see coils of barbed wire and armed guards atop the ramparts. The steepled towers that, like dunce caps, once graced its forty-foot walls have been lopped off. There's a visitors' parking lot below the wall facing the boulevard. I ignore it and pull into the fenced lot beside the river, the one marked Official Business Only. I save everybody a quarter-mile walk by parking in the inner lot. Whether it's summer or winter, that last quarter mile can be brutal. Sun blazing down on your head or icy wind off the river, or snow or rain or damp fog creeping off the water, and nothing but one high, gritty wall that you don't want to hug no matter how much protection it might afford. I drive through the tall gate into the official business lot because even if the weather's summery pleasant, I want to start the visit with a small victory, be one up on the keepers. Because that's the name of the game and chances are I won't score again. I'll be playing on their turf, with their ball and their rules, which are nothing if not one-sided, capricious, cruel, and corrupting. What's written says one thing. But that's not really the way things are. Always a catch. Always an angle so the published rules don't literally apply. What counts are the un-written rules. The now-you-see-it-now-you-don't-sleight-of-hand rules whose function is to humiliate visitors and preserve the ab-solute, arbitrary power of the keepers.

Onto whose lot we trespass. Pulling as close to the visitors' building as possible. Not too close because the guard on duty in the kiosk adjacent to the stairs of the visitors' annex might feel compelled to turn us back if we break into the narrow compass of his alertness. Close but far enough away so he'd have to poke out his head and shout to get our attention.

I find a space and the kids scoot out of their seats. Tish's girls are with us so we used the *way back* of the station wagon. For safety the rear hatch unlocks only from outside, so I insert the key and lift the lid and Danny and Jake and Tameka scramble out to join the others.

"We're in a parking lot, so watch for cars!" I shout after them as they race down the broad center lane of the parking area. What else can I say? Cramped in the car for the past half hour, they're doing now what they need to do. Long-legged, snake-hipped, brown children. They had tried to walk in an orderly fashion, smallest one grabbing largest one's hand, lock step, slowly, circumspectly, progressing in that fashion for approximately three steps before one tore away and another followed and they're all skipping and scampering now, polished by the sun. Nobody sprints toward the prison full tilt, they know better than that, but they get loose, flinging limbs and noise every which way. They crunch over a patch of gravel. Shorts and T-shirts make their bodies appear vulnerable, older and younger at the same time. Their high-pitched cries bounce off the looming wall. I keep my eyes on them as I lock the car. No real danger here but lessons, lessons everywhere, all the time. Every step and the way you take it here on enemy ground is a lesson.

Mom and Judy walk side by side, a black woman and a white woman, the white one tanned darker than the black. They add their two cents' worth of admonitions to the kids. Walk, don't run. Get Jamila's hand. Be careful. Slow down, youall. I fall in behind them. Far enough away to be alone. To be separate from the women and separate from the children. I need to say to whoever's watching—guards, prisoners invisible behind the barred three-story windows partitioning the walls, These are my people. They're with me. I'm responsible. I need to say that, to hang back and preside, to stroll, almost saunter, aware of the weight, the necessity of vigilance because here I am, on alien turf, a black man, and I'm in charge. For a moment at least these women, these children have me to turn to. And I'm one hundred percent behind them, prepared to make anyone who threatens them answer to me. And that posture, that prerogative remains rare for a black man in American society. Rare *today*, over 120 years after slavery and second-class citizenship have been abolished by law. The guards know that. The prisoners know. It's for their benefit as well as my own and my family's that I must carry myself in a certain way, make certain rules clear even though we are entering a hostile world, even though the bars exist to cut off the possibility of the prisoners seeing themselves as I must see myself, striding free, in charge of women and children, across the official lot.

· · ·

Grass grows in the margin between the spiked fence paralleling the river and the asphalt lot. Grass clipped harshly, uniformly as the bristle heads of convicts in old movies about prison. Plots of manicured green define a path leading to steps we must climb to enter the visitors' building. Prisoner trustees in ill-fitting blue uniforms—loose tunics, baggy, string-tied trousers a shade darker— putter at various make-work jobs near the visitors' entrance. Another prisoner, farther away, near the river edge of the parking lot sidles into a slate-gray Mercedes sedan. A pudgy, bull-necked white guy. When he plops into the driver's seat the car shudders. First thing he does is lower the driver's side window and hang out his ham arm. Then full throttle he races the Mercedes engine, obviously relishing the roar, as pleased with himself as he'd been when the precise, solid slam of the door sealed him in. If the driver is hot shit, big shot for a few seconds behind the wheel, he'll pay for the privilege soon enough when he adds the Mercedes to the row of Cadillacs, Oldsmobiles, and Buicks he must scrub and spit shine for the bosses.

Another prisoner leans on a push broom. The asphalt walks are spotless, but every minute or so he advances the broom another foot, punching its bristles into the gray surface as if his job is not to keep the path clean but punish it for unmentionable crimes against humanity. Others sweep, rake, and supervise. Two or three trustees have no apparent duties. They are at their ease, talking and smoking. A lethargy, a stilted slow-motion heaviness stylizes their gestures. It's as if they inhabit a different element, as if their bodies are enfolded in a dreamy ether or trapped at the bottom of the sea. I watch the prisoners watch the kids mount the steps. No outward signs betray what the men are thinking but I can feel them appraising, measuring. Through the prisoners' eyes I see the kids as sexual objects. Clean, sleek bodies. Young, smooth, and supple. The coltish legs and high, muscley butts of my nieces. The boys' long legs and slim hips. They are handsome children, a provocative banner waved in front of men who must make do with their own bodies or the bodies of other men. From the vantage point of the blue-uniformed trustees on the ground, the double staircase and the landing above are a stage free-world people must ascend. An auction block, an inspection stand where the prisoners can sample with their hungry eyes the meat moving in and out of prison.

But I don't have their eyes. Perhaps what they see when the kids climb the steps are their own lost children, their sons and daughters, their younger brothers and sisters left behind in the treacherous streets. Not even inside the walls yet and I can sense the paranoia, the curtain of mistrust and suspicion settling over my eyes. Except for the car jockey and a runner outside the guards' kiosk, all the trustees in the yard are black, black men like me, like you. In spite of knowing better, I can't shake the feeling that these men are different. Not just different. Bad. People who are dangerous. I can identify with them only to the extent that I own up to the evil in myself. Yeah. If I was shut away from the company of women, I'd get freaky. Little kids, alley cats, anything got legs and something between them start to looking good to me. Yeah. It's a free show when wives and mamas tippy-tap up them steps. And I'd be right there leaning on my broom taking it all in. I don't want to feel angry or hostile toward the prisoners but I close up the space between myself and my two women, glad they're both looking good and glad they're both wearing slacks.

It's crazy. It's typical of the frame of mind visiting prison forces on me. I have trouble granting the prisoners a life independent of mine, I impose my terms on them, yet I want to meet their eyes. Plunge into the depths of their eyes to learn what's hidden there, what reservoirs of patience and pain they draw from, what sustains them in this impossible place. I want to learn from their eyes, identify with their plight, but I don't want anyone to forget I'm an outsider, that these cages and walls are not my home. I want to greet the prisoners civilly as I would if we passed each other outside, on Homewood Avenue. But locks, bars, and uniforms frustrate the simplest attempts at communication; the circumstances under which we meet inform me unambiguously that I am not on Homewood Avenue, not speaking to a fellow citizen. Whether or not I acknowledge that fact I'm ensnared by it. Damned if I do, damned if I don't. I'm not wearing funny blue clothes. I walked into this zoo because I chose to: I can return home and play with these children, make love to my woman. These privileges, which in my day-to-day blindness I often don't even count as privileges, are as embarrassing to me, as galling in this prison context as the inmates' state of drastic deprivation must be to them. Without speaking a word, without having ever seen each other before, we know too much about each other. Our rawest, most intimate secrets are exposed, there's no room for small talk. We can't take our time and proceed in the gradual give-and-take, willed unveiling natural to human interaction. This place where we meet one another is called the slammer and sure as shit it slams us together.

People don't so much meet as explode in each other's faces. I say "Hi" to a tall guy who looks like somebody I might have played ball with once. He wasn't anybody I knew but he could have been. One ballplayer knows every other ballplayer anyway, so I said "Hi." Got back no hint of recognition. Nothing saying yes or no or maybe in his black face. The basketball courts where I sweated and he sweated, the close scores, the impossible shots, the chances to fly, to be perfect a second or two, or rise above the hard ground and float so time stands still and you make just the right move before your sneakers touch down again. None of that. No past or future we might have shared. Nothing at all. A dull, hooded "Hey, man" in reply and I backed off quickly.

Are the steps up to the porch landing iron or wood or concrete? I can't recall. I'll check next time. I feel them now, narrow, metal, curving like a ship's spiral ladder. My feet ring against latticed rungs. I can peer through the winding staircase to the ground. People can look up between the rungs at me. The first violation of privacy. Arranged so that the prisoners are party to it. One privilege conferred on the trustees is this opportunity to greet free-world people first. Form a casual gauntlet of eyes outsiders must endure. Behind the prisoners' eyes may be nothing more than curiosity, perhaps even gratitude toward anybody willing to share a few hours with a man inside. Envy. Concern. Indifference. Any or all of these; but my ignorance, the insecurity bred by the towering walls incite me to resent the eyes.

I don't enjoy being seen entering or leaving the prison. Enormous stores of willpower must be expended pretending it doesn't exist. For the hour or so of the visit I want to forget what surrounds us, want to free myself and free you from the oppressive reality of walls, bars, and guards. And other prisoners. I resent them. And need them. Without them it wouldn't be a prison. In the back of my mind I rely on the other prisoners to verify the mistake committed in your case. Some of these guys are bad, very bad. They must be. That's why prisons exist. That's why you shouldn't be here. You're not like these others. You're my brother, you're like me. Different.

A brother behind bars, my own flesh and blood, raised in the same houses by the same mother and father; a brother confined in prison has to be a mistake, a malfunctioning of the system. Any other explanation is too incriminating. The fact that a few twists and turns of fate could land you here with the bad guys becomes a stark message about my own vulnerability. It could easily be me behind bars instead of you. But that wouldn't make sense because I'm not bad like the bad guys for whom prisons are built. The evil in others defines your goodness, frees me. If it's luck or circumstance, some arbitrary decision that determines who winds up behind prison bars, then good and evil are superfluous. Nobody's safe. Except the keepers, the ones empowered to say *You go to the right. You go to the left.* And they're only safe as long as they're keepers. If prisons don't segregate good from evil, then what we've created are zoos for human beings. And we've given license to the keepers to stock the cages.

Once, on a previous visit, waiting an hour through a lock-in and count-down for you to be released to the visitors' lounge, I was killing time on the porch of the visitors' annex, resting my elbows on the stone railing, daydreaming at the river through the iron spears of the fence. An inmate called up to me. "You Faruq's brother, ain't you?" The man speaking was tall and broad-shouldered, a few years younger than you. His scarred head was shaved clean. He carried extra weight in soft pads on his hips, his belly, his cheeks. Like a woman, but also like the overweight lions in Highland Park Zoo.

I thought, Yes. Robby Wideman's my brother. Then I said, "Faruq is my brother," and expected more from the prisoner, but he'd turned back to the prisoners beside him, smoking, staring at nothing I could see.

A few minutes before, I'd noticed two men jogging along the river. I recognized their bright orange running shorts later as they hustled past me up the steps into the prison. Both greeted me, smiling broadly, the sort of unself-conscious, innocuous smiles worn by Mormon missionaries who periodically appear at our door in Laramie. Young, clean-cut, all-American white faces. I figured they had to be guards out for exercise. A new breed. Keepers staying in shape. Their friendly smiles said we'd be delighted to stay and chat with you awhile if we weren't needed elsewhere. I thought of the bland, empty stare of the man who had recognized me as Faruq's brother. Somebody had extinguished the light in his eyes, made him furtive, scared him into erecting a wall around his brown skin, trained him to walk and talk like a zombie. The healthy, clean sweat sheen on the runners' suntanned brows and lean muscled shoulders made me hate them. I wanted to rush after them. Smash them out of their dream of righteousness.

Up the steps, across the porch, through an outer lobby opening out on both sides to alcoves with benches and vending machines where trustees can visit with their families in a less noisy, less crowded setting than the general visitors' lounge. A short passageway next, ending at a floor-to-ceiling guards' cage. To the right of the guards' enclosure a steel-screened staircase. To the left a narrow corridor lined with lockers leads into the waiting room. I sign us in with the guard in the cage. Give him your name and number. He duly registers the information in his book. He's the one who initiates your release to the visiting room. He also holds the key to the rest room, keys to the lockers where visitors must store items not permitted inside the prison. It's a job and the guard treats it like most people treat theirs. Bored, numbed by routine. He wants things to run smoothly, to avoid hassles, and he's learned the best way to accomplish this is not to concern himself with matters beyond his immediate, assigned tasks. The larger scheme in which he participates is really not his problem. Like most of us he gets paid to do a job and the job's basically a pain in the ass and the pay is shitty so why ask for more trouble when you're underpaid for the trouble you got already. He resents having to explain why some people sit for hours and others get shuttled from waiting room to visitors' room in five minutes. He just relays through a loudspeaker the names and numbers another guard inside the prison phones to him.

P3468, Robert Wideman.

He knows it's not his fault some visits last three hours and others thirty minutes. Some days are busier than others. For him too. Fridays are bad. Attorneys always a pain. He wears a dull gray uniform and sits in a cage all day and has nobody to talk to except the con runner who lounges beside the cage or squats in the sunshine on the porch, freer than him, he thinks.

The guard in the cage doesn't run the prison. He just works there. He didn't rob nobody or stab nobody. He didn't pack his kids in a station wagon and drag them at dawn to this lousy place, so just have a seat, buddy. When they find Wideman I'll call you.

Once I counted the walls, the tall windows, estimated the height of the waiting-room ceiling. Eight walls, a ceiling twice as high as an ordinary room, four perverse, fly-speckled, curtainless windows admitting neither light nor air. I couldn't account for the room's odd shape and dimensions. Had no idea what its original purpose might have been or if it had been designed with any particular function in mind. The room made me feel like a bug in the bottom of a jar. I remembered all the butterflies, grasshoppers, praying mantises, and beetles I had captured on the hillside below the tracks. At least the insects could see through the glass walls, at least they could flutter or hop or fly, and they always had enough air until I unscrewed the perforated top and dumped them out.

The waiting room was uglier and dirtier the first few years we visited you. The same directive that ordered beautification of the grounds must have included the annex interior in its plan. A paint job—brown woodwork, baby-blue walls; new furniture—chrome tubing with pastel, vinyl cushions; a good hard scrubbing of the rest room to remove most of the graffiti—these rehabilitated what was most immediately insulting about the area where we waited for a phone to ring in the guard's cage and for him to call the name we wanted to hear over the loudspeaker. But the paint's peeling again already, flaking from pipes and radiators, drooping in clots from the ceiling. The vinyl cushions are faded, stained. In the *Ladies and/or Gents* the toilet seats are pocked by cigarette burns, graffiti has blossomed again. Wall art of a different sort decorates the main room. Murals tattoo the walls—a Chinese junk, a ship's wheel circling a clock. The most ambitious painting is above a bricked-in fireplace. A full-masted sailing ship plowing through marcelled waves. I wonder why it's only three-quarters complete. Was the artist released, the art program suspended because of lack of funds? Or did prison mayhem cause the picture to be left unfinished? A man beaten or raped or dead or consigned to the hole? A personality change, a soul too crushed even to fantasize anymore a proud clipper ship shouldering its way against sea and wind?

Our group occupies half the seats along one wall of the waiting room. The kids clearly don't belong here. Summer color glows in their faces. They are bright, alert kids somebody scrubs and cares about and dresses neatly. Both my boys sport shiny, digital watches on their wrists. But whose kids belong here? Who fits the image this room imposes on anybody who must use it? You said the prisoners complained about the state of the visitors' facilities and were granted, after much bullshit and red tape, the privilege of sprucing them up. But when it came down to supplies or time to work on the project, the administration backed off. Yes, you can fix up the place. No, we won't provide decent materials or time to do it. Typical rat-ass harassment. Giving with one hand, taking away with the other. If the waiting room's less squalid than it was three years ago, it's still far short of decent and it's turning nasty again. The room thus becomes one more proof of the convicts' inability to do anything right. We said you fellows could fix it up and look what a crummy job you did. We gave you a chance and you fucked up again. Like you fuck up probation and fuck up parole. Like you fucked up when you were on the street. And that's why you're here. That's why keepers are set over you.

I can hear the bickering, the frustration, the messages encoded in the tacky walls. It's a buzzing in my ears that never goes away inside the prison. Like the flies in the rest room waiting for the kids to start trooping in. Like the guard waiting to run his hand down in my mother's purse. Like the machine waiting to peek under everybody's clothes. Like all the locks and steel doors and bars we must pass through when they finally announce your number and name.

I drew the room once but I can't find the sketch. The picture was to serve as a jog for my memory. Documentation of the systematic abuse visitors must undergo from start to finish when they enter a prison. I knew that one day I'd write about visiting you and I'd need a careful blueprint of physical details, the things that bear so heavily on the soul. But it's not the number of doors or their thickness or composition or the specific route from the visitors' annex to the prison, not the clangorous steps and drafty, dank passageways and nightmare-size locks and keys, or the number of guards frisking me with their eyes or the crash of steel on steel ringing in my ears. It's the idea, the image of myself these things conspire to produce and plant in my head. That image, that idea is what defines the special power of the prison over those who enter it.

The process of implanting the idea is too efficient to be accidental. The visitor is forced to become an inmate. Subjected to the same sorts of humiliation and depersonalization. Made to feel powerless, intimidated by the might of the state. Visitors are treated like both children and ancient, incorrigible sinners. We experience a crash course that teaches us in a dramatic, unforgettable fashion just how low a prisoner is in the institution's estimation. We also learn how rapidly we can descend to the same depth. Our pretensions to dignity, to difference are quickly dispelled. We are on the keepers' turf. We must play their game, their way. We sit where they tell us to sit. Surrender the personal possessions they order us to surrender. Wait as long as it pleases them to keep us waiting in the dismal anteroom. We come (and are grateful for the summons) whenever we are called. We allow them to pass us through six-inch steel doors and don't protest when the doors slam shut behind us. We suffer the keepers' prying eyes, prying machines, prying hands. We let them lock us in without any guarantee the doors will open when we wish to leave. We are in fact their prisoners until they release us.

That was the idea. To transform the visitor into something he despised and feared. A prisoner. Until I understood what was being done, the first few moments at the threshold of the visiting lounge always confused me. There was an instant of pure hatred. Hatred lashing out at what I'd been forced to become, at them, even at you. The humiliation I'd undergone for the sake of seeing you poisoned the air, made me rigid, angry. I felt guilty for feeling put upon, guilty for allowing the small stuff to get inside me, guilty for turning on you.

That to get over first. And it's no simple matter in a noisy room crowded with strangers, in the short space of an hour or so, after a separation of months or years, to convince you and convince myself that yes, yes, we are people and yes, we have something to say to each other, something that will rise above the shouting, the fear, the chaos around us. Something that, though whispered, can be heard. Can connect us again.

You seem taller than you are. Long hands and feet where Mom used to say all your food went because you are like a horse and stayed skinny. Long legs and arms. In prison your shoulders have thickened. Your arms are tautly muscled from the thousand push-ups each day in your cell. Like Dave and Daddy and Grandpa you're losing your hair. The early thirties, but already your hair thinning, receding from your forehead. On top, toward the back, a circle of bare skull sneaks through if you don't comb your naps just right. Dave calls that balding patch we all sport our toilet seat. Other than that inherited sparse spot you're doing much better than I am in the keeping-your-hair department. More than most women, when you comb it out. When you plait it into braids and decorate each one with a colored rubber band, it gives you a modified dreadlocks look that emphasizes your high forehead and long, gaunt cheekbones. Bob Marley, or Stevie Wonder on his *Talking Book* album, or Albrecht Dürer's marcelled Christ. Faruq, the Muslim name you've chosen, is perfectly suited to your eyes. Burning. The terrible Turk declaring holy war on the infidels.

When you appear, I'm glad the kids are along. Happy that Judy insisted upon bringing them the first time we visited. You scoop them all into your long arms. All five squeezed in one hungry embrace. They squirm but endure the hug for your sake, then for their own as you press them to your need, to your strength, to each other. I'm grateful for the kids, cling to them as tightly as you do. Those are my children, your sister's children. We've brought the best of us into this godforsaken place. As you touch them, pick them up, and hug each one separately, the air is easier to breathe. You are their uncle, you are loving them, and for the moment that's all they need to know. Loving them because they're here, and loving the ones not here through them. That's all they need. All they ask. Jamila, the youngest, who's been here at least once every year of her life, hops up and down and squeals for another turn in your arms. Monique towers a foot above the others, a teenager suddenly remembering to be shy, awkward when you gather her last to your chest.

Look at my big girl. Look at her.

You grasp both Monique's shoulders and lean her back arm's length so you can get a good look too.

Ain't she growing. Look at this big thing. My little sweetheart's getting grown.

Her feet's bigger than Gammy's.

Hush up, Tameka.

Monique glowers at her younger sister. You better shut up, girl. A look full of the anger she can't quite summon up for you even though you're the one teasing and laughing louder than anybody. She turns back to you and a smile cracks the death-threat mask she'd flashed at her sister.

A bear hug and nuzzle for Judy. The same thing for Mom. Then we smack together, chest to chest. Hard the first time like testing shoulder pads before a football game. We grip each other's forearms.

We've made it. The visit's beginning. The room roars behind our backs.

About the Editor

Lee Gutkind, editor of *Creative Nonfiction*, a journal devoted solely to this genre, has performed as a clown for Ringling Brothers, scrubbed with heart and liver transplant surgeons, traveled with a crew of National League baseball umpires, wandered the country on a motorcycle and experienced psychotherapy with a distressed family—all as research for nine books and numerous profiles and essays, including the award-winning *Many Sleepless Nights*, an inside chronicle of the world of organ transplantation; *Stuck in Time*, which captures the tragedy of childhood mental illness; and most recently, *An Unspoken Art, Profiles of Veterinary Life*. His many essays and articles have appeared in the *New York Times Magazine, Sports Illustrated*, the *Georgia Review*, and *Prairie Schooner*. A professor of English at the University of Pittsburgh, Gutkind has pioneered the teaching of creative nonfiction, conducting workshops and presenting readings throughout the United States. Also a novelist and filmmaker, Gutkind is director of the Mid-Atlantic Creative Nonfiction Writers' Conference at Goucher College in Baltimore.